Natal. 2019

Lynne,

Thank you for sharing your gifts with us. I have searched for something special to gift you & could find nothing more personal than to share my story with you.

Grieving
by the
Numbers

Glimpses of Glory
by

Jan Teel-Nealis

Blessings upon you . . .

Grieving by the Numbers: Glimpses of Glory

By Jan Teel-Nealis

© Copyright 2018 Jan Teel-Nealis

ISBN-13: 978-1985823709

Printed in the United States of America

Presented by Captive Ink Media

Front Cover Design by Jennifer Reeve Lynch

Back Cover & Book Design by Charlotte Henley Babb

Praise for Grieving by the Numbers

"I got to know Jan shortly after her husband, Del's, sudden passing. I was amazed by her humble steady faith in her Heavenly Father's love while in the midst of such sorrow. In John 16 Jesus said, 'In this life you will have trouble, but take courage, I have overcome the world.' Over the following year, I witnessed Jan grieve courageously. As though she believed God's love was powerful enough to overcome, to heal, to redeem her families broken world.

Over the following year, Jan chronicled her and the family's journey through the valley of the shadow. She wrote candidly about pain and loss. She wrote lovingly about Del - his wisdom and sense of humor. She wrote with revelation about God's goodness, His faithfulness. And along the way she experienced and wrote down how God heals.

Jan is a gifted writer, a wonderful storyteller. She writes with wisdom and grace. Her words are an invitation into the love of God, an invitation into trust and intimacy. *Grieving by the Numbers* is a masterpiece on the healing and redemptive nature of God's love in the midst of sorrow. I am honored to recommend her book. I believe it will release courage and healing to all those who have experienced their own trouble."

Jason Clark

Author of *Prone to Love* and *God Is (Not) In Control*

Dedication

This book is dedicated to the offspring of Delbert Lewis Teel II: Nathaniel Andrew Teel, Joel Benjamin Teel, Bethany Hope Sigmon, and Jeremy Luke Teel and to their seed, both on this earth, in Heaven, and those yet to come: Leah Teel, Marcus Teel, Cadie Teel, and Elric Teel.

May the legacy of Delbert Lewis Teel II continue to be displayed in the hearts and minds of those you have fathered. May their seed come to know God early and may your love of God only be eclipsed by the love of God demonstrated in your seed to a thousand generations. It has been my genuine honor to have parented these souls with you.

I will see you on the other side in the twinkling of an eye.

Acknowledgements

There is no creative work ever fashioned that was not influenced by many voices. These voices shape us and become the catalyst for advancing through life. I would like to thank the first voices my ears ever heard, the voices of Albert and Betty Garner, my parents. Thank you for introducing me to the One Voice that I have been so thankful to have whispering in my ears for as long as I can remember. I would like to thank all the pastors, teachers, mentors, and friends who have helped challenge me and inspire me to go deeper into intimacy with God. My sincere appreciation goes to my siblings, Jerry, Rebecca, Diana, and Linda who have always been my biggest cheerleaders and constant anchors.

Reverend Barry Taylor helped to guide me into looking for the supernatural in every element of my life and these pages would not have been written without his influence. Dr. Bob Rodgers voice is woven into the tapestry of my life and walk with God. He helped me to believe, with every fiber of my being, that God is always good, and I can always expect miracles. To Lori Clifton, my thanks for being a covenant sister who stirs me to dream bigger and to take chances with the prophetic anointing that has always been mine to exercise.

To my beloved Pastors Mark and Julie Appleyard, you released me into my Divine destiny by making me teach, speak, and release what my ears were hearing from the realms of Heaven into the earth. You have inspired me to dream bigger dreams than I can possibly make come true, so that only with the help of Heaven, can I realize those dreams. The dialogue I hear inside my head these days often has an Aussie accent thanks to your beautiful voices.

Finally, my deepest gratitude goes to my Huckleberry friend, my Centurion, my second act, the Reverend Dr. Dale Nealis. Your devotion to me and love for me is humbling. May our second time around be greater than our first because we have increased in wisdom and know better than many that our days are numbered, and tomorrow is not promised. May we continually be fascinated with the wonder of our lives together as one in Him.

Foreword

My wife, Julie, and I have been pastors for the better part of twenty-three years. Throughout those years, the hardest, most heartbreaking, but most rewarding time we have shared with people during our time in ministry has been to walk with those who grieve, and we have learned some things along the way.

We have learned that grief is an intensely personal process. No two people will grieve the same way, or for the same length of time, or feel their grief at the same intensity. We have learned that grief, in the western world, is a culturally isolating process. We don't talk about it nearly enough because it's uncomfortable. Our patience with those going through it waxes and wanes according to the climate of our own feelings at the moment. The process that others go through as they embark on their grief journey is open to the judgment and criticism of both friends and family alike. We have learned that we typically tend to hide our grief because it's raw... and it hurts... and it's personal... and it feels so much better to not let anyone in to offer their opinion or give their advice.

Grieving by the Numbers: Glimpses of Glory offers a different perspective on grief. As pastors and friends of Jan, we have had the very great privilege of walking with her through this very intense, very personal journey. We have learned much from being invited into her process. We have been in awe of the goodness of God at every turn. And we have glimpsed His Glory as He has lavished it upon her in great, heaping helpings.

Jan has done everything differently. Opposite. Untraditionally. "Anti-culturally" if you will. Her courage to be open and vulnerable with this most tender time in her life has been rewarded with revelation and insight from Heaven that has brought healing and wholeness to her heart. Her resolve to let others into her process has been rewarded with a depth and richness of relationship with others that has been surprising. Her transparency as she traveled the journey no one wants to travel, has been rewarded with an authority to speak into lives of those who find themselves traveling this same unwanted, unasked for journey.

We are incredibly proud of this woman of God, and we pray with all our hearts that as you journey with Jan through these pages, your eyes will be opened to the wonderful way that our Heavenly Father turns beauty to ashes, and your ears will be tuned in to the gentleness of His voice as He leads you through your own journey into the healing and wholeness He has for you.

Mark and Julie Appleyard, Founders of Anothen

www.anothen.co

* * *

A friend of mine had contacted me about a friend of hers who had written a book about the death of her husband. She wondered if I would consider doing a foreword for the book. To be asked to participate in this endeavor would be difficult for several reasons. I did not personally know the author, and more importantly, it's a very difficult subject to address. I remember, I was somewhat taken aback at the first thought, then within my spirit, I felt total confirmation to accept this challenge.

Upon receiving the book a few weeks later, I was flabbergasted upon the very touching of the book, as my spirit felt an overwhelming presence of God. I knew this book had been written through the inspiration of the Holy Spirit which was leaping within me. Immediately the honor to be asked to be a part of this book was evident to me. As I started to read the first pages and chapters, there was such an anointing on the words as I paced the pages with such anticipation. My heart became captivated by such a force of love, and such a depth of despair, in a family that truly knew how to love each other through the best and worst of times.

There is such a bond of connection seen by this family to our Father's heart, as the story unfolds for the readers. It was truly overwhelming to be allowed to enter as a guest, and to see how they were held together by this magnetic force of such incredible strength, courage, and agape love like many have probably never felt, or ever being a part of, including me.

My life as a nurse can truly testify that there are many facets of death. It can be as beautiful as newborn babies receiving their first breath, or as heartbreaking to watch those who are losing a loved one struggle without the vision of Heaven. Most people cannot embrace this transition as a joy, but those of us who witness this ending of life as the beginning of eternal life, can grasp the fullness of this verse. We understand when God says our deaths are precious in his eyes (Psalms 116:15).

As the pages turned, Jan's tears became intertwined with my heart, which became one with this family, who had to travel through the shadow of death, like untold millions before them. The raw transparency of this family, who fought like warriors in some of the greatest wars for their patriarch, who had been a son, husband, father, friend, brother, coworker to many, is astounding. This man had now become a hero to all of the above, and now also to this stranger reading about his life.

The questions could develop in one's mind, "Why was this gentle soul ripped out of the hearts of many," and "How could they possibly march forward?" Here was a man who had done everything right, from his childhood and up to his ending breath. He surely walked in the greatest testimony of always serving the Lord Jesus, unlike many, whose testimonies are of being delivered from alcoholism, drugs, or sexual perversions and translated into the glorious light of Jesus Christ. One would have to surmise of him walking life as nearly perfect in the eyes of those who knew and loved Del Teel. By the end of the second chapter, most of us would desire to be more like him in so many ways, especially his intimacy with our lovely Jesus.

While learning about this man's heart, I kept thinking that surely this man had some flaws or issues that would surface in the next chapter; no one could be this perfect. The evidence throughout this book consistently showed no mistakes, regrets, or horrible secrets ever transpired. It was a steadfast flow of total love and devotion for his wife, his children, and all who knew and encountered this man of God, who desired the heart of Jesus. This man sought after the heart of his Creator like King David did. He became the sought out one! The one who everyone desired to be like!

We watch and wait on our Abba Father to display His faithfulness and eternal love to the many who were broken by the departure of Del Teel. Out of the tortuous debris of the shattered hearts of those who stood by this man, we see the glory of our Lord Jesus unraveling within the next chapters and throughout the book.

Papa God's love is poured out, in the midst of a tragedy on this family, which would forever mark those left behind as his beloved ones. One can almost see them tattooed on the palms of a loving Father's hands, who undoubtedly knew all the pain and anguish of giving up a "special one," so that all of mankind would be set free for eternity, when they gave their hearts to Him; so that they would be able to spend eternity with the One who had died for us because He loved us that much!

It was total brilliance by the Holy Spirit to adjust the scales of time, in a sequence that produced the common denominator by gathering the days, weeks, and months to align them with the numbers of days since this man left his earthly suit. It is encouraging for all to step forward into their hope of destinies as their own next act. We never forget the ones that have left earth, bound for our heavenly home; we just walk into the next chapter carrying them forever in our hearts while taking their wisdom, love, and legacy into others' hearts both now and for generations to come.

Because of this book, many will strive to become a great husband, father, wife, and friend to one another, like this man was. More importantly, we will strive for this perfection to our loving

Father, and His only begotten Son, by the leading of our comforter and teacher, our beloved Holy Spirit.

Grieving by the Numbers is surely a book that will alert the hurting who have lost their loved ones and teach us to allow our trust to be with our Father, in every situation of life, from birth unto our last breaths and to look forward with anticipation of an eternity in Heaven with those who have traveled on before us. To be the "Sought Out Ones," in someone else's life that leads them to the heart of Jesus, who loved them unto death.

"And they will call them 'The Holy People, The Redeemed of the LORD'; And you will be called 'Sought Out, A City Not Deserted'" (Isaiah 62:12 amp).

Karen Sumrall, Author of *Glory Filled* and *A Journey to Heart Throb Moments*, Minister, and Public Speaker

Prologue

The way that God uses everything in all of creation to speak to us fascinates me. I have always been captivated by the Biblical, or Spiritual, meaning of numbers. As the weeks unfolded after my husband's death, sometimes in a fog and sometimes in a rush, I began to listen to our Heavenly Father's voice sharing the significance of each week as it correlated with my grieving. Sometimes it was a memory and sometimes it was a character-building revelation. In the weeks following Del's sudden departure from this side of eternity, I began to write a weekly entry on my Facebook page reflecting on where I was in the process, and believe me, grieving is a process. You do not get over it. You get through it. You learn from it. You are shaped by it and forever changed by it. The loving Holy Spirit prompted me to publicly express my thoughts, helping me make it through the fog. Writing each week gave me a sense of purpose to march toward the goal of somehow, setting a marker stone at the end of that seven-day cycle. My sincere hope is that those who choose to walk down this path of remembrance with me will be blessed by these revelations and stories.

Reverend Barry Taylor, my former pastor and the founder of Liberty Ministries, was the first mentor to begin to bring revelation to me regarding the significance of numbers in the Bible. Although I had always felt God was communicating through the numbers in His Word, it was Reverend Taylor who taught me to look deeper. With his encouragement, I began researching how numbers tied into spiritual revelations in the Word of God. Those who practice Judaism have understood the spiritual significance of numbers for thousands of years. God's Word is rich in symbolism and revelation. My personal conviction is that His Word is perfect, and it is always speaking. It is a living thing, not a book of mere history and dead ideas. Although the Holy Bible is a completed work, God has never stopped speaking to those who are attuned to His call. We hear His Voice whisper in the splendid colors of autumn and the refreshing brilliance of springtime. We hear Him roaring in claps of thunder that make our hearts swell in response. We see Him in astonishing flashes of lightning that reverberate His majesty and splendor.

When I was a child, we were given paint sets and pictures of masterpieces that were only outlined in black and white, like puzzles. Each section had a correlating paint number to help you replicate the original artist's colors. They came with a palate of paints that corresponded to the numbers. At the end of your work, you would have created a piece of art that looked similar to the original. One found it hard to picture what the finished work would look like when only patches of color fragments were being applied to the hardened canvas, one chosen color at a time. The canvas was often ugly and distorted as the various shades that would make up the whole picture were applied. The practice of completing these canvas replicas was referred to as "painting by the numbers." So, it seemed fitting, since the unfolding of weeks were painting a new canvas in my life marked by the correlating numbers, to reference my journey as "Grieving by the Numbers."

Grieving by the Numbers was born of the simple act of journaling my sorrow in response to the way Father God was meeting me at the weekly markers every Thursday following that fateful day that Del returned to his Maker. After the first few entries, I had requests from others who were suffering the loss of a loved one to share what I had written. Before too many weeks had passed, I knew I had a book. May the entries and stories I share bring you hope, laughter, and comfort. If you have not yet met Father God, may you find His comfort toward this widow as an introduction to the kindest Person you will ever know.

Table of Contents

Introduction

My first memory of my husband is linked to a small church that my family and I attended from the time I was four years old. Housed in a humble building, Calvary Tabernacle Assembly of God was in Ballwin, Missouri, a suburb of St. Louis. As with most Sunday mornings, we started our day by gathering in a cozy Sunday School class where we were taught Bible lessons appropriate to our age groups. That particular Sunday, we had to combine classes because one of the teachers was absent. This was how I came to cast my eyes upon a handsome young man wearing a plaid short-sleeved shirt and sporting a bolo tie. (This was a very popular fashion statement among young men that season, as it was a throwback to cowboy days, most likely influenced by the abundance of television programming with an emphasis on the "Wild West.") I was enchanted. There was something in his teal-green eyes, his quiet demeanor, and his gentle spirit that took my heart by surprise. How can a little girl possibly know, at the tender age of nine, that she has met the one who will be her heart's desire for the rest of her days? I have no answer to this question. I will tell you that there was never another person who captivated my heart like this young man. My obsession with him only grew over the years.

When people would ask my beloved husband, known to me as Del, how he met me, he would not recount that scene in the Sunday School class. Instead, he would tell them, "My earliest memory of her was as a little girl with dark hair and dark eyes, playing the role of an angel in a Christmas play at our church." (This was the church where we first met.) By the time that memory was burned into his brain, I had been longingly chasing after him for two years! That play took place when I was eleven years old and I had been enamored with him from the time I laid eyes on him. He was four years older than I, a huge gap when the spread is between nine and thirteen years of age.

The play that Del was referencing had me assuming the role of an angel who admonished the other characters in the script to, "Bring to God the gold of which He is worthy, rather than the silver of second best!" How fitting words these would be for him to remember, as this was the standard that my late husband set. He was truly known as one who brought gold to whatever circumstance or situation he was challenged with in this life.

There is a story about Alexander the Great that reminds me of Del. Alexander was once passing by a beggar who cried out for assistance from the great conqueror. Alexander responded by tossing several gold coins in the direction of the beggar. His attendants questioned the generosity of their king, protesting, "Sir, copper coins would adequately meet a beggar's need. Why give him gold?" Alexander's response tells us much about his sense of nobility as he replied, "Copper coins would suit the beggar's need, but gold coins suit Alexander's giving."

This was the pattern of Del's life. He truly brought his best to everything he set his mind to do. He never settled for bringing silver or copper. He gave gold. When inducted into the National Honor Society (as Del himself was in high school), one is told that his or her motto in life is to be *noblesse oblige*, which means, *nobility obligates*. Del lived his life with this code of conduct.

As Alexander the Great faced death, his final request was to have the path to his burial covered with gold and treasures and to have his hands dangling outside of his coffin. His men respectfully asked him to explain his strange request, not wishing to fail to execute his final wishes, but concerned that his mind might be failing. He told them that his treasures could not save him, and he was leaving the world empty-handed, just as he had entered it. We all leave the world empty-handed, but we leave behind a legacy if we are faithful. Del was faithful. His legacy endures.

I am aware that we tend to deify those who have passed before us. I want my readers to know that the pages that will follow are a true depiction of a love story and my personal journey through grief.

Del and I had good times and hard times, as all couples do. Our solid foundation on The Rock that is Jesus, carried us through the trials, and the knowledge of The Father's always-good love enriched our relationship. Our Heavenly Father tenderly led me, week by week (and sometimes moment by moment), through the loss of the one for whom I felt I had been born into the earth. I so admired and respected him and thought that life would not go on without him. As many widows and widowers have learned before me, life does go on, with or without our permission.

Please join me as my love story, and the story of a life well lived, unfolds. Accompany me on my journey of discovery as I walked out of the darkness of my widow's mourning and into a day of becoming a bride again. You will behold the *Glimpses of Glory* that I was exposed to all along my tear-soaked path.

Chapter One: Our World is Shaken

October 9, 2013

Del awakened me while it was still dark. We were in the master bedroom of our home in Matthews, North Carolina. Del referred to it as our "forever" home. We gave it the name "Serenity," because that is what we had found in this place we had been renovating for the prior three years. The rambling ranch was only our second house since moving to the Charlotte, North Carolina region in 1984. My husband had worked for IBM (International Business Machines) for thirty-five years. He would tease that the acronym stood for "I've Been Moved," because of the company's tendency to transfer its employees to whatever location made the most business sense in any given season.

The gentle wakeup call from my normally quiet husband was unusual. I looked at the clock beside my bed; it read 5:30 a.m. He was dressed in his office attire (business casual) and looked as handsome as ever. He smelled of aftershave. I always loved being awakened to that fragrance and the way that it would linger in the room after he would leave for work each morning. As he gently touched my shoulder Del said, "I think I'm in trouble." I could tell that he was in pain, even in the very dim light coming from the bathroom that adjoined our bedroom.

Panicked, I was now fully awake. "What is it?" I asked, jumping out of bed.

"I'm gonna need some help." This admission was an astonishing one from a person who prided himself on independence and self-sufficiency. I knew this situation was critical.

"Do you want me to take you to the hospital?" I asked incredulously.

"I'm afraid so," came his quiet reply. There was a tinge of sadness in his voice, an expression of enormous pain, as he clutched his chest. I remembered the term "golden hour" as it related to heart attacks. I knew the first few minutes of an episode were critical and felt I could drive him to the hospital myself faster than an ambulance at that time of day. I threw on my clothes and a hat to cover my bed head. I pitched everything I thought I might need in the coming hours into a bag and jumped into my minivan. From the time he awakened me to the time I pulled up in front of the hospital, twenty-two minutes had passed. We both prayed all the way to the hospital, and I mentally relived the hours that led up to this frantic trip to the emergency room.

All that we had gone through the night before came flooding back to my mind. We had toured the under-construction home of our middle son, Joel, and his wife, Laura. My engineer-to-the-core husband took notes on little index cards of where every plumbing line and wire was placed in the still-open walls of the house. As he walked into each of the future bedrooms of our granddaughters, I heard him quietly musing, "So this is where they will view the world as they grow up." He walked into the living areas of the house and observed, "This is where their friends will come to see them," or "This is where they will be picked up by their boyfriends." He waxed melancholy at the thought of that prospect, and we both joked about how their daddy would be watching too. Del grew suddenly very tired as we were wrapping up our tour of the house. Our daughter, Bethany Hope, had just closed on her house that day too and was planning to move the following weekend. We had talked about going by to see her place afterward.

As we left the construction site of Joel's new house, I said, "You know, Bethany is going to want you to come and see her new place too."

"I know," he said remorsefully. "I just feel washed out. I need to get home and recover." My concern grew when we made it back to our home. I followed him as he walked back to his office. He sat down at his desk, reaching for the baby aspirin and popping one in his mouth.

"Is that the first one of those you have taken today?" I asked suspiciously.

"I don't know," was his reply. I didn't know if he truly couldn't remember or if he was trying to allay my concerns.

"Do you need to see a doctor? Are you going to be okay? Should we go to an Urgent Care?" We had gone over these questions before. No, he wouldn't see a doctor. Yes, he was going to be okay. He was just tired, he said, and needed to get a reset.

I went into the kitchen and made him some dinner. Since he didn't eat heavily when he wasn't feeling well, I opted for cream of rice for dinner. This was a meal I knew I could prepare quickly, giving him the much-needed energy that seemed to have drained from him during our little excursion. I kept hovering over him, but he appeared to be mellowing out and doing better. Del finished his dinner and said, "That was perfect!" He was always quick to express his appreciation, making even something as simple as a bowl of cream of rice seem like an extravagant meal. "I think I am going to go watch my soaps!" he said with enthusiasm. This is how he referred to his evening lineup of favorite television shows. Tuesday night was *NCIS* (*Naval Criminal Investigative Service*) night. The first episode was set in the Washington, D.C. area and the second was set in Los Angeles. Del loved the characters, and the stories were fascinating to him. He escaped to his evening's distraction and I engaged in other pursuits. Without appearing to be overly pesky, I kept going back and forth between my office and his just to chat with him and make sure he was recovering from his earlier energy drain. At about ten o'clock that night, he came into my office to sit with me and share a glass of red wine. Our habit was that he would pour one glass, I would take the first sip, and he would finish the glass. I said, "I think I am going to turn in early tonight." Del was a night owl who required very little sleep, and I had adapted to his ways over the years, so it was very unusual for us to go to bed before midnight. On this night, he decided he would go with me. I was relieved because I really wanted him to get some rest.

As we lay in bed, we went through what had become an almost nightly ritual. I said, "Thank you for choosing me, Mr. Teel!"

To which he would respond, "Thank you for saying 'Yes!'"

Next, I would express my concern, "Please take good care of yourself. You are not replaceable."

To which he would protest, "One day, you are going to marry some young buck and go on the adventure of a lifetime. I'm holding you back."

"Stop saying that! I don't want to go on an adventure without you!" I would declare sincerely.

On more than one occasion in more recent evenings, he would say, "You are going to be fine." It was as if he knew something was going to happen. I wrote it off as fatalism, but I had an uneasy feeling, especially on this night.

As I pulled up outside of the emergency room that morning, I told him, "Honey, you get out and sit on that bench and wait for me. I will park and join you." He didn't protest, as would have been his normal response. He got out of the car, but he just stood there where I had dropped him off. I scrambled to get back to him, and we walked through the doors of the emergency room. Del began to reach into his back pocket for his wallet to dig out the obligatory insurance card. I said, "Here, let me do that for you." He didn't resist my offer of help. As we walked to the registration desk to check in I said, "Can you please help me? I am pretty sure my husband is having a heart attack."

The young woman behind the desk looked at his insurance card and said, "I am going to need to see his driver's license." With annoyance at her lack of urgency, I went back inside the wallet to dig out his driver's license. In that moment of acute frustration, I caught a flash out of the corner of my eye of Del falling straight back onto his head like a tall tree chopped off at its base. I heard the loud bang as his head hit the hard surface of the hospital waiting room floor. I dropped beside his body and began to cry out, "Dear Jesus, please help!" Del's eyes were open, but he wasn't there anymore. Del had the most unusual eyes I had ever seen. They were a mix of blue and green. The inside was jade, and the outside rim was a deep blue. In that moment, all I could see was black. I could hear sounds coming from his body, but I felt his spirit leaving him. I felt helpless and at a loss. I had heard the medical term "fixed and dilated" before but had never seen it. My beloved was not in there anymore. I began to pray for him to return to me. I was contending for his return, wrestling with Heaven for a Divine reversal through earnest prayer, just as a boxer might contend for a heavyweight title. Something far more important to my world than a boxing title was hanging in the balance.

Medical staff began to scramble with a gurney and life support equipment as they wheeled him back into the examining rooms behind us. I followed as they took him through the doors, frantically texting my children and my church family to join me in prayer. I continued answering questions from the admissions personnel while simultaneously listening to the sounds of the nurses and doctors working on my husband and trying to bring him back to me. The sound of technicians calling out, "Clear!" followed by the erratic beeping of the monitors they had set up to give them needed feedback from their efforts haunted me. I could hear them calling out numbers. "What is the significance of those numbers?" I wondered. I heard the dreaded sound of them working to restore his heart, followed by the sounds of a rhythm being broadcast over a heart monitor they had strapped to him. I experienced momentary relief, followed by disheartening sounds as, repeatedly, they struggled to bring him back. I hung onto every breath and every beep being generated by the machinery that was working to bring him back to earth.

The admissions nurse asked me to join her at her desk. I wanted to stay outside of the room where Del was being attended. She promised it would only be for a moment. Her desk was directly across the hall from the examining room. I could still see the activity going on behind the sheer curtain, so I agreed. As I sat there answering her questions, my brother called me from St. Louis.

"What's going on there now?" he asked, frantically looking for an update while trying to remain calm for my sake. He and Del had been best friends growing up. This wasn't just his sister's husband. For Jerry, it was truly a brother whose life was ebbing away as he listened from afar.

As I tried to talk to Jerry, my son Joel arrived. I kept my brother on the line as the emergency room doctor stepped outside of Del's room.

"Mrs. Teel?" She awaited my affirmation that I was, indeed, Mrs. Teel.

"Yes. I am Mrs. Teel. This is our son Joel." I directed her attention to the fact that I now had support with me. What a great gift. I was so thankful to have my brother on the phone and now one of our sons standing beside me.

"Your husband is clinically dead," she said compassionately. Her words hit me like the force of a hurricane wind. While my mind was trying to process those words that seemed unfathomable, she went on, "We have tried to stabilize him and get a solid rhythm, but he is just not staying with us. I am so sorry."

Everything inside me screamed loudly, "NOOOOOOO!" Aloud, I simply stated, "God is going to give you wisdom and you are going back into that room, and you will get his heart going again!" I honestly don't know where that gumption came from at that moment, but her response was heartening.

She took a deep breath and said, "Okay. Thank you for that." She then retreated behind the curtain and started working on him again. We prayed. We pleaded. We waited. A few minutes later, she came out and said, "We have him stabilized enough now that we can move him to the hospital in Uptown Charlotte. The cath lab is his best hope now. If we can get an ambulance to take him there, we will make that happen."

Two men wearing blue paramedic uniforms with the familiar emergency response badges appeared just then and said, "We can take him." They had just ended a shift. As she debated whether to let Del go with them or await the designated ambulance drivers for that hospital, they said, "In the time that it takes them to get back here, we could be halfway there." She agreed and released him to their care.

Joel and I followed behind them back through the lobby where I had walked in with Del just a few minutes before. My daughter, Bethany Hope, and her husband, A.J., came in just as we were going out. Joel left his car and drove my van to the hospital. Bethany and A.J. followed. We were all in prayer and scrambling to let everyone we could think of know what was going on so that we had mighty forces gathering and bombarding the heavens on behalf of the patriarch of our family.

The trip to the facility in the center of Charlotte flashed by quickly. Joel and A.J. dropped Bethany and me off at the same place the ambulance had delivered Del a few minutes earlier. The two of them had to find parking spaces and we wanted to get inside and close to Del as quickly as possible. We waited for a while for the men to join us, but I wanted desperately to get upstairs to where they had taken Del, so a volunteer at the hospital escorted Bethany and me through the maze toward the cath lab upstairs. He was a kindly, older gentleman. Many of the volunteers in the hospitals in our region are retired men and women wanting to make a difference in the community. As we were ascending the elevator, I heard, "Code Blue, Cath Lab. Code Blue, Cath Lab."

I looked at Bethany and said, "That is your daddy." Somehow, I just knew that he was still struggling. Our senior volunteer looked at us sympathetically.

Bethany said, "Mom, it's a big hospital. That could be anyone."

"It's your dad," I said with absolute conviction.

Bethany Hope, our only daughter, had been named Bethany for the city in Israel where Jesus visited some of His closest friends, Mary, Martha, and Lazarus. The city of Bethany was where Jesus raised His friend Lazarus from the grave on the fourth day after His friend had succumbed to an illness. After His resurrection, Jesus departed the earth, ascending back to His Heavenly Father from the city of Bethany. Del had wanted our Bethany to devote her life to being a friend of God and had chosen her first name because of that association with the friends of Jesus. Hope, her middle name, was chosen because in the New Testament the Greek word *hope* means *a confident expectation*. Del had wanted a little girl so badly. He prayed for her conception. He had a "confident expectation" that she would be brought forth in the world. I was unsure about how I would mother a little girl. I knew how to raise sons, but I was concerned about how well I would do as the mother to a little girl. Del would declare, "You are going to have a friendship like no other mother and daughter have ever had. You are going to be the closest of friends!"

As we were making our way upstairs to join Del, I considered how his words had come true. We had a lovely daughter who had become one of my most treasured friends. Her life had infused ours with hope from the start. Here she stood, as my trusted friend and daughter, facing the most critical day that either of us had ever faced. Whatever the outcome, I was so thankful that Del had bombarded Heaven with his request to father this wonderful daughter.

My racing thoughts were interrupted by the senior volunteer's question, "What is his name? I will go and check on things in the cath lab for you and let you know what I learn," he offered kindly. After giving him Del's name, we both thanked him and made our way to a waiting room. A few minutes later he returned to us and said, "It was your dad, but they are working on him and that is a good sign. They wouldn't be working on him if it was too late. Keep a good thought," he encouraged us and then departed.

A few moments later, we received word that our pastor and his wife were already in the hospital and looking for us. Mark and Julie Appleyard had migrated from Australia with their three children and founded a small church in Waxhaw, North Carolina, a few miles south of Charlotte. I had been attending services there for a little less than a year, but my heart was bound with theirs from the start of our acquaintance. Their charming Aussie accents and kind hearts ushered peace and comfort into the atmosphere. We were then joined by our church's worship leader, Nathanael Whittenburg. My sons Nathan and Jeremy came as quickly as they could to join us as we continued to pray for our beloved patriarch while he was being attended to by the medical staff. Now all our children were with me, along with some of their spouses, as we waited.

After what felt like days, but had only been a few hours, we were all gathered into a conference room by the cardiac surgeon who had been working on Del. His demeanor was professional but emotionally detached as he stated, "Your husband is gravely ill. We have taken extraordinary measures to stabilize him. He now has a pacemaker to regulate his heart. We also put in several stents." He went on to explain other gadgets and systems they had put in Del, and on him, that made him sound like a bionic man.

I told the surgeon, "The engineer in Del would be fascinated by the technology you are using to assist him, but the other part of him is going to be horrified when he awakens to discover all of the hardware that is now in his chest."

I tried to infuse some humor in the matter, but I was remembering all the conversations Del and I had over the course of our years about how horrified he would be to go out of life in this manner. He was explicit about not having anyone in the room with him if he were ever in a hospital, except for me. He had told the children his desire regarding this matter. He had said that having anyone besides his wife in his room would be the equivalent of having someone come into his bedroom without knocking or being invited. Because of his very deliberate wishes, I did not have anyone accompany me as I made my way back and forth from the Intensive Care Unit room where he was being treated to the waiting room, where his family and friends awaited news of a reversal.

This was my Facebook post during that time of waiting:

October 9, 2013

> I am overwhelmed by the kindness that has met me in this moment of crisis. For those who don't yet know, my beloved husband had a massive heart attack this morning. We were in the lobby of the emergency room when it happened—God's amazing provision! His heart has stopped multiple times and they told me at one point that he was clinically dead. God has chosen to give us a different report. He is in the cath lab now having his plumbing worked on. He has been there for about ninety minutes. Please keep him in your prayers and know that GOD IS ANSWERING OUR CRY!

As I made the trips back and forth from the waiting room where my friends and family had assembled to Del's hospital room, where a staff of several medical personnel attended to his needs throughout the hours that stretched into the long night, I reported on the numbers. There were multiple sets of numbers I was receiving from those who were working on our beloved patriarch to bring him through the dark of night. At one point, we were told that his blood pressure was too low. The staff had brought in a special dialysis machine to help when his kidneys began to shut down, but his blood pressure needed to go up for the cutting-edge dialysis machine to work. We all gathered in the waiting room and began to pray. As we prayed, the numbers changed. His body was responding to the prayers. More friends and family gathered, and we had a small congregation there, praying not only for Del, but for the others who were there in the hospital and in need of a touch from Heaven.

Later in the night, Del's temperature began to go up. The nurses and doctors told us that is was critical it go back down. We prayed and called out the numbers. My youngest son, Jeremy, was there with his wife, Elizabeth. At one point during the evening, she began to call out the numbers in prayer and command that his temperature go down. The thought occurred to me, "Has the prayer mantle slipped from Del's shoulders onto Elizabeth's?" I had never seen this side of the warrior bride my son had married. She was fierce, passionate, determined, and sincere in her prayers. I was inspired to slip away a few minutes after her very powerful prayer and check on Del. His temperature was dropping again. We had sign after sign that the numbers were going the right way.

Each Wednesday evening, we had a midweek service at our home church, so Mark, Julie, and Nathanael had to excuse themselves and tend to the rest of the flock who would be assembling at Crossroads Church in Weddington. Assuring us that they would have the congregation join us in petitioning Heaven for Del, they left us with a parting prayer asking God to give us strength and courage to continue to stand and believe for a good report from the doctors.

Around 11:00 p.m. that evening, Mark and Julie returned along with another former pastor, Barry Taylor. Barry had been with us for hours earlier in the day but had gone back to his home in Denver, North Carolina. None of our spiritual leaders could sleep knowing what a fierce battle we were waging in prayer for Del. I watched in fascination as Julie would hover over each family member, lighting like a dove, to minister comfort and hope. Julie had been a practicing midwife before leaving Australia. In this country, her accreditation wasn't recognized, leaving her to become a practicing doula instead. Her years of consoling and comforting women in the throes of childbirth certainly served her as she gently offered words of encouragement, in her lilting Australian accent, to each of us assembled in the room.

Pastor Mark offered words of encouragement and strength as well. He told us tales of miraculous healings he had witnessed in similar situations. He told us humorous stories too. Pastor Mark is a marvelous narrator. He knows how to captivate an audience with his antics, making him a treasured preacher. He shared tales of victories from the past that we could hold onto in these hours of uncertainty.

As night slipped into the wee hours of the morning, I encouraged everyone to go home and get some rest. I was going to sleep on the floor of the waiting room. There were so many technicians gathered around Del's room that the only place I could stand when I stepped inside was at the head of his bed. I would put my hands on either side of his face and pray and speak over him for a few minutes and then slip out again so that I wasn't interfering with the work they were doing for him. Bethany and A.J. decided to stay with me and sleep as much as possible on the hard floor of the waiting room. Just as she had stood with me through so many of my life challenges, Bethany would not leave my side that night. She was as exhausted as any of the others, but if Mom was staying, she was staying.

When Bethany was a little girl, she would get up in the wee hours of the morning, make her way to our bedroom with her blanket in her hand, and curl up on the floor at the end of our bed. She was so concerned that she would miss seeing her daddy off to work early in the morning, that she would place herself in a position so as not to miss him while he was going through his morning routine. He knew she was waiting for him. He would always be careful where he stepped if he got up in the middle of the night, knowing she was likely at the foot of his bed. She would typically tumble down the steps after him in the morning and wave at him from her perch in the living room window as he backed out of the driveway to head off for his workday. Seeing her curled up on the floor of this waiting room reminded me of all those nights she had awaited his awakening as a little girl.

Joel and Laura had gone back to my house at one point during the night and picked up some things for me to be more comfortable in the waiting room. While walking through the house, Joel said that he felt Del's spirit following him around. At one point, he stopped and said aloud, "You can't be here, Dad! You need to get back to the hospital and get inside your body." He said that he sensed Del at the back door when he was pulling away, seeing him off as he always did when the children would visit. A deep sense of dread washed over him.

Early the next morning I entered the room to check on Del again. I hadn't been there for a while as my body had finally allowed me to rest, sleeping fitfully for a couple of hours on the floor of the waiting room. It was quieter now. There were only two technicians working with him, and as I stepped inside, I saw that the numbers were quite good. His blood pressure was good. His heart rate was good. His temperature had actually dropped below normal. A heater had been placed on his body to keep it warm now. I said, "Wow! Things look so much more promising this morning! His numbers are good," I declared.

The young nurse looked up at me and said, "Those numbers are deceiving. They aren't telling you everything. His pH levels are way off. We need to see some major improvements." I decided she was just giving a negative report, and I was having none of it. I was going to focus on all of the good numbers. I went back to the waiting room and told Bethany and A.J. how encouraged I was by what I saw. They were both relieved. They decided to head downstairs and get some breakfast and bring something back to me.

I posted the following on my Facebook page:

October 10, 2013

Weeping endures for the night, but joy comes in the morning! Del's fever is GONE! His blood pressure is perfect. His heart rate is good. Next prayer request is that his pH level goes to 7.5 and his oxygen rate goes up. God is fighting for us, pushing back the darkness.

Just after I posted this, the young doctor who had worked with Del the night before and who had come in regularly to our prayer vigil, came out to see me accompanied by the nurse with whom I had spoken just a short time earlier in Del's room. The doctor appeared to be of Middle Eastern descent. His English was perfect, though touched by an accent that revealed that it was not his native language. He looked around the waiting room and asked, "Where has your family all gone?" I told him most had gone home for the night and my daughter and her husband were downstairs getting breakfast. He looked at his watch and said, "This won't wait." He sat down beside me and said, "Your husband will not survive this incident. We have done all that we know to do to bring him back to you, but he has grown much worse overnight and his organs are shutting down." He waited for only a moment to allow me to process what he had just told me before continuing. "I am going to ask you to sign a DNR (do not resuscitate) directive. If his heart stops, it would just be cruel to start it again."

It felt as though all the oxygen had been sucked out of the room. I sadly shook my head, tears beginning to form as I said, "Del already signed one of those. He has a living will and health care directive that states that we are not to use heroic measures to sustain him if there is no reasonable belief that he will be able to live without the support of artificial means." I choked out the words, having rehearsed them in my head over and over during the night, hoping never to speak them aloud.

"Your husband must really love you and your family to have signed such a directive," he offered compassionately. "I have never seen any family fight harder than yours did to hold on to someone. It was a beautiful thing to watch, but it is the right thing to let him go peacefully." I was touched by his thoughtful words, but the severity of them washed over me like a pounding wave. The Lord was my banner and I felt Him holding back the waters so that I could breathe, but my head was barely above the waterline. Bethany and A.J. walked back into the room. My daughter began to cry out in utter agony. The sound of her heartbreak was one of the most painful sounds I have ever heard. If anguish has a sound, it was embodied in her response to the news that her daddy was slipping away from us. We called all of the children and told them to come to the hospital immediately. They all began to gather, and I went back to be with Del.

The things your mind does during these times are astonishing. Something within me kicked into overdrive, and I began to see things very clearly. I was lifted into a place where I felt as though I had superpowers. There were things that would need to be taken care of regarding this transition. One of them was that I knew I needed someone with me when I stood beside Del and watched him take his last breath. I told Joel, "I know you promised your dad that you wouldn't come into his hospital room, but I really do think he would forgive you if you stood with me as he goes."

Joel's response was amazing. He said, "I actually told Dad that I wouldn't agree to that because if we ever came to a time like this, I wouldn't just be there for him, I would be there for you too." I was astonished and relieved at this news. He hadn't shared it with me the previous day but had waited until I reached out for the support. Joel had been with Del and his family when Del's mom passed away three years earlier. It seemed fitting to have him with me. I also asked to have Del's eldest brother, Dennis Teel, with me for those last moments. They both agreed and joined me by Del's side.

The technicians waited until we had assembled to begin to unplug each of the machines that had been artificially supporting Del's body. The cardiologist who had performed the surgery on Del the previous morning came into the room and checked Del's eyes. He told me that he felt Del had been brain dead since the previous morning following the initial heart attack. "When Mr. Teel was first admitted yesterday, his pupils were dilated to the point that we considered that he might be beyond our help. We thought that, perhaps, it was the extraordinary number of drugs that were used during his initial resuscitation to which he was responding. Not knowing for certain, we did put forth our best effort to give him every chance to come back around. That being said, I do believe your husband has been brain dead since yesterday." I felt as though he was sharing this information to reinforce that we were making the right decision in ceasing further life support. That statement was consistent with what I had seen the previous day when I felt as though Del's spirit had left his body. Joel's feeling as if Del's spirit was inside our house when he had gone there the night before was likely quite accurate, as I had felt he had truly left us that morning in the lobby of the hospital when his body had fallen like a tree being felled.

Del's death, as recorded by officials on that date, didn't come loudly or with any fanfare. I held his left hand as we watched the monitors. This left hand was the hand that had worn a wedding ring, reflecting his marriage covenant with me. His hands had given me such joy and strength. His hands had nursed our children when they were hurt and had folded in prayer to ask for God's blessings. These were the hands that had stroked my head when I gave birth to each of our four children and had comforted me when I lost our fifth child. These were hands of love. These were hands of diligence. As I stood beside him on this day of transition from my world to another, unseen world, I understood that it would be the last time I was going to feel warmth in his hands on this side of Heaven. I heard Joel's quivering voice, somewhere in the distant fog of my thoughts, say, "That's it. He's gone."

"How do you know?" I asked uncertainly, as his statement brought me back to the finality of this sacred moment. I just couldn't comprehend that this was really the end, and he had slipped away so quietly. He was a gentle soul in life and in death.

I asked the medical staff, who had been monitoring him for so many hours of this vigil, if they could keep his body warm long enough for my other children to join us. I wanted them to have an opportunity to say goodbye if they so desired, now that Del was gone and we would not be violating his wishes. There were only two attendants in the room at that point. One was the nurse who had joined the doctor a short time earlier to deliver the dreadful news that Del wasn't coming back to us. The other was a young man who shared that he, too, had lost his father only a few weeks earlier. They assured us that they would take away all of the cords and tubes and clean Del up and bring us back inside to say goodbye again, without the trappings of the artificial machinery that had kept us from drawing near to him previously.

We left the room and assembled back in the larger waiting room where friends and family had gathered once again. I asked each of the children if they wanted to go back inside and touch their dad one last time. Jeremy, my youngest at twenty-five years of age, expressed a desire to do so, but Bethany and my eldest, Nathan, decided to only come outside the room where his body would be waiting and not come inside with us. Pastor Mark joined us for this poignant moment.

As we entered the room, Pastor Mark went to the top of the bed where I had held my vigil for more than twenty-four hours. Mark stands at over six feet tall. He is prematurely gray but has the huge brown eyes and enchanting smile of a young boy. When faced with sadness, a sweetness envelops him that speaks of the hope of Heaven. He anointed Del's head with oil and kissed him on his forehead. He then said, in that beautiful Australian accent of his, "It is my honor to grieve with your family, brother. You are leaving such a legacy and it is my honor to grieve with them." I saw tears begin to swell in his eyes as he made this beautiful and bittersweet gesture. He didn't know Del well, except through the connection he felt through God's Spirit. Joel, Jeremy, Pastor Mark, and I stood there for some time, drinking in the moment. In the hallway outside of this room stood the rest of our family. They all wept, as did we. After a time, the sounds of sobbing and the need to comfort my other children caused me to turn to the hallway to share in their sorrow. I turned away from Del's earthly vessel, knowing this was the last time I would touch his warm flesh. My heart felt as though it had been turned inside out.

As I stepped into the hallway to join my grieving family, I was astonished to see that there was a beautiful tray of elaborate food prepared and waiting for us. (This is a gesture of benevolence that the hospital staff and volunteers do for the family of those who have passed. The staff said they could take it into the larger waiting room to share with those who were there to support us. I agreed it would be fitting.) I was so touched by this simple act of kindness and comfort. It was the beginning of such strange contrasts for me during my grief journey. The understanding by those who have traveled this road before us that we would still need to have sustenance in the midst of our grief, and the knowledge that none of us would have our wits about us enough to do anything to address that need had prompted this very kind deed. The beauty of this gesture, so perfectly thoughtful and precious, was at war with the atrocity that prompted its necessity.

Standing outside his room, as Del had taken his last breath, a sweet melody began to play over the public speaker system within the hospital; a lullaby signaled that a new baby had just been born into the world. The hospital played it softly to alert the world that a new life had just arrived on the planet. I wondered if Del's and the new baby's spirits passed one another in the halls, as Del was leaving and the little one was coming into the world.

As we returned to the larger waiting room, condolences were shared, and we formed ideas about our next steps. Death interrupts all of your plans. Death trumps other engagements, reducing that which was seemingly urgent into the category of trivial. Death creates chaos, yet it is all a part of the cycle of life. Somehow, through the fog of grief and disbelief, there are decisions that must be made and plans that have to be executed. Who will prepare his body for burial? Where will his remains be laid to rest? How will we pay for this expense? And how, standing in the center of anguish my heart has never known before this moment, am I supposed to make these kinds of decisions with any level of competence or certainty that I am doing the right thing? Normally, Del is the one we would have turned to for counsel regarding such weighty matters. He wasn't here any longer. This was the beginning of a journey that would have us leaning into our Heavenly Father's arms as never before.

The prayers of saints around the globe carried us through the hours that followed in a way that was tangible. There is no other explanation but that of supernatural grace that spread like a blanket over us to help guide us. As those assembled at the hospital asked, "What can we do to help?" I had a clarity so succinct and so otherworldly, it can only be described as supernatural.

Turning to my sister-in-law, Diane Teel, I asked, "Could you get a cleaning service to come and clean my house before my family begins to arrive?" The words had barely left my lips before she was on the task. Several of Diane's close family members had passed in recent years, and she was acutely aware of both the emotional and physical support that would be needed in the coming days. I was thankful for her assistance and the absolute knowledge that she wouldn't rest until she had someone assigned to the task.

I asked others assembled to help Bethany hire a moving company and a truck to facilitate moving her and A.J. out of my house, on that day, to their new house. "What would you think of having your things moved today so that we can have a place for family to come and stay at my house and your new house too?" I asked her, as we started making plans for our next steps in the process. Bethany seemed relieved.

"Yes. I need to stay busy," she agreed. "Some of my best friends are here with me and we have plenty of support to make this happen," she concluded. A short time later, my family overheard Bethany calling the moving company that she had scheduled to move her that following weekend. "Yeah. I need some assistance today. My dad just died on me...without my permission. So, yeah. I am going to need to make some changes to our schedule." In true Teel fashion, she was trying to make light of the most devastating loss of her young life, for her words were tinged with both humor and bitterness.

Jeremy and Elizabeth (Bess) were walking behind her. In disbelief, Bess exclaimed with a small bit of humor herself, "Did she just say what I think she said?"

To which Jeremy replied, "Yep, I believe she did." He knew the heaviness his sister was feeling, and he recognized her attempt to immerse herself in the task before her, rather than succumb to the waves of grief that were trying to carry her under. She was attempting to live up to her name. She was doing all that she knew to do to bring hope to the horror that was now unfolding for all of us. If infusing hope meant moving her earthly location from one house to another on the same day that her father was moving from his earthly home to his Heavenly home, she would roll up her sleeves and set her mind and heart to the task.

Bethany and A.J. had sold their previous house that February and had planned to buy another one right away. Instead, they had put in offer after offer and had been unable to secure a new residence. We had invited them to stay with us while they found a new place. I was a real estate professional and knew that it was just a matter of time before we found the right home. Instead, it became comical how the doors kept slamming shut. In the meantime, they stayed with us. At one point, they had decided to build a new house, and we had agreed to have them stay during construction.

After an amazing foreclosure became available and they won the bid, Bethany and A.J. abandoned the plan to build and just awaited the closing date on the gently used residence instead. Little did we know, that those precious eight months would give Bethany the gift of time with her dad and give her husband the gift of getting to know his father-by-love in a way that would have been more difficult had we not been sharing the same space for those eight months. They had planned to make the transition into their new home that weekend but, with many people coming to be with us during this time, we would need the extra house to lodge them. I also knew that my daughter, whose love for me is fierce and unrelenting, would have a hard time moving out of the house and leaving me alone. Intuitively, I knew that the best thing I could do for Bethany on this day of profound loss was to give her a task to put her hand to and a place to call her own. My instincts were rewarded when Bethany called me later that day and told me about an experience she had in the backyard of her new home that would bring me assurance I had done the right thing in insisting that she move on that day. (The details of her Divine encounter are revealed in Chapter Two.)

As news of our loss reached my family in our hometown of St. Louis, my youngest sister, Linda Mason, posted the following on her Facebook page:

October 10, 2013

Despite our prayers and pleading with him to hang on, Del decided to go on and be with Jesus today. He has been a part of my life as long as I can remember.

At age five, I decided that he was the perfect man. He was funny, handsome, caring, giving, and always gentle with his words. He loved God and adored my big sister. He was the measure I would use to compare every other man, from that day forward. My sister was the luckiest girl in the world! While growing up, I spent summers laughing until my sides hurt at his countless puns and silly jokes, forever trying my best to understand that engineer language he spoke. And watching him shamelessly flirt with my sister. All the while, learning what true love looked like. Then, one day, I met James. Finally, a man who could stand up to the "Del" ruler. And, would you believe it, they spoke the same language? Through the years, our families have spent wonderful holidays and vacations together; all of which have included countless hours talking, laughing, and mining for moments. I have a lifetime of memories, and all because he taught me that life truly is not measured by the breaths you take but by the moments that take your breath away.

And, yes, laughing until you can't breathe counts. I can't wait to see him in Heaven and watch those shoulders shake with laughter. So, until we meet again, my childhood hero, my brother, my friend...

Chapter Two: Preparing for Farewell

I can't remember how I got home from the hospital that afternoon. I just know that I somehow found myself back in the bedroom of my home and I needed a shower and a space to cry that wasn't in the presence of anyone but God. As I walked past my bed, I grimaced at the thought that I would be sleeping in it alone from now on. Walking straight into my bedroom closet, I put my arms around Del's clothes and began to sob, taking in deep breaths and trying to fill my senses with his fragrances still lingering there. I wondered how long that fragrance would last. How many days, weeks, or months would I have this place of refuge to go to and still feel him near me?

I managed to push myself into the shower. I remembered a scene from the movie *The Big Chill* in which one of the characters had powered herself through the process of a funeral for someone with whom she had a deep connection. Afterwards, while others visited in her house and she was left to the solitude of her shower, she allowed her tears to mingle with the water and released the waves of sorrow that came rushing over her. I repeated that scene in the privacy of my bathroom, weeping in exhaustion and immeasurable anguish.

After my shower, Joel and Laura arrived with our two granddaughters, Leah and Cadie. Leah was a somber and thoughtful five-year-old. Her sister, Cadie, was only two months shy of her second birthday. Joel and Laura wanted me to tell the girls about their Grandpa Del's passing. They all gathered in my bathroom, sitting on the floor beside my dressing table. I had managed to shower but had not been able to get through my entire routine. My hair was still wet. I kept trying to put my makeup on, only to cry it all off again. How do you tell your precious grandchildren that their Grandpa Del would not be a part of their lives in a physical way any longer? Would they truly grasp the concept of death? I knew Cadie was too young to understand. Leah, on the other hand, would comprehend it to some degree. I just didn't know to what extent. I started with a question, "Leah, do you know what has been going on with your Grandpa Del?"

She was very solemn as she nodded her little head and said, "Yes. He has been in the hospital because he was sick."

"Yes. That's right. Well, he was very, very sick. The doctors did everything they could to help him, but they couldn't fix his heart. Grandpa went to Heaven this morning." My words were measured and felt so completely inadequate. They sounded hollow and far too trite for the significance of what I was attempting to communicate. "He is now with Jesus and with your little brother, Marcus." (Joel and Laura had lost a son to miscarriage when Leah was a toddler. She understood the concept of death and separation from someone you love, to a degree. I wanted to put it in such a way that she would be able to picture her Grandpa Del playing with her little brother. The vision of Del playing with Marcus was comforting to me and I hoped it would comfort her as well.) "So, even though we won't be able to see him anymore or touch him, he will still be in our hearts and he will still be looking down on us from Heaven. Do you understand?"

Her little head, covered with fiery red hair, merely nodded in response, taking it all in and processing the words she had just heard. Suddenly, the full weight of this revelation hit her little heart. Turning into the arms of her parents, Leah began sobbing with great heartbreak. Cadie didn't understand what was happening, but she went over to her big sister and said, "I sorry, Leah. I so, so sorry!" She didn't know what she was trying to comfort her big sister over, but she knew that things had just gone terribly wrong. We all wept, once again, each of us going into our own internal rooms and trying to find a way to make sense of our loss. We grasped for anything that would help us to cope and continue to function.

Laura said, "Cadie is saying she is sorry because usually when Leah cries, it is because of something Cadie has done." We smiled at the thought that Cadie was apologizing for something she did not do, but felt the need to do so, just in case this was somehow her fault.

Around that time, someone came into my room and said that we had visitors who had just come to offer condolences to us and share in our grief. It was too soon for my heart. I just couldn't face anyone outside of this intimate group who shared Del's DNA and his life. Although protocol may have demanded that we arise and greet those who had come, my heart and soul could not be moved to attend to those actions in that moment. I just shook my head in protest and said, "I just can't!" My family departed to convey the message that I wasn't receiving guests quite yet and to thank them for their kindness in coming to offer their support. I needed time. "How much time?" I wondered. "When would I be able to see anyone outside of this safe haven and cope in a coherent manner?" I found grief, in that moment, to be exceptionally selfish and demanding in its own way. I was too weary to fight the torrent of emotions.

The children left me to finish getting dressed for whatever this day would mandate. I continued to converse with God in the solitude of those moments through prayer and meditating upon His Word. I recited Psalm 23, "The Lord is my Shepherd. I shall not want..." To my amazement, a peace began to flow over me, and a resolve began to arise. I felt a bubble of grace permeate the atmosphere. The prayers of the saints in Heaven and on earth were carrying me, supernaturally, through each moment. I began to push through the rest of the day, moving toward a dreaded appointment. Eventually, decisions were going to have to be made about what we referred to as Del's "earth suit" and how we would properly bring honor to his memory. Preparations needed to be completed for the arrival of friends and family who were coming from our home state of Missouri.

While some of my family were gathered at our home, Bethany and her husband were busily moving their possessions from their storage unit and the room that had, for the past eight months, housed them with her dad and me. Many friends came to gather around them and make the task lighter. Bethany's sorrow was intensified by the knowledge that her dad would not get to see her new home and give his approval. As she moved through the process of unpacking and setting up her house for the family she would be accommodating the next day, she opened the birthday card she had been given on her birthday just a few days earlier. She had saved it to read later because she had wanted to read it when she was alone and savor the message she knew her dad would have written within. She felt as though the words he had penned within the card were prophetic, as if he were telling her what was coming.

"Happy, Happy, Happy Birthday, my daughter! You have been stretched a bit this year, but that's okay. It was to prepare you for the year ahead. You are stronger, wiser, more empathetic...May you be a grace and HOPE dispenser during this 30th year! Love, Dad."

A flood of emotions swept over her, and she stepped out onto her new patio to gather her thoughts and quiet the storm she was feeling. Then, a little to her right and a few yards away, Bethany saw something wondrous.

Bethany's new home backed up to a large pond with a huge water fountain in the center. She was particularly looking forward to sharing this feature with her dad who loved ponds. As she stepped out to have a quiet moment of reflection and listen to the sound of the moving water, she saw her dad at the edge of her yard overlooking the pond. She froze in awe and wonder, taking in the sight that Heaven was granting. Her dad had his back to her. In this vision, he was wearing blue jeans and a red checkered shirt, clothing, that in the past, had always made him look cheerful and ready for an adventure. She could only see his profile as he was looking up at someone to his left. He was smiling and talking in a most animated fashion and nodding his head in approval. His face reflected joy and peace. She couldn't hear his words or see the person to whom he was speaking but, in that moment, she knew he had seen her new home and was stopping by on the way there to let her know that she had his approval. It was a splendid gift to her heart. She wanted to go and hug him, but the vision vanished, leaving only its memory to embrace and to share with all of us at a later time. A Heavenly visitation from her dad was just one of the many Divine hugs that we would experience in the unfolding of Del's departure.

That evening, my youngest son and his wife went into my bedroom and turned down the covers. Unbeknownst to Jeremy and Elizabeth, this act of kindness was a nightly ritual Del and I shared. If he came to bed before me, he would turn back my covers for me and remove the abundance of pillows we had at the head of the bed when it was fully made. Joel and Jeremy had scattered yellow Post-it notes throughout my bedroom and bathroom with sweet messages to warm my heart in the lonely hours they knew would lie before me. As everyone else left, Jeremy and Elizabeth stayed behind, insisting that they weren't leaving until I was under the covers and sleeping soundly. As I lay there that evening, my thoughts wandered to what life would be like totally alone. I had never lived alone. I had gone from the cover of my father's house to live with my step-grandmother just before I turned seventeen. My parents had relocated, and I had remained in the school district where we had lived most of my life. (I only had four months of high school to complete before I graduated.) Del and I were married just after I finished high school, so I had never lived alone. I couldn't contemplate that fact for too long, as exhaustion overtook me, and I fell into a troubled sleep.

The next morning, I awakened to the task that I had dreaded. My dear friend, Kathy East, came to join me for what I had to do that day. Kathy and I had met in a church Del and I had attended when we first moved to Charlotte. She had one of the most beautiful singing voices I had ever heard outside of a music studio. We had served on worship teams together throughout the years. We had spent many hours together as our children were younger, learning how to parent. We had visited one another's hometowns to meet our families—hers in West Virginia and mine in Missouri. She had been woven into the fabric of my life and had loved Del dearly. She had been beside me during the vigil at the hospital. She had been there when I made the decision to have a certain, well-known, funeral company take possession of Del's body to prepare it for burial. Kathy had arranged to go there with my family that morning and make final preparations for his viewing and life celebration.

When we arrived at the appointed mortuary that morning, we were escorted into a room with samples of urns, funeral program stationery, and other trappings of the industry. A funeral director, dressed in a somber business suit and wearing an equally somber demeanor, greeted us and we began the dreaded task of making final arrangements. Not certain of the proper protocol, but wanting desperately to know where they had taken Del, I asked, "Is my husband here in this facility now?" I didn't know if his body had been prepared yet, but I knew that they should have had ample time to have taken him from the hospital, and I wondered where he was. The evening before, as I had wrestled with sleep, I wondered what was being done with him.

I was shocked when the gentleman replied, "Your husband's remains have been taken to a processing center." He named the location, which was an extremely undesirable area of our city on the west side, typically known as an industrial and blighted area. To learn that Del's body was not located in this small town of Mint Hill (only about three miles from me) but had been taken to a remote location across town, was my undoing. I was simultaneously angered and dismayed by the words, "processing center." The thought that I had entrusted something so sacred to these people who had treated it so callously was almost too much to bear. I had a hard time focusing during the process of making all the other choices that were required of me. The unsettled feeling that I had already chosen badly by having what I now perceived to be an incompetent provider take possession of Del's body left me feeling defeated. We made the preliminary arrangements with the funeral home and then headed to the place where Del's remains would be interred.

One of the greatest gifts to me in this involuntary mission to which I was sent was the fact that Del and I had already discussed where we would wish to be buried at the end of our days on earth. One day, we had been out exploring a rural area of North Carolina, just outside the city of Charlotte. During our explorations, we came across the most unusual cemetery either of us had ever seen. The grounds were tucked back in the woods and looked more like an enchanted forest than your typical burial place. We had driven through the hallowed soil of this sacred space and I had ventured to ask him where, within the graveyard, he would prefer to be laid to rest. There were a few flat monuments made of bronze and a few raised mausoleums. The loveliest places were those made of stone and etched with loving epitaphs to those who had departed. Del and I had both expressed the desire to be laid beneath the canopy of trees in the monument section of the cemetery.

When we drove to the offices of the burial ground, we learned that it was operated by a funeral home directly across the street from where we intended to lay Del's earth suit to rest. As we walked inside, the paint was a cheerful yellow and there were large brass, gleaming light fixtures. The Williamsburg-style interior décor greeted me with a sense of comfort and elegance, and it felt like a home. There were live, colorful birds in the foyer singing their songs of praise. Del would have been fascinated both by their beauty and their song. I felt like I was visiting a mixture of our present house and our timeshare townhouse in Williamsburg, Virginia where we had been vacationing every spring for several years. We had amassed an abundance of sweet memories in Williamsburg, a fact which made this place immediately evoke a precious sentiment. A great sense of what is known as "buyer's remorse" overtook me when I saw where we could have had Del's life celebration service if only I had known this was an option.

I turned to Kathy and said, "Oh, I love this place. It feels so much better to me than the place we just left." She agreed. "I wish I had known this was an option. But maybe it isn't? It is so beautiful and likely a lot more expensive," I mused.

"You know what?" she said, "We won't know if we don't ask."

We went into the offices to discuss what our needs were going to be for the interment. My beloved friend got up and went to inquire if we could arrange to have Del's body brought to this new place and cancel the other plans. She came back smiling. "They said they do it all the time. It is no problem," she assured me.

I turned to Robert, the compassionate young man who was going to help us pick a burial plot. "Do you know how your rates compare to the rates of the funeral home that has his body now?" I asked. The question seemed a cold one to ask, but I knew my husband's desire to not be unwise over his final arrangements. He had always joked with me about being thrown into an old pine box. I didn't want to be irrational in my grief and make more mistakes, as I felt I had made by having the other funeral director prepare his body.

"We are a family owned and operated business," he said. "The other place is a corporately-owned entity. I think you will find that we are significantly less expensive than our competition," Robert assured me with a sympathetic smile. I was hopeful as he started sharing his packages with us and we determined that, indeed, it was thousands less and the quality of service far exceeded what we had planned to experience with the other funeral service. I was so thankful for the boldness of my friend to take matters into her hands when she sensed how much better this place fit our needs and our desires than the former one. How gracious our Father God was to provide a friend who came alongside and contributed her strength and wisdom when we were too distraught to navigate these uncharted waters.

After we settled on the funeral arrangements, my heart was lifted. I could feel that grace bubble surrounding me once more. We headed across the street to determine where we wanted to pick a family plot. My son Joel said, "Where did Dad always want to sit when we went to church?"

I laughed and said, "Toward the front right and as far over as he could be so nobody could sit beside him, and he could escape without disturbing anyone."

"Okay," he rationalized. "Let's find that spot here in this place."

Robert said, "I know just the place." The young funeral director led us up the hill and toward the edge of the forest. He was warm and engaging but filled with compassion as he shared the wisdom of this option and his vast experience in helping families deal with loss. "If you choose this place, nothing will ever be placed beside him. This boundary is as far as we plan to develop this side of the grounds. The forest beside this is not conducive to placing more grave sites. We will be leaving this as a green space. Nobody will ever be buried beside your dad if we put him on the edge of the forest as far right as possible," he said as he looked toward Joel.

"You know," I said, "It occurs to me that your dad always slept on the right side of the bed, so I will be laid to rest one day to his left, just as I always have in life." This decision was another small comfort. We all agreed it was perfect and Del would approve. His only neighbors would be the wildlife to his right. It was the perfect place for my privacy-loving, introverted husband.

We returned home, and my son Jeremy began to reach out to Del's coworkers who were scattered in offices in Boston, New York, Ohio, and France. Del had spoken with his scattered coworkers frequently by phone, but they were rarely physically in one another's presence. He had worked for IBM for most of his career but had retired from IBM in 2010 after thirty-five years of service and started working for a French company, Dassault Systemes. This change caused him to have a wide array of international coworkers and a cross-cultural community to which he was learning to adapt

A dear friend of mine, Cheryl Yutzy, lived about an hour north of me in Mooresville, North Carolina. She had been unable to be with me during the time we had held our vigil in the hospital, but she called and said she was coming to stay with me until my parents and siblings arrived. She said she was going to sleep beside me that night so that I wouldn't be alone in bed, adrift in a sea of sorrow. I was so touched by her offer. She packed her bags and told her husband she was staying with me as long as I needed her. This loving sacrifice of hers prompted me to do something that would have otherwise been excruciatingly painful. I decided I needed to wash my sheets in preparation for her coming. As I stripped my bed and headed to throw the bedding into the wash, I was sad and glad, simultaneously. I viewed her arrival as a gift that gave me the courage to do what may have otherwise taken much longer, but it was also speeding up the process of letting go of the familiar. Del always kept a handkerchief in his pocket. I took one from his dresser drawer, doused it with his aftershave, and put it under my pillow to remind me of his fragrance as a consolation for washing his fragrance from my sheets.

That night, as Cheryl and I lay in the dark, I rehearsed all the events that had unfolded over the past forty-eight hours. She listened compassionately as I felt the full weight of the words I was sharing. Del was gone.... I was a widow.... Life was never going to be the same.... God is good.... His love has been steadfast.... He has seen me through this storm thus far, and He will see me through to the end of this life.... I miss my husband.... How in the world am I going to do life without him?

As each evening passed and a new morning dawned, I was in awe that the world hadn't stopped turning. The sun was still shining, and birds were chirping. The squirrels scurried around the lawn, collecting their nuts and burying them in secret hiding places. People were still going about their business as if they didn't realize that one of the most precious gifts ever bequeathed to this planet had been called back to his Maker. One of Del's favorite songs had been "Did the Lilies Cry to Say Goodbye to You?" The lyrics ask the question regarding the death of Christ. The notion that creation was aware, even if humanity was not, that a great sorrow had come upon the earth, was compelling to him. I thought of that song on this new morning as I prepared for the arrival of my family from Missouri and continued working on Del's homegoing celebration. I tried to focus only on the task before me and keep my mind off the unanswered questions about what our future would hold. My steadfast hope was that, although I didn't know what the days ahead would look like, I knew my Father in Heaven already held all of my days in His hands. That hope sustained me.

Chapter Three: The Gathering

The evening of the visitation and receiving of friends and family (to express their condolences and support) arrived. I had some private time with Del for a few moments before inviting others within the sacred space of this hushed atmosphere that evening. Del's body was lovingly prepared for burial, and each of the items selected for his send-off was chosen for its special significance. I had brought a favorite navy-blue suit for him to wear. His dress shirt was a robin's egg blue color that he had favored for special occasions. My one regret about that choice was that his lovely eyes were now closed in repose and one couldn't see just how well the color of the shirt brought out the color of his eyes. I knew he wasn't there, but I studied his every feature intently, trying to emblazon it into my memory. I studied his long eyelashes and thought about the story of how he had been playing with fireworks as a child and had singed them off, to his mother's horror, only to have them grow back even longer and thicker. I studied his hands, flashing back to a similar scene when his dad was taken to Heaven twenty-one years earlier. I had studied the rugged beauty in the hands of Del's father, Delbert Lewis Teel Sr. His hands told a story of how he had loved and provided for his family of nine for so many years. He had toiled at raising a garden to feed his family. He had toiled at raising a Godly seed by modeling what it was like to live a life of devotion to his Heavenly Father, following after the precepts he had learned from reading God's Word in Holy Scripture. He had folded those hands in prayer and had often tenderly placed his hands upon his children and grandchildren and lifted up prayers of intercession for them while on the earth. I could hear the echo of Dad Teel's sweet voice saying, "I sure do love you!" Even now in this hour of loss, I could hear Dad Teel's tender words.

Del had followed in his father's footsteps. His hands weren't filled with the calluses that his father had boasted. Del had made his living and provided for his family through the use of that beautiful mind of his, but his hands had been a source of strength and comfort for me and for his family, just as his fathers had been to him. Del had still mourned his dad and had just been talking about missing him a few days before he, himself, was taken home to be with his Heavenly Father and his earthly father and mother. All of the saints who had gone before Del were now welcoming him to his true home in Heaven. The Bible refers to those faithful saints who have crossed over as the "cloud of witnesses" (Hebrews 12:1). Del was now in that cloud. He would now only be a witness to our lives here on earth.

As a part of the tribute to Del, we left small, white index cards on tables throughout the funeral home on which people could write messages to Del. His sudden death had left people feeling like they had things they wanted to say to him. Because Del always had a pocketful of cards like these to take down notes, we left them for people to write their messages. We then placed the cards inside his suit-coat pocket. The children wrote the possible names of his future grandchildren. Others just wrote their goodbye notes to him.

Instead of a standard guest book, we scattered engineering notebooks throughout the venue to allow folks to leave messages for Del's family. Del kept a library of engineering notebooks to help him jot down thoughts about work and record his personal musings. Seeing Del with one of his notebooks at a gathering of colleagues on one occasion, a coworker had once asked him, "Can I touch it?" nodding toward the notebook Del kept tightly within his grip. "I feel like it is the Holy Grail. Maybe I can get some of your genius inside my head if I touch it." Del had been humbled by the words and by being the object of good humor, but he had held those sacred journals close to him. I had known that Del kept notes inside the scrolls about important dates, such as his vacation days. Anytime I couldn't remember an important date or when we had something done at the house, I knew that I could pinpoint the approximate time and go to Del to have him look it up in one of his journals. Until his death, I had never intruded into the privacy or perceived sanctity of the contents of any of the pages. Now, however, we were finding that we had to look within the pages of his personal journal to seek out answers to passwords and encrypted messages to access important information.

Each of us was amazed as we glanced through the pages. First, we were looking for answers to specific questions about passwords but, as we perused the contents, we were hungrily searching for a new message from the pages. We longed for a new point of connection with the one to whom we had so often turned for wisdom and counsel. We saw within the books, which spanned over two decades, notes such as, "Joel got his driver's license today!" "Jan returns from St. Louis today," "Nathan begins Lee College," "Bethany got engaged!" "Jeremy graduates UNCC today!" "It's a girl! Leah was born!" "Cadie was born today!" Most of the personal notes were written in the margins of his journals, while the majority of the notes inside were work-related. One of our sons remarked, upon pouring through the pages, "Dad lived his life in the margins!" The observations were both interesting and poignant.

Del loved bottled mocha Frappuccinos. We would buy a case at a time for him from Costco. He referred to them as his "brown juice." In honor of his homegoing, we had placed iced mochas throughout the venue for guests to drink in honor of him. As I saw the mourners carrying their little bottles throughout the evening, I flashed back to a scene that had happened just a few weeks earlier in our kitchen.

I was standing at the kitchen island with my head down, studying real estate documents, when Del passed through on his way to my office to get one of his bottles from a small fridge we kept specifically for his mocha collection. He stopped, turned toward me, and pointed at me with an intense look in his eyes. "Janet Lynn," he said, "I love you!" He had said the words often enough before, but something made me freeze frame this dialogue as if my brain were taking a small video clip of the interaction and my spirit was saying, "This is important. You are going to need to remember this moment."

I pushed all other thoughts aside, pointed my finger back at him, and responded, "I love you, Delbert Lewis Teel! I love everything about you! I love your smile. I love your eyes. I love your ways!" He quietly chuckled, his shoulders shaking slightly as he turned to continue his task of retrieving his cold treat. I stood there wondering what made this moment different than any other of our ongoing flirtations and affirmations. Something inside of me was telling me this interaction was important. I needed to remember this precious interlude. The thought of that sweet moment came back to me, softly caressing my memory, as I interacted with those who had come to comfort us on this evening of visitation.

I shared this memory with Bethany and she too had been in a similar moment with her dad in the kitchen. The interaction had happened just a few weeks earlier when her dad said, "Can I have a hug?" as he was walking through in the middle of a task and saw her standing there.

"Of course!" came her quick reply. As he held her for a few moments, something in her heart told her this was different. She lingered a little longer, trying to push away the thought that this might be a goodbye hug. There had been other instances where she felt he was trying to prepare her for his possible departure. She would encourage him to take better care of himself. "I need you to be around a long time. My kids are going to need to know their Grandpa Del!"

Del would look at her, somewhat regretfully, and say, "I have lived a good life. I have been really blessed."

She would respond with, "Say, 'So far,' Dad! 'I have lived a good life—so far!' I am going to need you to be around a long time." A wistful look would cross his face and she would be left with an uneasy feeling that he was not going to be around as long as she would have hoped. Her brothers had partaken in similar conversations with their dad. She felt that a part of him knew that he would leave us prematurely and he was doing all he knew to manage our expectations, just as he would do in his nightly ritual with me.

There were groups gathered throughout the funeral home that evening sharing stories, jokes, and memories, listening to Del's family as they recounted their own shock at the suddenness of his departure. Some were quietly weeping; others were laughing at the retelling of one of Del's silly puns or at the shenanigans of Del's comedy-inclined sons. At one point during the evening, Del's sister-in-law, Diane Teel, came to me and had me sit down, asking me to close my eyes and listen to all of the sounds coming from the gathering in that place of mourning and sadness. She said, "Do you hear the laughter and the sadness, the quiet voices and the loud ones?" I nodded. She continued, "All of these sounds are rising into the atmosphere and going into Heaven where each sound is a musical note. The musical notes are all rising and coming together and forming a beautiful composition that is Del's song." Del loved music, especially well-written compositions. The notion of this musical composition floating Heavenward brought me comfort.

The next day I would be presented with a song written by one of the music directors at our local church, Cheryl Vought. She called her new composition, "Del's Song." Having never heard the conversation I had with Diane that evening, Cheryl had simply sought the Lord early the next morning about the music she would perform for Del's homegoing service. Father God gave her this new worship song. She presented me with the words and music after the service only one day after Diane had made this declaration.

During the time we were receiving those who had come to comfort us, I looked up and saw two familiar faces in the crowd that made my heart swell with gratitude. While Del and I had lived in Lexington, Kentucky from 1974-1981, we had many folks in transition live with us. Del would say, "Sometimes people need a bridge to get from point A to point B and we can be that bridge." Two such roommates were Vicky Miller and Kathy Crawford. Vicky had moved from Kansas following a brief engagement to one of the members of a musical group called *The Living Sound*. She had followed him during his transition from ministering to a career in music. Although they remained good friends, they had broken their engagement and Vicky had stayed with us for about eighteen months, directing the nonprofit daycare center that was run by our local church. During this time, her good friend Kathy had moved in as well. Kathy was one of the musicians at our local church and a cherished friend to Vicky. She had introduced Vicky to the man who would become her husband. We became empty nesters after their great companionship, but we loved that God had woven us into the tapestry of their lives for however brief a season. We had not been together since Del and I left Kentucky in 1981. We had stayed in touch over the years, but I hadn't physically seen Vicky since then. Kathy had managed to visit a couple of times from her home in Louisville, but Vicky had moved to Kansas, and we had never been able to coordinate a visit. These two faces before me, as I was receiving mourners that evening, were a particularly precious gift that brought me comfort in a special way.

Again, I was struck by the two forces that seem to be at war during mourning. The beauty of the love and connection that brought my friends to stand beside me in this hour of need stood alongside the sadness that this sudden loss is what it took to get us back in the same space. I was so delighted to see them but saddened that Del wasn't with us to bask in this reunion. Kathy and Vicky had been planning an outing together when the news reached them of our battle for Del's life and his subsequent death. Vicky had flown to Louisville and joined Kathy. Instead of following the itinerary they had been planning, they got into their car and drove from Louisville to be with us for Del's homegoing celebration. God sent them to me to help me during this time of mourning. They had known a different version of Del than many of those who had gathered around us in the years we had been in the Carolinas. They had known Del in the season of his beginnings. They had come to be witnesses to the legacy he had left behind far too soon. We would share some private time later that evening when they returned to our home and sat in Del's office chair to feel connected to him.

There was a grace that held me like an iron clamp during that evening. As I received family, friends, old neighbors, new neighbors, friends of my children, coworkers, real estate clients, and many others, I felt a peace that passes human understanding. I was thankful for all of the loving support. I never knew how much it means to those in mourning to have people come and present themselves before those who are facing loss to say, "I acknowledge that you have just suffered a great loss. I stand with you in this hour to declare that you are not alone and that you are justified in your sorrow." They don't say it in those words, of course. They say things like, "I am sorry for your loss," "He was such a good man," "We are praying for you," and "Let us know if you need anything." Some words were awkward and poorly chosen. Other words cut straight into my heart and offered a balm that was unspeakably kind. This experience taught me how important it is to those who suffer a great loss to have others simply be there. It isn't what one says, but the spirit they bring that offers hope.

By the time the evening was wrapping up, Del's family members had come from Missouri, Kentucky, and Wisconsin. My family had joined us from Missouri, as well. Everyone cooperated to find places for each person to stay, and I retreated back to my home to spend another night alone in our marriage bed, falling again into a fitful sleep and asking God to see me through another lonely night. I was so thankful that I hadn't fallen apart. I was thankful that His saints were holding all of us up in prayer. The waves of love from Heaven just enfolded me and carried me through until the early dawn.

Chapter Four: A Life Well-Lived

I awakened to the new day reflecting on what we were doing eight days before. Bethany and her husband, A.J., had been celebrating her thirtieth birthday in Orlando, Florida, but were coming back into town for a family gathering to mark the occasion that evening. We had planned a small party for her with some of her favorite people. We gathered at an Italian restaurant in Matthews called Fontanellas. We had chosen the place because they had a special party room. Bethany thought her immediate family, already a very large number, would be there to celebrate, but we also had added a few others to the mix. Our former pastor and his wife, Barry and Linda Taylor, our present pastor and his family, Mark and Julie Appleyard and their children (along with a favorite aunt who was visiting from Australia), and Bethany's best friends, Kurtis and Becky Dziki, all joined us to celebrate her special day. We pulled the tables together and put Del in the center, directly in front of where Bethany and A.J. would be seated. The evening was lovely and perfect, generously sprinkled with hilarious laughter as her big brother Nathan had shown up in his full Renaissance costume, still playing the character of Prince William of Wonka.

Nathan had been running late that evening and had called to say he would be stopping at his apartment to shower and change after having attended the second day of the opening weekend of his favorite event of the year, the Carolina Renaissance Fair. The fair is a place where one may step back in time to a period of knights and ladies, kings and queens, and is highlighted by jousting tournaments and crafts from the medieval period. There are many performers such as comedians, musicians, acrobats, and storytellers who help enhance the "RenFair" experience. I told him to just come dressed as he was because the children would all love it. His dad had never seen him wearing his costume or playing his character. Del had always avoided crowds and had never felt compelled to attend the local fair, known here as "Fairhaven." Nathan had been a fixture there for many years, where he acted as a "playtron" instead of merely a patron, or attendee, of the fair. The locals who develop a character and participate in enhancing the full medieval experience for others are known as playtrons, playing a recurring role and remaining in character. Nathan had formerly been known as Sir Milton of Bradley, games keeper of the royal court. He wore mesmerizing puppets that looked like real animals on his shoulders. He operated the puppets through a clever set of levers in his hand. Although he kept the puppets, he had exchanged the persona of games keeper for Prince William of Wonka, and became known to all the ladies of the court as the purveyor of chocolate confections. He carried chocolate Doves and chocolate Kisses in his apparel to share with the playtrons and the patrons, as well as the royal court.

I watched that evening as Del delighted in Nathan's storytelling and how he had held the youngsters captive with his enthralling jokes and the puppets on his shoulders that seemed to move independently of him. Nathan was reveling in the fact that his dad got to see why he loved doing this so much. We all laughed until our sides hurt.

On the days leading up to the funeral, Nathan had come to me with a concern related to his RenFair community. Some of the closest people in the world to him were in town for the Carolina RenFair season, but they didn't have the appropriate attire to wear to a funeral. They had their working clothes for setting up and breaking down their booths at the fair and their costumes to wear during the weekend of the fair, but nothing in between. I told him that he should tell them to come to the funeral in their costumes. Since we had never gotten his dad to come to Fairhaven, we would bring Fairhaven to him, just as Nathan had done on that evening of Bethany's birthday celebration. I told him he should dress in his costume as well so that all the RenFair players would feel a part of something that was supporting him. He was delighted to share the news with his RenFair friends and hoped that a few would accept the invitation to attend. I wished for the same thing as well.

I went into my closet and considered what to wear. Nathan had his costume and I truly longed to put on something other than my widow's garments. I remembered the scripture about donning "a garment of praise for a spirit of heaviness" (Isaiah 61:3). Sincerely wanting to celebrate Del's victory rather than my defeat, I had told everyone to wear something in the teal color. Del had rehearsed the term, "If you can't fix it, feature it!" to us so many times, that I had adapted the teal color in all of my real estate logos, cards, and signs. Although our last name was Teel, many thought it was Teal, so we just rolled with it. In his honor, most of my family opted to wear teal as a sign of solidarity. I had a closet full of it, but I wanted to choose something befitting the occasion. My older sister, Rebecca, cautioned me about wearing anything that I loved on that day because she was concerned that I would never wear it again since I would associate that garment with my sadness. Thankful for her counsel, I made my selection and prepared to move into the rest of my day.

I had asked one of our worship leaders, Cheryl Vought, to lead worship for the service that day. I didn't know that she, herself, had lost her dad just a few months before in an eerily similar way. I didn't know that she was paying it forward. The one song I knew I needed to hear first that day for Del's service was written beautifully by Katie and Bryan Torwalt. These words were my heart's cry for that day. I knew that this would set the atmosphere and invite the presence of God to permeate our service and our hearts in order to endure what we still had to face, not just on that day, but on those that would follow.

Holy Spirit

There's nothing worth more that will ever come close

Nothing can compare, You're our living Hope

Your presence, Lord

I have tasted and seen of the sweetest of loves

Where my heart becomes free and my shame is undone

Your presence, Lord

Holy Spirit, You are welcome here

Come flood this place and fill the atmosphere

Your glory, God, is what our hearts long for

To be overcome by Your presence, Lord

Let us become more aware of Your presence

Let us experience the glory of Your goodness

My family gathered around Del's earth suit one last time before the service that would mark the final tribute to his life. We each said our goodbyes in our own way. I was asked if I wanted a few minutes alone with him but declined because I felt that it would be difficult to tear myself away if I was left alone with him in those quiet moments before we headed out for his service.

Robert, the funeral director, lined us up to follow the casket out of the side room and through the hallway toward the chapel where the service was to be held. He looked at Nathan as he was arranging all of us and said, "I think you are going to be quite pleased." I thought this was an odd thing to say, solely to Nathan.

I was placed directly behind the casket. My dad stood beside me on my left and my granddaughter Leah held my right hand. We began our long walk behind Del's body in the procession. My head was down as I walked behind him, deep in thought and fighting hard not to sob out loud. Suddenly, as we rounded the corner, I saw a sea of color begin to bow as wheat in the wind. An array of brightly clad Renaissance Fair players, all wearing their regal finest, were bowing and curtseying as Del's casket came toward them. Now I understood what Robert had been trying to tell Nathan. Not only had his friends come, they had come en masse to pay tribute. Almost fifty of the players were represented, with Queen Bettina, a special friend of Nathan's and a fellow believer, right there in front. I left the procession and headed to her to offer my sincere thanks for the honor they were all paying to my husband and my son. Beside her stood the pirate king, Scott Spyglass, one of the most beloved of playtrons. He said, "Your son is a prince among us and that makes his dad a king. It is altogether fitting for us to be here to pay him this honor." I was humbled and amazed. As I returned to the procession, I thought about what it must have been like when Del entered Heaven's gates and was greeted by the courts of Heaven. I am sure Heaven applauded.

Walking down the aisle behind the attendants, I was thinking that the last time my dad and I had walked down the aisle of a church to join Del at the front had been our wedding day. Somewhere deep inside me, I cried out to Heaven, "This isn't the way it was supposed to happen. Del was supposed to be with me when I lost my dad. This is all wrong!" I remember thinking, maybe one day Dad can walk me down the aisle again to another love. Though a fleeting and far-off dream, the thought did cross my mind amid a torrent of others on that day.

Cheryl Vought and another dear friend, Lori Clifton, began to lead the congregation in worship and the Holy Spirit descended upon the room, filling our hearts with comfort and peace. My sons eulogized their dad, aided by a carefully crafted letter of tribute Bethany had written and gifted to Del the previous Father's Day. The letter spoke for her and clearly reflected her heart and her sentiment about her fallen hero. As Jeremy introduced the letter, he said, "Bethany was the lucky one." He meant that she had actually expressed to her dad, on this side of eternity, how much she admired him and how much he meant to her. She had written it, printed it, and had it framed for him. Del had placed it among the other trophies in his office. That day, its heartfelt words served as her eulogy to her father. The letter was read into the record for all of Heaven and earth to hear.

He's the Kind of Man

He's the kind of man that stops and makes you think

Beyond the surface of things

He's the kind of man who will do without so that a stranger can do with

He's the kind of man who does things in secret as to not receive credit

He's the kind of man who takes the time to examine things for what they are,

not for what they seem

He's the kind of man that makes other people want to be better

simply by being around him

He's the kind of man who does things in excellence, not for pride, rather because his Father placed that standard in his heart long ago

He's the kind of man that makes a person laugh when they feel like crying

He's the kind of man people strive to be like

He's the kind of man legacies are made of

He's the kind of man the Father loves to hear speak

He's the kind of man the Father loves to watch

He's the kind of man that makes the Father laugh and smile with "That a boy!" on His face

He's the kind of man that "gets" the Father

He's the kind of man that is one of a kind and

He's the man I'm honored to call father and friend.

I love you, Daddio! You're an inspiration and in case you didn't know how much I love and respect you, the above are a few examples of why. You're stronger than you know and admired by more than you know. Your life may not be what you imagined but be assured, your Father and family are VERY proud of you and SO honored God picked US to be YOURS!

(Written in loving tribute to her father, by Bethany Hope Teel Sigmon.)

Elizabeth, Jeremy's wife, also wrote a letter expressing her heart to this man who had quietly won her heart with his gentle ways and soft approach.

October 14, 2013

Dear Dad,

Today I call you that for the first time because I realize now that's what you are to me. Though you found me a self-centered 16-year old, you still claimed me as something much more subtle. We had a soft shuffle from around the corner, a sweet genuine smile with a quirky but always welcomed, "Hey, Lady!" (often with mochas for two in your hands). We had an unspoken understanding that if the rug was ripped out from underneath me, you would be there. Like you always were, the man of velvet steel.

Yes, that was us. And you loved me from the very beginning. Though you never made the push for me to love you back. Slowly but surely you became an unmovable pillar in my life. And I did love you and I do love you.

After you went home to Glory, I could hardly breathe. It was, and still is, surreal. At first I thought my tears and cries were for the hearts breaking all around me, but very quickly I realized that pain was my own. That ache was my own. And though I never called you dad, I knew you had always called me daughter.

Today I see your legacy. Today I feel you here. I see you in Jan, who you loved with a depth Nicholas Sparks could never put into words; in Nathan, whose heart for people matches that of your own; in Joel, who always voiced what you were thinking (and often without a filter); in Bethany, who has your fighting spirit and loyalty she would have only learned from your example, and in

Jeremy, who still brings joy and laughter even in the darkest moments.

I look at this family, your family, and I see your heart I see your smile I see your faith and I hear your laughter. And I know you are here.

Look at what great things that have come from you, Dad. And though we are bending in this hurricane all around us, we will not break. We are your greatest accomplishment. We are your family. We are the Teels. And it is a privilege to count myself among them.

Your daughter,

Elizabeth

Afterwards, reflecting back on what Elizabeth had shared, my other daughter-by-love, Laura, stated, "She said perfectly what I was feeling."

The boys also read letters, emails and notes from colleagues of Del's from IBM and Dassault Systems. Some of his French coworkers sent their sympathy and one entry stated, "Your husband was a delicious man!" I don't know if she meant to say sweet or delightful, but either way, she got it right. He was a delicious man. He was sweet and thoughtful.

They read from emails sent by online gamers who referred to Del as "Mr. Fraggle" because of a server he created to form an environment where children and adults could play in a community that was secure and monitored by someone known online simply as "The Pedestrian." In the guise of The Pedestrian, Del would monitor the activity to assure it remained a safe place for his children and others to play. I thought the server only had a handful of players, but I was astonished when condolences came in from around the world from those who had been affected by his presence and his forethought to create a protected place for children to play online. One of the mourners sent word that he was now playing online with his child with the same kind of thoughtfulness and diligence for safety that Mr. Fraggle had demonstrated to this community when he was a young player. One wrote, "I was homeschooled and didn't have much of a social life, but Fraggle became my family." One said, "I didn't have a dad. Mr. Fraggle was my dad." Many other messages were read into the service as a loving tribute to those who never met Del but who were impacted by his selfless service in a quiet corner of the world.

Joel is affectionately known in our family as "Mr. Inappropriate." We all joke that he should wear a T-shirt with that label as a public service announcement. If it comes into his head, it is often coming out of his mouth. His expressed thoughts particularly know no bounds if they will bring a laugh. The occasion of his father's eulogy was no exception. Joel was in heightened form as he kept laying out puns that his dad would have found amusing, even if inappropriate, saying things like, "You are a lucky stiff, aren't you?" as he looked down at his dad's casket. He then said, "I know, 'Go to your room, Joel!'" Knowing Del's humor, he would have found Joel's witticisms hysterical. On a more serious note, however, Joel said these words, "I now understand why Dad never ventured too far from his office. You see, when Dad met you, he fell in love with you. He took responsibility for you and your well-being. He thought it was his job to look after you once you were in his close circle. He didn't let too many people in." He then added, "Maybe it was because he couldn't afford all of those mochas!" We all laughed but there was truth in his summation of the character of his dad.

Before sharing a message of comfort that day, Pastor Mark Appleyard had the ushers pass out Dove Chocolate Promises to all those in attendance. Each brightly-colored foil wrapper has a message written inside. As Pastor Mark unwrapped his sweet confection and ate it in front of the attendees, he said, "Isn't it good? Can't you just taste the chocolatey goodness? Did you read the message inside?" He likened the sweetness to the love of God. He said not opening up and partaking in this treat's foil-wrapped goodness is like not responding to the Biblical directive that says, "Taste and see that the Lord is good; How blessed is the man who takes refuge in Him!" (Psalm 34:8). He encouraged all of those in attendance to consider tasting of the Lord's sweetness and accepting His free gift of salvation and love.

At the conclusion of the service, Cheryl Vought began to play and sing a song I had never heard before. I wanted to stay and linger longer, but protocol demanded I follow the casket as we prepared to take Del's earth suit to its final resting place. (The precious melody was the one that she would gift to me later that day and tell me that she had entitled it "Del's Song.") We were ushered to the limousine in front of the funeral home and then followed the hearse across the street to the interment service. I was, again, so thankful for the close proximity of the cemetery, and that we weren't making a cross-city drive. We had a few chairs set up for my family by the gravesite. Two family friends were there and began singing the song, "Oh, How He Loves." That was one of Del's favorite songs and sentiments. As we sang him goodbye and the brief service ended at the grave site, Nathan's RenFair folks gave out a loud proclamation in true RenFair style. "Inasmuch as the father of Prince William of Wonka has gone to meet his Maker, we lift up our voices and cry Hip, Hip, Huzzah! Hip, Hip, Huzzah! Hip, Hip, Huzzah!" The ground trembled with their gloriously, loud cheers and Heaven applauded once more; it was a fitting send-off. At my instruction, the funeral director invited all of those in attendance to feel free to return to our home, Serenity, to enjoy a time of fellowship, food, and reflection.

Upon arrival back at Serenity, I was astonished at the amount of food everywhere. The counters, kitchen island, and tables were all covered with food. I had asked my beloved neighbor Sheila Rhoney if she would oversee the matter of acquiring food for the gathering. She is a caterer and had catered several special events for us over the years of our acquaintance. Instead of attending the funeral, she had stayed behind to attend to the food. I didn't know how many to expect but thought I could always freeze what we didn't use. I said to her upon seeing the bounty, "Oh, my goodness! You outdid yourself this time."

She shook her head and said, "This wasn't me. This is from your church family, neighbors, and friends. I didn't have to do much except to find a place to store it all." I was amazed, God knew we would need it as somewhere close to 200 people came back to the house that afternoon to continue to share fellowship and reflect. Truly this was a bittersweet reflection on the kind of life Del had lived. The joy of knowing that he was far better off where he was now than we were as we continued to muddle through, gave us enormous peace.

Queen Bettina and her court arrived and set up temporary quarters on the deck at the rear of our yard. My sister, Linda, snuck out to get a picture of the royal court enjoying their feast when she realized they had all bowed their heads as Queen Bettina was leading them in prayer for our family. The scene was so touching, just another sweet kiss from Heaven and another reminder to me to live my life from Heaven to earth.

Chapter Five: Supernatural Provision

As the services were over and our families began to depart, my sister Diana Kaye Johnson decided to stay behind for a while as the rest of the family returned to Missouri. She knew this transition was going to be hard. She said she needed a rest from her hectic life at the Arlington Hotel she owned in DeSoto, Missouri with her husband. I needed a companion and she had always been there with me when we were young. Del used to describe her as a big heart on legs. That was his way of paying tribute to someone whose kindness and caring nature was extraordinary. She truly is a remarkable woman filled with compassion and empathy for those who are hurting.

Over the course of the next few days, Jeremy took time off from work to help me manage the finances and put things in order. Helping me gave him something tangible to set his hand to do in the wake of the great void created by Del's absence. Jeremy was directly responsible for positioning me in a manner that allowed me to maintain my lifestyle after Del's passing. During his internship at Northwest Mutual in his last days at the University of North Carolina in Charlotte, Jeremy convinced his dad to take out supplemental insurance. The policy wasn't huge, but it was enough to assure that I could be comfortable and not have to leave the house that Del and I had referred to as our "forever" home. God's Divine provision and kind hand in my finances became more and more evident with each passing week.

Jeremy had always been a planner and a strategist. In this regard, he was very much like his dad. Although Jeremy loves to make folks laugh (and will do almost anything to achieve that goal), he is a thoughtful man with a vision toward long-term goals. Jeremy had attended community college for a few years while simultaneously working as a volunteer firefighter and exploring varying fields of study, including insurance and real estate. He didn't want to settle for whatever was easiest to achieve. He wanted to be passionate about his career. When he was accepted into the Belk School of Business at the University of North Carolina in Charlotte, his dad was so proud. Jeremy's admission into this program was a high honor, one that required that students maintain a high GPA to keep their seats in this prestigious program. Jeremy wanted to be in a career that would provide security for his future family and his desire to do so had also gifted me with security and peace.

During the time we were trying to make a plan of action to settle all of Del's affairs, I reached out to the benefits coordinator to find out what portion of the life insurance I needed to set aside to pay the extraordinary medical bills I knew would follow Del's stay at the hospital. When I reached the coordinator and explained what I was trying to do, she told me that two things had prompted an unexpected benefit. She stated that because Del had checked into the hospital, and because he had spent the night, a special condition had been met that allowed there to be absolutely no deductible whatsoever. All of his medical bills were covered! I never knew such a benefit existed. I reflected back on my insistence that the emergency room doctor revive Del's heart. Because she had responded favorably to me, we had been allowed to keep Del with us for twenty-eight hours and that triggered this unexpected benefit. God knew about this advantage, even if I was ignorant of it. He didn't allow us to hold onto Del but, even then, He was making provision for us in a way that only reflects more clearly how very kind He truly is to us.

One of the other provisions had been in the making for years and had only come into focus in the weeks leading up to Del's leaving. When I had first started my career as a real estate agent in Lexington, Kentucky in the late seventies, I was what is now known as a "fixer-upper." I would buy houses that nobody else wanted and, with a little imagination and hard work, turn them into something everybody desired. Del and I would move from house to house as we renovated them. He would tell everybody that I had wheels and handles on all our furniture because we moved so often. (We moved four times in eighteen months, with eight weeks being the record time for us to be in one house before I sold it for the next one.)

In the aftermath of the meltdown of 2008, I had adapted my business model to incorporate the skills I had attained in the early part of my career to now serve investors, as well as traditional buyers and sellers. I would help them identify a good investment property, assemble the resources to have the house renovated, then stage, market, and sell it for them. At the end of the process, I would get a commission for my efforts. Often, it was a very small amount in relationship to all the work that would go into doing this for clients. Del would say, "You need to be getting those profits for yourself instead of the little tip at the end of all your labor." I would tell him that cash is king in this industry and, without it, I couldn't play in that game.

In an effort to find a solution to the need for funding, Del had encouraged me to take my daughter and her husband to a real estate investment seminar in Anaheim, California in August 2013. In this seminar, I networked with investors who were willing to finance whatever deals I found in any part of the country. They would share in the profits, and I would be positioned to earn more than just a small commission for my efforts. I learned how to buy properties in any part of the country, not just my own limited market. Del and I formed an LLC (Limited Liability Corporation) when I returned from California and started to pull together an action plan to start buying investment properties. Before the ink was dry on the pages, Del was gone. His life insurance and his insistence that I learn how to do these investments without fear had left me postured to be able to sustain my business even without the partnership of other investors. Again, God knew what was coming and He was positioning me in ways that far exceeded my comprehension.

While I was preparing for one of our investment sessions in California, I was in my room listening to worship music when the song, "In Your Arms" by Meredith Andrews came over my Pandora station. In that moment, I was absolutely captivated. As I listened to the words, I got onto the floor and began to weep in worship and adoration. There was a mixture of melancholy and gratitude that had overtaken me, just as that which had met me previously when Del had stopped on his way to grab his mocha to declare his love. I didn't understand the sadness, but I just began to declare the words in faith over whatever storms were brewing. In the days after Del's passing, I remembered how stirred I was by these words and I sang them over and over. The song speaks of turning the world off and replacing the noise that has drowned out His Voice, which was once so clear.

One morning while my sister, Diana, was still with me, we had a few friends over. My dear friend Kathy East was among the group of ladies who had joined us for coffee that morning. She informed us that her sister was going to Ireland in a few months and that God was doing amazing work there. She said that the old wells of revival were being renewed, and she wished she could go there too. I heard someone at the breakfast table say, "I am going to Ireland in June for Del's birthday and Father's Day and I am taking my kids with me." As soon as I heard it, I realized the words had actually come from my mouth. The thoughts never passed through my brain. I just said them out loud, as if my voice box was projecting someone else's thoughts other than my own.

Kathy responded in astonishment, "Really?"

I smiled lamely and said, "Apparently so." I was equally astounded and having an internal dialogue that went something like, "Are you crazy? You can't take your kids to Ireland! You just lost your husband. That would take something like $25,000 to take this family to Ireland. You don't have that kind of money. What are you thinking?" I have no idea how I decided the amount needed to go to Ireland with all of my children would be $25,000. I thought I had plucked the figure from the air.

The conversation moved on, and I am sure that the ladies at the table were convinced I had lost my mind. Ireland was not on my bucket list. I had a passport at Del's insistence but never had any plan to leave the United States. I figured that there is so much to explore in my own country that I would never have a reason to go elsewhere. My children had traveled extensively. Bethany had been to Israel. Nathan had been to Germany. Joel had traveled to the West Indies and Europe. Jeremy loved to explore our own country and had honeymooned in the Cayman Islands. I was content to hear about their exploits and leave the globetrotting to them.

As the days unfolded following that unrehearsed declaration regarding Ireland, I kept getting emails and Facebook notifications about things related to that country. I went into Del's office one day to attempt to clean up a bit and found a lovely book filled with pictures of the Irish Islands. The picture book had been a gift from Joel to Del that I had never seen before. Joel had gone to Ireland in the summer of 2001 on a short-term mission trip with some friends. He had a wonderful experience there and I had totally forgotten about the link to this land. St. Patrick was the patron saint of the university Del had attended in Rolla, Missouri. I had done a light piece about St. Patrick in a journalism class while in school, but never really had done much research about the true history of the man. As my Facebook feed kept bringing up things about him, I dug further and learned that he was affectionately known as "the apostle who raises the dead" to some of the Irish converts.

As the signs kept pointing to Ireland, I said a prayer, "Father, if you want me to go to Ireland, I will go. You just have to provide $25,000 for the trip." I am glad I was sincere in my prayer because a few days later, a check for $25,000 appeared in my mailbox. The check was for a life insurance policy Del had with IBM which I hadn't known existed, nor was it a part of our financial plan of action in the event of his untimely death. So, I assembled my family and told them what I was feeling about going to Ireland for Del's birthday and Father's Day. (Del's birthday was June 18th and usually was right at or around Father's Day every year. I knew this was going to be a hard year to face those two events.) The oldest, Nathan, was ready to go. My second born, Joel, couldn't go because he had two little ones that wouldn't be able to handle the demands of an extended vacation on a tour bus in Ireland for over a week. (Joel had already been to Ireland and his wife had lived there for several years during her childhood, so they weren't as captivated as some of the others.) Bethany's husband had just taken a new job and couldn't go due to the lack of vacation time available for the venture. But my youngest son and his wife were also on board with the plan.

After figuring out the funding, I gave a lump sum to Joel and Laura and to Bethany and A.J. I told them that they had to spend it on an extravagant trip that would make their dad happy. Del used to teasingly tell the children when they asked if they could participate in a special event or trip, "Okay! You can go. Just don't enjoy it!" He meant just the opposite, of course. He used to revel in sending the children on adventures and then hearing about them later. Therefore, when I gave them the money, I made it conditional. They were not to spend it on something that they needed because there would always be a need. They had to treat this like found money and make amazing memories with it.

Bethany decided on a trip to the Rocky Mountains in Colorado, a place her daddy loved. She rented a house for a week that backed up to Pikes Peak, one of the places where Del had an encounter with God's creation that had moved him beyond words. He had said, "As I sat in the Rocky Mountain National Forest, I felt like I could just sit down and die here. I have seen beauty that is too much for my heart to contain." He had hiked many trails and had been drawn to the raw beauty of that place, even contemplating a move to that state while employed with IBM on more than one occasion.

Joel and Laura took their girls to Disney World and had a lovely time making memories. They were able to use one of our timeshares for their lodging needs, so they had enough money left over for a down payment on a trip to Paris for their tenth wedding anniversary the following spring. Del would have been delighted by how they all used this funding to make special memories to last a lifetime.

The story of my adventure in Ireland, and how it changed the course of my life, will follow in a later entry. I wanted to mention it now as a part of the unfolding of the supernatural provision Father God made for us at every step of our journey. As we were grieving, we were met with such abiding kindness and provision, it helped to know that Father was guiding us, and it felt like Del still had a hand in things. Maybe he was still influencing things from a higher place. This knowledge brought all of us abiding comfort and peace.

Chapter Six: Emerging from the Fog

As I marked the weeks after Del's passing, I was in a fog. I was sleeping very little. My children were also suffering from insomnia and having tormenting dreams. Jeremy had a dream in which he walked into his dad's office and saw him sitting behind his desk. Relieved, he rushed into his dad's embrace and said, "You really scared us!"

Del returned his embrace and said, "I know. It scared me too!" As Jeremy looked around his dad's office, he saw that many books and shelves had been removed, and only a small fraction of what had been there before was present in the room. Then the dream ended. I told him that, perhaps, God was trying to tell him that if his dad had returned, he wouldn't have been the man he had been before. We grasped for meaning in every dream and among every written scrap of paper that we could find in his office.

Before I knew it, the weeks had become a month. I wrote the following post on my Facebook page on the fourth week after his passing.

November 7, 2013

Four weeks ago today... How is that even possible? The world didn't stop spinning. My heart continued beating. Laughter and worship continued to be heard on the earth. My beloved is just on the other side of a door that I cannot yet walk through. Until we are reunited, our family will continue to treasure the years that his life enriched ours. We will keep reminding ourselves of what joy he is experiencing in the arms of Father God and that he is enjoying eternity without restraint. We will continue to love as we were loved and create an enduring legacy to

please our Heavenly Father and our beloved husband,
father, grandfather, brother, uncle, cousin, and friend...

In a fleeting moment, a whole month had passed. The aftermath had kept us busy. Meeting with funeral directors, ordering headstones, coordinating with insurance agents, closing accounts, slowly disassembling a lifetime of collecting and memories had kept us occupied. The reality of this new paradigm was beginning to sink in.

One week slipped into another and the goal of posting each week kept me journaling. Every Tuesday night I would think about what I had been doing at that exact time a few Tuesdays before, and how I might have done things differently if I had known it would be my last night to lie beside him in my bed. I would approach every Wednesday with dread, because only a few Wednesdays before, my world had been tattered. Thursday mornings around 10:00 a.m., I wanted to run away from all the clocks because their ticking marked yet another week without him. Slowly, however, Father God graciously met me on those weekly markers and started giving me a voice and a hope. He gave me comfort and a perspective that allowed me to make it through another week. I started looking forward to what He would share with me. Often, those revelations would come between midnight and 2:00 a.m. on a Thursday morning.

When I was a child, we were given paint sets and pictures of masterpieces that were only outlined in black and white, like puzzles. Each section had a correlating paint number to help you replicate the original artist's colors. They came with a palate of paints that corresponded to the numbers. At the end of your work, you would have created a piece of art that looked similar to the original. One found it hard to picture what the finished work would look like when only patches of color fragments were being applied to the hardened canvas, one chosen color at a time. The canvas was often ugly and distorted as the various shades that would make up the whole picture were applied. The practice of completing these canvas replicas was referred to as "painting by the numbers." So, it seemed fitting, since the unfolding of weeks were painting a new canvas in my life marked by the correlating numbers, to reference my journey as "Grieving by the Numbers."

The following section of the book are entries are adapted from my Facebook posts and will only be interrupted by the insertion of what was going on in our world outside of the marking of these weeks. These entries will include our travel to Ireland and the supernatural signs and wonders that met us there. It will also include a romance that began to emerge toward the end of my one-year chronicle. I hope that you will join me as I share with you my grief journey.

Just as the messy splotches of paint on the canvas were pointing toward the replication of a masterpiece, so my grief journey has been messy, disorganized, and excruciating, but it has also been filled with wonder and hope. *Hope*, in Greek, means, a *confident expectation*. Father God doesn't disappoint. What seems to be a mess from our perspective is being used to accomplish His masterpiece. His works are not replicas. His are pure genius and incredible originals. You are one of His works, and so am I. You are now invited to join me on this passage from mourning to dancing, from sorrow to joy, from despair to a confident hope.

Chapter Seven: The Journey Toward Hope

As promised, I will now share a compilation of numerical meanings, and adaptions from my social media posts during the first fifty-four weeks after the loss of Del.

Week One: Unity, Singularity, Uniqueness

In God's Word, we read, "Hear, O Israel: The Lord our God, the Lord is One" (Deuteronomy 6:4).

He is One, yet He is comprised of three parts: The Father, The Son, and the Holy Spirit who is lovingly referred to as The Comforter. These three operate as one. Jesus said He could do nothing by Himself. He only did what He saw His Father doing (John 5:19-20). There was no action He took outside of that which was authorized and demonstrated by His Father in Heaven. Isn't it astonishing to think that the greatest sacrifice that has ever been demonstrated, in all of creation, was first modeled by the Creator himself? Jesus said of the Holy Spirit, in John 14:26, "But the Comforter, which is the Holy Ghost, whom the Father will send in my name He shall teach you all things, and bring all things to your remembrance, whatsoever I have said to you." In short, The Father says, "This is my son in whom I am well pleased..." The Son says, "I do all to glorify the Father..." The Holy Spirit says, "Let me teach you of the Father and the Son..." All three cooperate as one and their love for one another is indivisible, just as the number one is indivisible.

The presence of this Comforter is my only hope as Father reveals Himself to me in new ways along every step of this grief journey.

Week Two: Witness, Division, Difference

Every important assignment in the Bible seemed to require at least two parties to bring a witness or testimony. There were two angels sent to Sodom and Gomorrah, two spies were sent to Jordan to scout out the city, and Jesus sent his disciples out two by two. God's Word says, "Two are better than one because they have a good reward for their toil" (Ecclesiastes 4:9).

There were twelve spies sent into the Promised Land to scout it out for the Israelites. Of those twelve, only two came back with a good report. Only two saw the land from Heaven's lens and said, "We are well able to take this land." The others felt they were grasshoppers in the sight of their enemy. Only two saw the truth. Only two lasted through the forty years in the wilderness as the other spies and all their other peers passed away, leaving only those who would stand with them and look at what lay before them through Heaven's eyes.

As a woman who had a faithful companion and co-laborer for the length of forty years, I can tell you two are better than one. What I have learned through this broken path, however, is that we are never alone. God promises He will never leave you nor forsake you. Jesus said, "I am with you always..." Sometimes you see Him in a glimpse of something lovely that takes your breath away, a blooming flower in an unexpected place, a rainbow after the rain, a sunset too amazing for description. Sometimes, you feel Him in the arms of friends and family who bring you hugs and support through your moments of despair. Sometimes you hear His Voice through your pastor on a Sunday morning or through the kindness of a stranger just giving you a greeting or a sweet smile. I have seen Him, heard Him, and felt Him all along my path. Although lonely, I am never alone. Although widowed, He is always my cover and my comfort. He will take me into the Promised Land of Heaven one day, where my beloved companion has already gone.

Week Three: Divine Fullness, Completion, Perfection, The Trinity

Three is the minimum number required to establish a pattern. We see this number repeated continuously throughout the scriptures. We see it first in the establishment of the Godhead: Father, Son, and Holy Spirit. We see it in the forming of mankind as being made up of three parts: body, soul, and spirit. We see it in the establishment of the Tabernacle of Moses. He formed an Outer Court, Holy Place, and a Most Holy Place (The Holy of Holies). You can see the pattern of threes throughout the Word of God and it is a divine invitation to unlock His mysteries and look for Him in new and more intimate ways.

As one who has knowledge of spiritual matters, I can know in my mind that my best friend of more than forty years is in a better place. I can know that he has gone on to delight in his reward. But, this body of mine is longing for his touch, his hugs, to see his nods of affirmation (when I share something I know he would appreciate) or hear his gentle laughter as we enjoy a moment of mutual amusement. This three-part human experience can be filled with overwhelming emotions as my spirit longs to connect with the eternal, but my flesh is still anchored to this earth. I lean into the Trinity during these days of sadness and look for the comfort that can only be found by keeping a Heavenly perspective while walking in this earthly body.

Week Four: Creation, Earthly Completeness

There are four directions: north, south, east, and west. There are four seasons: winter, spring, summer, and fall. Four is the number of the great elements on the planet: fire, water, air, and earth. Four is also seen in Heavenly worship as the book of Revelation describes four creatures: one is like a lion, one is like an ox, one has a human face, and one is like a flying eagle.

In my time of sorrow, God has revealed Himself to me as the fourth man in the fire, as we saw in the book of Daniel. The three Hebrew children were thrown into a fiery furnace so hot that the men who threw them inside were consumed by the heat of the flames. What the king saw when he looked into the fire was astonishing. He said, "Didn't we throw three men into the fire? Yet, I see a fourth man and he looks like the Son of Man!" I have to wonder, every time I read this passage how it was that the king would know what the Son of Man might look like? Did Heaven open and reveal to him this wonderful knowledge? The three Hebrew children came out of the fire with no harm and even the ropes that had bound them had burned up, leaving no char or marks on them, only freedom.

May God take all of us through our fiery trials and tests in the earth with the revelation that the Son of Man is with us in the fire. May we walk away from our testing with no smell of smoke and no evidence of past hindrances that bound us.

Week Five: God's Grace and Preparation for What Lies Ahead

November 14, 2013

Today marks the five-week anniversary of my beloved husband's going home date. God's Biblical number five is the number for grace. (Grace is the unearned FAVOR of The Lord.) His grace and mercy have met us at every turn. They have covered us like the morning dew. The past two weeks have been difficult because it is harder to reconcile ourselves to the knowledge that we won't hear his voice or feel his tender touch or witness his gentle ways this side of eternity. When we are saddened by that great loss, we are comforted in the CERTAIN knowledge that we will see him again and that he is having a blast on the other side of that threshold we will all step over one day. He is not constrained by physical or emotional limitations. He is singing at the top of his lungs. He is dancing. He is playing with our child and grandchild. He is worshiping at the feet of Jesus. He is cheering us on. He has always been our number one fan and he is now unlimited in his vantage point to be a witness to all of life's events simultaneously. "To be absent from the body is to be present with The Lord!" (2 Corinthians 5:8). We rejoice in his triumph even as we sorrow at our great loss. As his family, we invite you to open your heart to God's great love if you have not yet received this amazing gift. I know that He gives us unspeakable joy and peace that passes understanding because we are already one with Him, which means that Del is only a whisper away.

Week Six: The Number of Man, Release from Bondage

November 21, 2013

Six weeks. The number six represents mankind. It was on the sixth day that God created man. His law states that a man will work six days but must rest on the seventh day. A Hebrew slave could be sold into bondage but could only be enslaved for six years before being set free. None of us know when our Father will call us into His rest, but we do know that our time on this earth will have an end and we will be reunited with those we love.

Six weeks ago today, my best friend, husband, confidant, and the wisest man I have ever known was called Home. The amazing grace of God has been so very tangible in our lives. We have had some challenges to get through, but He has covered us at every step. The outpouring of love, prayers, and support by family, friends, and others is more helpful than you may know. The Kingdom of Heaven is touching the earth in every kind word, deed, and smile directed toward our wounded souls. I am so thankful and humbled by these expressions of compassion. Del has left me with four of the most precious gifts as the best proof of his love in his children, Nathan Teel, Joel Teel, Bethany Hope Teel Sigmon, and Jeremy Teel. Together, we will weather this storm. We will grow in wisdom, compassion, and love. We will continue to do everything we do for the glory of God and in EXCELLENCE, as Del always did. We will continue to advance the Kingdom of God until we meet Del again in a place that is more enticing now because he is there awaiting us.

Week Seven: Completeness and Perfection

November 28, 2013

Seven weeks. Seven is God's number for completeness or perfection. He created the whole earth in six days and then rested on the seventh day to provide a pattern for us to learn how to rest. His Word in the book of Revelation tells us at the seventh trumpet sound the first resurrection of the dead takes place, a finish to our salvation. Del already had his first trumpet call and he has entered into his rest with the saints who have gone before him. We are abundantly thankful to know that we will see him again.

This marked our first Thanksgiving without Del:

Seven weeks ago today, my beloved passed into Heaven's embrace. The days without him have been sad and facing a holiday season void of his physical presence is challenging . . . but GOD... (Pastor Mark Appleyard always says to pay close attention to words that follow the phrase, "but GOD.") Our Heavenly Father has provided His grace sufficient. He has been our Strength in weakness. He has been our Comforter in sorrow. He has been our Shelter from the storm. He has surrounded us with Kingdom-minded folks who have continually wrapped us in their prayers and compassion. They are His hands and His feet. They are His heartbeat. We are so very thankful for each of you who have whispered a prayer or stormed Heaven's courts on our behalf. We are thankful for the text messages, Facebook messages, phone calls, and even the warm wishes from a distance that never go any further than from your heart to God's ears. We are thankful that we had such a rich deposit of love in our lives for the years we had with my beloved Del. I am honored to have been his life mate and the mother of his children. He taught us how to anchor our lives in the most important relationship we can embrace, one with our Eternal Heavenly Father. His absence in our midst as we gather today will be an acute ache that is unfathomable; but knowing that he is present with God in Heaven, where he is witness to the places Father is preparing for us there, is a comfort that brings us joy. During his final hours on earth, before suffering the fatal heart attack that led to his death, he was walking through the construction site of Joel and Laura's new home. He was videotaping everything for their records. In the same way, I am sure that he is now drinking in the amazing dwelling places that the Master Builder is creating for those who love Him. He always wanted to walk ahead and make sure things were going to be just right for us, just like Jesus! Happy Thanksgiving, beloved friends and family. May this season of thanks spill over into each of our lives and become a lifestyle we embrace with a purpose every moment God gives us on this side of eternity.

Week Eight: New Beginnings

December 5, 2013

Eight weeks. The number eight is symbolic of new beginnings in God's Word. The Greek word for Jesus' name translates into the number 888.

I find it hard to believe that it was eight weeks ago today that the most important person to ever walk into my life walked out of it. He has crossed over into Heaven's embrace and awaits our reunion when we will once again continue our great adventure side by side. The Grace that has wrapped itself around us has been nothing less than amazing. That is how Father God does things, always in excellence, always with loving kindness. People tell me that I am the strongest woman they know. I am not. I am as weak as a newborn baby (and I sometimes cry just as incessantly). The glory of Kingdom life is that we have this promise that He delivers to us in the form of our "daily bread." He promises that His strength is made perfect in our weakness. I can abandon the strength of my own flesh and trade it for His perfect strength. I can cling to the promise that I will be with Del again sooner than my mortal mind can conceive. I will continue to walk in integrity and build the legacy Del has left behind to the glory of Father God, who is the Giver of Life and from Whom all blessings flow. He is my PEACE!

Week Nine: Divine Completeness

December 12, 2013

Nine weeks. The number nine symbolizes Divine completeness. It is fitting that on this ninth week without my beloved soulmate and best friend, we should be celebrating the completion of the home that he toured with me the night before his fatal heart attack. Tonight, our family assembled at the new home of Joel and Laura. (They have named it Providence.) We enjoyed reminiscing and discussing Del's wonderful legacy. We missed Nathan's good company. (Thank you for serving Crossroads South, Nathan, and all of the wonderful family of musicians who lead us in worship there weekly.)

Status Update

December 15, 2013

Leaving our Sunday morning fellowship today, I was alone in my vehicle, reflecting on how much my Heavenly Father loves me. Tears were streaming down my face in gratitude for His amazing love. I felt His arms of love around me this morning when Bailey, the young daughter of our worship leader, Cheryl Vought, came by and gave me a huge hug. I heard about His love when Lisa Ann Giovanniello introduced her twin little girls, Olivia and Sophia, to me (formally) so that they would put a face with the name. Lisa would mention me as, "Miss Jan from church," for whom they prayed nightly. I received a gift from His hands when our guest speaker, Jason L. Clark, gifted me with an advance copy of his new book, Prone to Love. I am surrounded by His love every day and in so many ways.

Sometimes I recognize it, but I know He loves me, even when I miss His love notes from Heaven.

Week Ten: The Completeness of Order or Wholeness

December 19, 2013

Ten weeks. Today marks the ten-week anniversary of Del's departing this earth for his Heavenly home. Spiritually, the number ten in God's Word is representative of wholeness or completion. Del departed us on 10/10 and it was in the tenth hour of the day. His favorite book of the Bible was the gospel of John. John 10:10 says, "The thief does not come except to steal, and to kill, and to destroy. I have come that they may have life, and that they may have it more abundantly." I am saddened by the gaping hole that has been left in my heart by his departure, but I rejoice to know that he is enjoying an abundant afterlife in eternity with the only constant we are promised. For Jesus also promised, "I will never leave you, nor forsake you." He is with us. He is in us. He is for us. What a blessed hope we cling to that those who have departed us on this side of the veil are with Him on the other side. He is merciful and true and His love for us is rich and boundless.

I mailed out our Teel Christmas newsletter a couple of days ago. Del loved the tradition of updating our friends and family with the year filled with news from our adventures. It was something he loved to collect, and he would read them to help him remember how our lives were unfolding. The newsletter this year was a major effort to write, but I hope it will bless those of you who take the time to read our annual novel.

Status Update

December 22, 2013

Our first wedding anniversary—it would have been our fortieth!)

Today I celebrate my fortieth wedding anniversary. It will be my first without my beloved, Happy Golucky (a.k.a. Mr. Fraggle, a.k.a. Delbert Teel). I slept in the house of his older brother and his wife (Dennis and Diane Teel) last night at the beach, and it was the best sleep I have had in weeks! I am thankful for the amazing marriage I have had with Del and the offspring of our love, Nathan, Joel, Bethany Hope, and Jeremy Luke. I am thankful for our expanding family and for the wisdom I learned from Del through all of our years. I am thankful that he inspired me to seek a relationship and intimacy with Our Heavenly Father at an early age. I cannot imagine living through this loss without the anchor of my absolute conviction that I will see him again on the other side of this veil we call life. God's loving arms have been holding me through every sorrow. He speaks to me gently through moonbeams dancing on the crashing waves, through the laughter of our children, through birds that soar above us singing His praises. We have a full evening planned and I know that God will arrange for Del to peek through one of Heaven's portals to smile down upon us as we have our *Walk to Remember* in one of the places where the movie thus named was filmed!

Week Eleven: Disorder and Chaos

December 26, 2013

Eleven weeks. The number eleven represents disorder and chaos. How fitting that this number should land the day after we have made it through some very tender firsts without our patriarch.

Eleven weeks (seventy-seven days). I wonder when I will stop counting the days and weeks and moments without my beloved husband. We have made it through our first Thanksgiving, the first wedding anniversary, and now our first Christmas holiday without his gentle presence and good humor. Wiser folks than I assure us it will get easier once we make it through all of the firsts without him. The emptiness is excruciating. Our laughter was more tempered this season, our heartache more tender.

Del always made Christmas wondrous, from wrapping presents in funky packaging to hiding the gifts and sending us on the hunt for treasures. He always wanted the children to remain children for as long as possible. In that spirit, I purchased toys for our boys this Christmas. My Christmas highlight was having my grown children running through the house with Nerf guns, shooting each other as our two granddaughters each chose an uncle to assist by retrieving the "bullets."

I often wonder what amazing things our Heavenly Father has prepared for us when we come home to His house. Does He sit and revel in the laughter of His children as they take in the splendor of what He has prepared for them? I am quite sure He enjoys it in Heaven, but it also touches His heart when we recognize His good gifts here on earth and thank Him for them. He is good. He is kind. He is for us. He is closer than the mention of His name!

Week Twelve: Divine Order and the Family of God

January 2, 2014

Twelve weeks. The Bible tells us that there is a tree in Heaven that produces twelve kinds of fruit twelve times a year for the healing of the nations. We have just completed a twelve-month cycle and celebrate a new beginning in 2014. Today marks twelve weeks since Del drew his last breath on earth. I wonder if he has tasted the fruit of that tree in Heaven yet? (He always loved fruit and exotic foods.) May the year 2014 be a fruitful year for all of us. May we bring Heaven's light and life to this earth for the healing of the nations.

Week Thirteen: Redemption and Blessings

January 9, 2014

Thirteen weeks. The number thirteen strikes fear and suspicion into the heart of many. Biblically, it is a number of great promise and blessing. For me personally, it has always been a number that represents redemption. The picture I have posted was from a car going through my house on Friday, June 13, 1980. God miraculously moved all of the inhabitants out of our house just moments before this happened. The amazing thing is that everyone walked away, even the driver, without major injuries. The insurance not only paid to rebuild our home, it was better after the accident than before the accident. So many miracles, signs, and wonders came out of what could have been a tragedy. I could write a book about it...well, maybe just a magazine article. Lol!

Today marks thirteen weeks since Del went home to Heaven. I can focus on my loss or I can focus on God's promise that blessings will be born of this tragedy. I choose to believe in God's always good love. I choose to believe that the best is yet to be. I know it won't look like the past. (Nobody could ever fill the void that my precious husband has left.) The future, however, can be rich with joy and blessing as we focus on how faithful God has always been to create something wondrous out of our sorrows. He is not finished with us. We have a Kingdom to advance and a message to be delivered. He is good. He is kind. His mercy endures forever!

Week Fourteen: Deliverance

January 16, 2014

Fourteen weeks. Fourteen weeks have passed since I have seen the face of my beloved Del or heard the sound of his voice or felt the touch of his gentle hands. I was fourteen years old when my parents allowed him to start courting me. (Yes, that is what they called it when you are too young to date, but you can sit with one another in church and write to one another while your "steady" is away at college.) Del used to say, "Marry them young and raise them right!" Of course, he was just teasing. We were so fortunate to find love at such an early age and to have our lives centered around our relationship with Christ. Del was my mentor and my inspiration. I was a mediocre student until we became a couple, and I wanted to live up to his standards. I found a news article in his belongings this week that was from the local newspaper in our hometown. The article listed the honor roll students. My name was there on the list and he had circled it. (I didn't even know until this week that it had been published in the paper, much less that Del had saved it.) The number fourteen represents deliverance or salvation and is used twenty-two times in the Bible. "Fourteenth" is found twenty-four times in scriptures. The fourteenth day of the first month is the Passover when God delivered the firstborn of Israel from death. Passover was a foreshadowing of His deliverance that was coming from His firstborn son, Jesus. His death delivered all of us who receive this gift into eternal life. I mourn the loss of my beloved and miss his good-natured ways every day. I rejoice in the knowledge that Jesus paid the price to secure Del's eternity with Father God and that I, too, will one day be with him on the other side. Until that day, I will continue to strive to make Del proud and hope that one day I will find my name on God's honor roll.

Week Fifteen: Covenant and Favor

Thanks, my Facebook friends and family, for allowing me to use this forum to express myself as I find my way along a path I have never walked before. Your prayers and kindness have helped to steer me. Blessings upon you.

January 23, 2014

Fifteen weeks. The number fifteen represents Covenant, Cover, Divine Grace. A covenant is not a contract. In a contract, we identify parties who agree to certain elements in a transaction. In covenant, we agree to change our identity. Just fifteen weeks ago today, my beloved husband departed this earth. I was destined to be in a covenant of marriage with him as his wife and enjoyed that identity for forty years. Although he has gone ahead of me to see Father and enjoy his reward early, I still have an identity that is tied to that marriage. My beautiful family is the fruit of that covenant.

Jesus has called us all to engage in a Divine romance and an eternal covenant. He paid the price for that eternal covenant on the fifteenth day of the month in the fulfillment of His Passover destiny.

Fifteen is three times five (3 x 5 = 15). The Biblical number for excellence is three and five is the Biblical number for grace. Grace is the unmerited, unearned favor of The Lord. As I enter this fifteenth week of mourning, I am easily overcome by emotions that blindside me. I was standing in Lowes (purchasing more lock sets so I can keep Serenity locked down like Fort Knox), when it occurred to me that Del will never again be on the other side of that door to come to my rescue when I lock myself out of our house. I tried to keep my composure as I made my purchase and explained the reason for my unexpected tears to the bewildered young lady behind the register. She asked, "Can I give you a hug?" She came around and held me for a moment to comfort me in my grief.

Favor: When a perfect stranger reaches out her arms to bring you comfort in the middle of Lowes because she wants to ease your pain.

Favor: When your baby sister (Linda Mason) is fighting for her life in a hospital, 700 miles away, and folks who have never met her start bombarding Heaven with intercession for her because they know how dear she is to me.

Favor: When you can't figure out what your adorable grandchildren have done to the settings on your television to make it malfunction and you pick up the phone to call your personal Geek Squad (Nathan Teel), and he sets it right in moments.

Favor: When you find random love notes left in unexpected places by your sons (Joel and Jeremy).

Favor: When your daughter (Bethany Hope) frets over whether you have had both your physical food and your spiritual food and makes sure to bring you liberal doses of both.

Week Sixteen: Love and Loving

January 30, 2014

May you know the blessing of walking in the identity of one who is highly favored by God in this new covenant of unconditional love!

Sixteen weeks. There are sixteen names for God given to us in the Old Testament which relate to His love for His children. (Even those sixteen names don't begin to adequately depict how great His amazing love is toward us.) In the New Testament there are sixteen attributes associated with genuine love articulated in 1 Corinthians 13, "Love is patient, love is kind, love does not envy, love doesn't parade itself, love is not puffed up, love doesn't behave rudely, love doesn't seek its own, love is not provoked, love thinks no evil, love doesn't rejoice in iniquity, love rejoices in the truth, love bears all things, love believes all things, love hopes all things, love endures all things, love never fails." (Substitute the word God in place of the word love and read that again. Yes, He is all those things and more.)

In the book of first John, the sixteenth time John uses the word love it is used in the context, "There is no fear in love..." The Bible tells us that "God is love."

For Del and me the number sixteen has always held a special meaning. Del and I were four years apart in age. We had four children. Our children were all approximately four years apart in age. Every fourth year, for only sixteen days, we were all divisible by the number four. We made it a family tradition that during those 16 days we would have our picture taken. When we look back over our family portraits throughout the years, we will always know how old each of the children were by taking one of the numbers and adding or subtracting the number four.

Since Del went to his eternal home, sixteen weeks have passed. The acute sorrow is diminished as we embrace a new future without his perfect placement in our lives. Our pastor has invited us to dream again. The songs from Heaven are drawing us into a place of rest in His good dreams for us. Recent lyrics birthed into the earth by our worship leader and local Christian composer, Cheryl Vought, resonate with my heart: "Awaken my soul. Awaken the dreams that you have always dreamed for me. Open my eyes. Let me catch a glimpse of Heaven opening." The certainty of Father God's "always-good love" for us (as Jason L. Clark so beautifully puts it in his writings) propels us forward with the assurance that better days are before us. These are not the days I had envisioned for myself, but His grace is sufficient for each new day. I rest in the certain hope that my family will be comforted. We will dream with Father God and cling to the knowledge that He has a perfect plan for all of our tomorrows. Del was such a wonderful reflection of Father God's heart toward us. Although Del is absent from our lives, Father God will never leave us nor forsake us. As we quiet ourselves in His love, Wisdom and Comfort come to meet us. We are prepared for following the pattern set for us by Del and, most importantly, by Jesus. He only did what He saw His Father do and He only said what He heard His Father say.

"Show us the ancient paths, Father. Teach us to follow hard after You, in joy and in sorrow, in abundance and lack. May we learn to set our affection on You, as You have set Your affection on each of us."

Week Seventeen: Indivisible Love, Vanquishing of the Enemy, Victory

February 6, 2014

Seventeen weeks. Seventeen, the number of weeks it has been since I shared my beloved's bed, since I laughed at his corny jokes, or listened to his wise counsel. Seventeen is the seventh prime number, which means it is not divisible by any other number. Seventeen is the sum of two perfect numbers: seven and ten. Biblically, seven is the number for spiritual perfection and ten is the number of ordinal perfection. They combine to represent the perfection of spiritual order.

In Romans 8:35, we see the question posed, "What can separate us from the love of Christ?"

Seven things answer the question: "Shall tribulation, or distress, or persecution, or famine or nakedness, or danger, or sword?"

That list is followed by verses 38 and 39 which reflect ten things that cannot triumph over the love of Christ with Paul's declaration: "I am persuaded that neither death, nor life, nor angels, nor principalities, nor powers, nor things present, nor things to come, nor height, nor depth, nor any other created thing, shall be able to separate us from the love of God, which is in Christ Jesus our Lord" (Romans 8:38-39).

The number seventeen also represents "vanquishing of the enemy" and "victory in Christ." God vanquished sin through the death and resurrection of Christ. Jesus was raised from the dead on the seventeenth day of the first month.

In the "Love Chapter" (1 Corinthians 13), the seventeenth time the word love is used it states, "The greatest of these is LOVE!"

As I live in the aftermath of a loss so painful it defies reason, I am comforted to know that this is a temporary state. Nothing can separate me from the Love of God, and I will one day be reunited with my beloved Del as we are joined in the company of all of those who have gone before us in the presence of the one Who is LOVE. I know that He is for me. I know that He is with me. Nothing can separate me from His love and His presence. Not even death can separate me from God's precious love. Seventeen. A number that is indivisible. Just as it cannot be divided, so we who are in Christ are also indivisible. We cannot be divided by or separated from His love. Cherish this truth, as I do when my heart is lonely, and I am seeking comfort. I close my eyes and rest in His arms, knowing that He is holding me and carrying me through my darkest hours. Better days are before me because He is holding all of my tomorrows. When I can't trace His hand, I can trust His heart.

Week Eighteen: Life or Slavery (Choose LIFE!)

February 13, 2014

Eighteen weeks. This date marks the eighteenth week since I lost my beloved's presence on this side of eternity. I see him frequently in certain expressions on the faces of his children. I hear his wisdom being echoed in their voices as they counsel one another. I hear his compassion as they comfort one another during a particularly tough day. I live in this house we named Serenity, gifted to me because of his lifetime of striving to provide good gifts for his family.

In scripture, the number eighteen has two significant meanings. In the Hebrew breakdown of the number, it means "life." The strange thing is that it also means "slavery." This is a paradox when I read the reflections of theologians and scholars on the meaning of this number. These two meanings seem so far from one another.

God's Word says that He sets before us life and death and He encourages us to "Choose Life!" (Deuteronomy 30:15,19). For me, life outside of Christ is slavery. He has set us free from the bondage of sin and death. Jesus laid down His life and then rose again so that we would see the pattern that we are to follow. Del was a wonderful role model for me from my youngest days. He modeled a selfless life that was devoted to others. He has now been set free from the responsibility of carrying his family and their needs. He has left that in the capable hands of Abba Father, whose very name is El Shaddai (the God Who is MORE THAN ENOUGH).

May we all choose life over slavery. May we all strive to follow the Supreme-Pattern-Son, Jesus, as we spend our days on this planet advancing His Kingdom and honoring Him for all of His precious gifts. I am honored that He chose me as His daughter and He calls me His beloved. I am also honored that, for four decades, Del and I enjoyed the journey as one.

Week Nineteen: Faith in God's Perfect Judgments

February 20, 2014

Nineteen weeks. In the Bible, the number nineteen is symbolic of faith and hearing. Nineteen is also symbolic of Divine order and judgment. In our family, Del was always the keeper of order and his judgments were sound and wise. For nineteen weeks we have journeyed through this life without the wit and wisdom of our family patriarch. On this warm, spring-like day, I ventured into the cemetery where we laid my beloved's earth suit to rest. I sat on the bench that we bought to enjoy moments of reflection and considered the man whose impact compelled me to come and quietly rest. I know he is not there. Still, I find comfort in these quiet moments. I wonder what he would think of how we have navigated through these uncharted waters. He was such a contemplative soul. He was always the quiet strength behind each of us. He was the voice of reason and the reminder to look to the Word of God for our answers to life's questions. Nineteen. In Hebrews 11 we are given examples of nineteen people or groups, who "by faith" overcame every obstacle because they believed in the promise of a better tomorrow. Many patriarchs of the faith are named in that passage including Abraham and Sarah, Moses, Joshua, Rahab, David, Samuel, and the prophets. They believed that He Who had called them was able to keep all of His promises to them. By faith, I know that one day God will call forth all of those souls who have found their rest in Him. His Word declares, "For the Lord Himself will descend from heaven with a shout, with the voice of an archangel, and with the trumpet of God. And the dead in Christ will rise first. Then we who are alive and remain shall be caught up together with them in the clouds to meet the Lord in the air. And thus, we shall always be with the Lord" (1 Thessalonians 4:16-17).

Until that glorious day, we will continue to listen for the still, small voice of our Heavenly Father and follow hard after Him. He is our Wisdom. He is our Strength.

Week Twenty: Waiting and Expectancy

February 27, 2014

Twenty weeks. Today marks twenty weeks since my beloved has left the life we built for a life on the other side of eternity. In the Bible, twenty is symbolic of both waiting and expectancy. When Del and I started our family, he wanted to have a daughter. We had been blessed with two wonderful sons, but he felt that our family unit wasn't complete. We learned that the name *Hope* in Greek meant, *a confident expectation*. When we found out that we were pregnant again (before the modern age of certainty when you could read an ultrasound to determine the gender of the unborn child), I only hoped for a girl, but he was confidently expectant that the child I was carrying inside of me was, indeed, the fulfillment of his fondest hope. And then we waited. The pregnancy was a difficult one, and I was housebound the final few weeks. We were met with challenges in our personal, spiritual, and professional lives in those weeks before the arrival of our Bethany Hope. We had been a part of a local church that had become cultish and had asked us to leave when we questioned some of their methods, leaving me with absolutely no moral support during this trying time. Del was working in the biomedical labs at IBM and finding that the culture of the workers was putting the processes at risk. He was forming a proposal to suggest that IBM sell the business and abandon their pursuit of this particular business endeavor, possibly putting his own job at risk. So many trials were facing us during that season, but her arrival negated all of the hardship of those long months of waiting, and those other challenges grew dim in the brilliance of her smile and the delight of her daddy with his little girl. God later added an additional son to our family, Jeremy Luke (whose name means "God will lift up" and "Light").

Life presents challenges. I am now in a state of both waiting and expectancy. God's Word says we do not live as those who have no hope (1Thessalonians 4:13). I know that the time of my delivery into the arms of Heaven has not yet come, but I wait expectantly for that day when I will join my beloved again and we will continue to enjoy sweet fellowship. For all of the days that God blesses me with on this side of that veil, I am determined to live confident in my expected end. One day, I will join the saints who have gone before me in that Great Cloud of Witnesses. Until that day is upon me, I will lift up the light of His Kingdom and rejoice in His sweet fellowship and His always-good love!

Week Twenty-One: Time and Spiritual Maturity

March 6, 2014

Twenty-one weeks. Today marked the twenty-first week of trying to figure out how to do life without Del beside me in the tangible realm. His presence is still felt everywhere. He has left his tender marks throughout our home and in the love and laughter that are manifested in the hearts of his children. They embody his spirit and they were his finest achievement. Del was twenty-one when we were married. I was twenty-one when we lost our second child to a miscarriage at six months gestation and when I took that grieving and decided to throw my energy into getting my real estate license. Out of that loss, I found a new direction. I am still trying to figure out how to leverage the loss of his precious companionship and love into something that makes sense. Twenty-one. The number of weeks it has taken for the shock of his loss to go from acute pain to a constant ache and longing.

Biblically, the number twenty-one marks "time." When Daniel was in Persia he prayed, and an angel appeared to him and told him that God had heard his prayers as soon as he had lifted them. There was a great war in the heavenlies, however, that delayed the angel coming with God's answer for twenty-one days. Twenty-one. It is also the product of seven (spiritual perfection or maturity) and three (Divine perfection) multiplied (7 x 3 = 21). When I submit my will to His Divine care, He multiplies Himself in my life and I align myself to achieve spiritual maturity (perfection).

Today I found a paper Del had written that he entitled, "The Eternal Family." Del had been taken up in the Spirit and had seen things that he was reluctant to share. (For some people to be "taken up in the Spirit" means that they had an experience where it was as if they were in a dream, even though they are fully awake. I believe this is what happened to Del on this occasion.) I am thrilled that he finally decided to write them down. A portion of his experience was that he was taken into the foyer of Father God's house. While there, he saw children playing in the light of God's presence and declaring to their mother, "Mom, there are no shadows here!" (No carnal nature.) He felt the wind of God's glory stirring all around him. He could smell the fragrance of God's grace. He described it as a kaleidoscope of fragrances, many new, and some familiar. He said, "Oh, Father, You gave us those fragrances so we could smell You!" He then said, "I shouldn't be here!" as he fell to his knees. Father God knelt down and pulled Del onto His knee and then opened His hand. Del described it like this: "It seemed like I was looking into infinity. I could see stars there. I did not understand all that I was seeing, but there was one thing I could understand. Right there in the middle of His hand...my name...it was RIGHT THERE!"

I know that God has each of us in the palm of His hand. Our walls are ever before Him. He has good plans for each of us. Is it any wonder Del decided to stay once he was back in Father's lap again? I know that there is a tsunami of God's love that is going to invade the earth soon and we will all experience the WIND OF HIS GLORY, THE FRAGRANCE OF HIS GRACE, and the LIGHT OF HIS PRESENCE as it pierces the darkness.

Week Twenty-Two: Sons of Light

March 13, 2014

Twenty-two weeks. Twenty-two, the number of weeks it has been since I walked into a room and held the gaze of someone whose eyes adored me, the number of weeks since we exchanged a glance from across a room and instantly knew what the other was thinking and smiled in silent acknowledgment of that understanding. Twenty-two. The number of weeks since I poured out my heart to someone who loved me unconditionally and always wanted to know everything about my day. Twenty-two. Del and I were married on the twenty-second of December. Our marriage had its challenges. We learned how to give more grace to one another in our weaknesses and to focus on, and honor, our individual strengths. We learned to walk in the Light of His Word. The more Light He poured out as we sought His guidance, the more we learned to love. Twenty-two. In God's Word, we see the number twenty-two as symbolic of light. There are twenty-two letters in the Hebrew alphabet. There were twenty-two books in the Aaronic/Levitical Old Testament, the Light of God for Israel. There were twenty-two generations from Adam to Jacob (renamed Israel by God)! The book of John mentions light twenty-two times. On the twenty-second time John uses the word, he quotes Jesus as he says, "I have come as a light into the world so that everyone who believes in Me may not remain in darkness" (John 12:46).

This week I closed on three houses in three different counties, one in North Carolina and two in South Carolina. I have asked for God's favor and the Light of His guidance as I attempt to find properties to fix and flip to replace my husband's income. His promise to me is that He will direct my steps. Sometimes there is only enough light to take the next step. He speaks to me through His Word. "Thy Word is a lamp unto my feet and a light unto my path" (Psalm 119:105). He speaks to me through signs and wonders. He speaks to me through the wise counsel of friends and seasoned experts. Above all, He speaks to me in my heart. For, although I have lost the precious, engaging eyes of my beloved husband, the eyes of my Beloved Father are always upon me. He loves me better than anyone and He knows me better than anyone. His love is deep and unconditional. His love is immeasurable. He is for me. He is my Light and my salvation. Though my steps are cautious, I know He has promised to guide me. I rest in that promise, for He is worthy of my trust!

Week Twenty-Three: God is with Us, Abundance

March 20, 2014

Twenty-three weeks. Today marks twenty-three weeks since I lost my soulmate to Heaven's realm. This week has been difficult as I have observed my "going steady" anniversary without him beside me to reminisce about that magical evening forty-three years ago when he asked me to wear his high school ring. To me, this day was even more exciting than the day we became engaged, as it was the fulfillment of my fondest dreams to have this precious soul actually consider courting me. I had fallen in love with him when I was nine years old and he was thirteen. I had chased him around like a little puppy dog for years. (He called me his little sister. LOL!) He had gone away to college and I started writing to him every day. We shared our daily challenges and he discipled me in the things of The Lord. He inspired me and made me want to be a better student and a more devoted believer. I wanted to make him proud of me and his influence helped me to go from a mediocre student to an honor roll student. His spiritual life and devotion to prayer made me long to know Father God more.

The number twenty-three. In God's Word, this is the number for both abundance and death. Those two things seem like opposite ends of the spectrum to me. One of the most moving chapters of the Bible is Psalm 23, the shepherd's psalm, which begins, "The Lord is my Shepherd. I shall not want" (Psalm 23:1). This declaration speaks to abundance, painting a beautiful picture of a relationship that is both intimate and sure. "Thou anointest my head with oil; my cup runneth over" (Psalm 23:5). Just as the shepherd knew how he cared for the sheep under his care, he parallels how his Heavenly Father cared for him in the same manner. The final portion of this chapter ends with, "Surely goodness and mercy shall follow me all the days of my life; and I will dwell in the house of The Lord forever" (Psalm 23:6). Del now abides in His Father's house. He lived a life that was drenched in the goodness and mercy of our Good Shepherd. My comfort each day that I am away from him is found in the knowledge that Father God has Del in His great house with

Him. Del is reveling in the presence of Abba Father. Of this fact, I have no doubt. I don't begrudge him this joy. If anyone deserved to go home early and enjoy his reward, it was Del. He loved us well and he was well-loved.

Week Twenty-Four: Heaven and the Heavenly Servants

March 26, 2014

Twenty-four weeks. This week has brought challenges to our family as we have marked the twenty-fourth week since our beloved Patriarch's passing. We have all stumbled across "land mines," emotionally speaking. March is a month filled with significant dates for us. All three of our sons, our first grandchild, and two of our daughters-by-love were born in this month. Additionally, St. Patrick's Day and March 19th were also special days for Del and me. Because we were married only three days before Christmas, we decided that our "Going Steady" anniversary (March 19th) would be when we would celebrate our relationship so that we weren't crowding Christmas. We plan and God laughs! Preparing for March was even more expensive and hectic than December. Lol! I couldn't reminisce with Del about the significance of all of these special dates or the tender hearts that were joined to ours in the form of three amazing and Godly men or their wives and children. I could, however, lift my voice in thanks and worship for the gift of our family (and the gift of our only daughter who came to us in the autumn of the year because she wanted her own month).

My heart has been more and more centered on Heaven these days as I consider what Del is doing and seeing. As we touch his belongings and try to respectfully handle his personal effects, I am reminded that he no longer has an opinion about those things. They are so inferior to the stuff of Heaven. He always told us to embrace a "30,000-foot view" when we were analyzing a problem. His view far exceeds the 30,000-foot altitude now.

The spiritual number for Heaven and the priesthood is twenty-four. In the Book of Revelation, John describes twenty-four Elders who sit on twenty-four thrones in Heaven, each wearing a crown. They are continually bowing down before the Throne of God and worshiping Him. I once heard a woman give a testimony about being taken up into Heaven and seeing the Elders there. Her description of them tickled me, as it made them seem less fierce and more like Jesus. She said that in Heaven when you meet one of the twenty-four Elders, you instantly know who they are because they are always asking how they can serve you. They live to serve and draw pleasure from serving. I am reminded of the Words of Jesus when He said, "Whoever desires to become great among you, let him be your servant" (Matthew 20:26). I have seen days when Heaven has touched the earth. I have lived in moments of excruciating pain and unspeakable joy colliding. Del is gone. The memory of him lingers and I immerse myself in reflection, but I also know that he set the stage for us to carry on. I feel he is pulling strings in Heaven that are affecting us on earth so that we can do just that. On St. Patrick's Day, I submitted an offer for a house I have been trying to purchase for about two months, each time with a rejection. Located at Ocean Isle Beach, the house is about a mile from the ocean and backs up to Lake Joel. I had a specific number I didn't want to exceed. I had submitted at least twelve offers on it. The one I submitted on St. Patrick's Day was actually about $4,000 under my previous bids. I was just informed that the seller accepted my offer. When I found out about it, I felt like it was another kiss from Heaven.

Del was a wonderful provider while he was here on earth. He spoiled all of us with his generosity and his servant's heart. He learned that generosity and kindness by keeping the 30,000-foot view and trying to model his life like Jesus did. Jesus only did what He saw His Father do. Del wanted to be just like Jesus. He didn't always meet the mark, but he came closer than any man I have ever known. Is it any wonder that we miss him so very much? Jesus said when He was about to leave to go back to Heaven, "It is expedient for you that I go away: for if I go not away, the Comforter will not come unto you..." (John 16:7). We have been comforted to know that Del is in a wonderful place. And we have been comforted by the sweet presence of God's Holy Spirit as we journey through each day by His grace and His goodness leading us.

Week Twenty-Five: Grace, Favor, Redemption

April 3, 2014

Twenty-five weeks. As of today, we have muddled through twenty-five weeks without the wit and wisdom of one of the most gentle, unselfish, and tender-hearted men God ever created. His absence is felt daily, and so is his profound influence. I see him in his children's faces. I hear him in the wisdom that they dispatch. I laugh at their good humor and hear his puns oozing out of their beings. I find myself talking to him throughout my days, mostly telling him how much I miss him. I am frequently telling Father God how much I miss Del too. Father knows my heart is longing for Del's sweet presence. As I articulate to Him all the things I miss in a long and wistful list, I am reminded again that all of those attributes were just minuscule fragments that were reflecting Father's love toward me. He uses people to love us and to mentor us and to express His heart toward us. The number twenty-five is the number for favor and redemption, Biblically speaking. The number for grace or favor is five. When you multiply five times five, you have grace upon grace. I have always been astonished and humbled that a heart like Del's could be captured by my love. I never felt worthy of the man I married, but I always knew that nobody on earth could love him more than I did. Something about Del captivated me when I met him. I believe that I saw Jesus in Del and that association made me love him. Del's love and devotion to me changed me for the better. I always wanted to honor and respect him and make him glad that he chose me to be his life partner.

As I consider the gift of that love that was mine for more than forty years, I am also aware that The One Who gave that gift of love is still with me. He never leaves me. He never forsakes me. He is my eternal beloved and I am His. Again, how amazing is it that One, who is PERFECT, can love someone such as me and, yet, He does! GRACE is "unearned, undeserved FAVOR," a gift of God! One of the definitions of *favor* is *to be approved by someone; partiality*. Jesus paid the price for my redemption. His loving sacrifice brought me the gift of God's favor, His partiality, His approval. Del loved me so well, and I thanked him often for choosing me and for loving me. But

Father has an even higher love for me. He has redeemed me. He has called me by my name. I am HIS! The favor of God has rested heavily upon me and my family through these weeks of grieving and loss. It is assuring to know that this gift of unmerited grace will continue to be the banner under which we live out all of our days until He calls us home. Maranatha! (Greek: The Lord is Coming!)

Week Twenty-Six: God's Love and Adoration, the Name of God

April 9, 2014

Twenty-six weeks. We have reached the six-month mark from the date of Del's departure from his earth suit. In many ways, the loss feels much fresher than six months. In other ways, it feels like an eternity since I looked into those beautiful eyes that held my gaze from our first meeting. His eyes were gentle and kind, much like I picture the eyes of my Jesus. His eyes held a love for me which I have never seen reflected in the eyes of any other person on this earth. My parents, siblings, children, and friends love me, but not in that unique way that was reflected in the eyes of my beloved. Twenty-six. In Genesis 1:26 we read the account of God saying, "Let us make man in our image..." I believe that the "us" in that passage was a conversation between The Father, Son, and Holy Spirit.

As a family, the Trinity created mankind in their image, both male and female. The numeric value of God's name in Hebrew, "YHWH" is twenty-six. Since the twenty-sixth verse of the first chapter of His Word has Him infusing His precious image into mankind, what is He trying to show us in this revelation? I believe that the love and adoration that He holds in His heart for each of His children is greater than any love we can ever experience in human form. If we could gaze into His eyes, we would see such pools of liquid love there that our hearts would melt within us.

God gave the Torah (the first five books of God's Word) to Moses in the twenty-sixth generation of mankind. (From Adam to Moses there were twenty-six generations.) In this collection, God began to reveal His heart toward mankind and His loving and merciful nature as our Creator. There were twenty-six generations from King David to Jesus Christ, the heart of God born into a fleshly body to bring redemption to all of mankind. In the form of His Beloved Son, God revealed Himself to us as a loving Father, worthy of all of our affection and devotion. Jesus said, "The Son can do nothing of Himself, but what he sees the Father do; for whatever He does, The Son also does in like manner" (John 5:19). Twenty-six. It is also the Biblical number for The Gospel (Good News).

Del used to write me love letters. We exchanged letters daily while we were courting when he was one hundred miles away attending college. I read them over and over. I still have all of our letters from our courtship. God has written us a love letter too, His Word. He also sent us a love letter in the form of His Son to show us how far He would go to reconcile us to Himself. I long for the day when I can behold the eyes of my beloved Del once again, but I know that when I hold the gaze of my Beloved Father I will know that Del's love for me was just a small deposit borrowed from Father God. He loves me best. I am His favorite, and so are you!

Week Twenty-Seven: The Fingerprint of God

April 17, 2014

Twenty-seven weeks. I am tardy in posting my reflections on the twenty-seventh week of life without Del. I have done a lot of soul searching since his departure, and especially during this Holy Week when we acknowledge the PASSION of Christ the Beloved. I have been looking for the fingerprints of God in all of the elements of the unfolding of this new season for our family. Twenty-seven. That number is the Biblical number for the very fingerprint of God. Three times nine equals twenty-seven (with three being the number for both the Trinity and excellence, and nine being the number for spiritual completion).

We lost Del to Heaven's realm in the autumn of the year. We have now passed through winter with all of its woes. I heard many people state that it was the coldest winter they ever recalled enduring. My father lives in St. Louis and has endured many harsh winters but declared that this one was RELENTLESS.

Relentless. That word is usually connected to things that are unpleasantly plaguing someone, but I have learned to embrace it as one of Father God's most endearing qualities. He is relentless in His pursuit of the creation of a love story unique to each of us to share with Him.

Last evening my family gathered at our home here at Serenity to celebrate a belated Easter dinner together. We found joy in one another's company, even as we laughed and cried about some of Del's endearing attributes. A few of us watched some old home movies because we longed for the sight of him and the sound of his voice. After everyone had left the house, I put in one of the oldest videos of our family that I had. Del had captured a Christmas gathering that included his parents, a second birthday celebration for Jeremy, a fourth birthday celebration for Bethany, a thirteenth birthday for Nathan, a special trip to Kitty Hawk with Joel, and many other precious moments. I was fascinated to see the world through the lens of the cameraman. The images he focused on tell you a lot about his priorities. Del was always there behind the camera, trying to preserve moments for future reflections. I am sure he thought we would be enjoying them together one day in our dotage. Instead, I was watching alone, hungrily longing for the cameraman to step in front of the camera so that I could see his face and hear his voice. I was thankful for the precious images he had captured, but also fascinated to observe his heart as he took time to frame each person in so many of his sessions and speak to them directly so that they would address the camera and future generations. They didn't know that is what they were doing, but he knew.

Father God can sometimes seem like the elusive man behind the camera. Sometimes we don't hear His voice or see His face, but His fingerprints are everywhere. The vibrancy of this brilliant, green spring is His voice assuring us that life will be renewed again, and the cycle will go on. The lovely, Carolina, blue sky sometimes makes me wonder if He painted it that color so that we might know what His eyes look like. His fingerprints are truly everywhere, but especially upon my own heart as He has lovingly carried my family through this transition with the delicacy and tenderness that only a loving and faithful

Father could exhibit. Our journey into the unknown continues with the assurance that He is capturing these images in His own, Divine way for us to enjoy at a future date when all becomes clearer.

Week Twenty-Eight: Eternal Life, Our Great Hope

April 24, 2014

Twenty-eight weeks. The only person in the Bible to be given the description, "a man after God's own heart," was David, the psalmist/worshiper/warrior/king (Acts 13:22). He is mentioned in twenty-eight different books of the Bible. The number twenty is symbolic of waiting and expectancy and the number eight is the number for new beginnings.

For many years now, I have listed most of the houses I put on the market by adding the number 888 at the end. If a house was valued for $150,000, we would list it for $150,888. If it was $199,000, we would list it for $199,888. When asked by my clients why I chose such a strange number, I tell them that I am declaring that they will have a new beginning and I am doing it three times because three is the number for excellence. I am declaring that they will have an excellent, new beginning.

Week Twenty-Nine: Departure

May 1, 2014

As we reflect on the twenty-eighth week since Del has left this earth with all of its encumbrances, we are believing in a new beginning somewhere in the future with him. We wait with expectancy and hope for a new beginning. Del is already living that promise. As we are fully in the springtime of the year and watching new flowers and trees filling the earth with each new day, awakened to another season to shine with their glorious praise to the Creator who made them, we are made aware of the cycle of life and that seasons come and go on the earth. While he was here, I am convinced that, like David, Del was a man after God's own heart. May we strive each day to make it our quest to be a people who are chasing after God's heart as we wait in hope and expectancy for our new beginning.

Twenty-nine weeks. The number of weeks I have been processing the most pivotal moment in my life continues. As I wrestle with the implications and aftermath of a life without my heartthrob, I consider the Biblical character of Jacob in this twenty-ninth week and how he wrestled with The Lord. His name is mentioned in scripture twenty-nine times. He was renowned for being the only human who physically wrestled with The Lord. God's Word tells us that his night of wrestling ended in two profound changes in his life. God changed Jacob's name to Israel just before the break of dawn. His identity was forever transformed by this mysterious and supernatural encounter. The joint of his hip was also touched, causing him to have a distinct limp afterward so that, on the occasions that Jacob might forget his new identity, there would be a physical reminder of a spiritual change. He would no longer be "Jacob the Supplanter." He was now Israel. Now, when one called his name, they were declaring, "God prevails!"

When Del departed this natural realm, my identity changed. I was no longer able to mark the box "married." I was now faced with marking the box "widowed." I was no longer part of a couple. I was single and alone. My family and friends surrounded me and kept me going, just as I am sure Jacob's surrounded him after his encounter with The Lord that marked him forever. I am sure they asked why he now limped. God's Word states that Jacob's descendants never ate the tendon attached to the socket of the hip in memory of Jacob's transforming encounter. After that sacred time with The Lord, his twelfth son, Benjamin, was born. His family was not complete until after he had a change of identity. The number twelve is the number for Divine order and family. In the birthing of that son of destiny, Jacob lost his beloved Rachel. Her parting made the two sons born to him by her all the more dear to him.

I am looking for His Divine touch in my life. I am looking for His purpose as I am wrestling with an uncertain future. Like Israel, I know He has bigger plans for me than I can now see. I am destined to stake a claim in the Promised Land He has prepared for me. Del used to declare over me (to our children), "I love hanging out with this lady and watching how God moves for her." If I am limping a little in the aftermath of my struggle without Del's declarations (that God is always moving on my behalf, even in the tiniest details of my life), my faltering gait is just a reminder that my destiny is still being written. He has called me by a secret name. For now, I embrace His special name for me, "Beloved." For though I am now widowed, I will forever be the Bride of Christ.

Week Thirty: The Blood of Christ, Redemption

May 8, 2014

Thirty weeks. The nation of Israel mourned Moses' death for thirty days. Their mourning marked a time of transition into a new era under new leadership. Moses was the only leader Israel had ever known, and now he was gone and Joshua (symbolic of Jesus) was taking his place. Jesus and His cousin, John the Baptist, started their ministries at the age of thirty. In the lineage of those who were set aside to serve the priesthood, thirty was considered the time that they were of full maturity, both physically and mentally, to serve in the temple. At age thirty a man was considered mature enough to be commissioned as a soldier in the armies of Israel. Joseph became second in command to the king of Egypt at the age of thirty. David became king over Israel when he was thirty. This is also the number that symbolizes the blood of Christ and the betrayal of Christ by Judas for thirty pieces of silver.

Because it is the product of three times ten (3 x 10), thirty is also symbolic of Divine order in excellence. It can mark just the right moment in God's Divine plan for us. I don't know if it was a part of God's Divine plan for Del to leave us far too soon for our liking or comfort, but I know that He still has a plan for all of our lives. He has a plan for each one of Del's sons and his daughter. He has a plan for their seed as well. I humbly await the unfolding of that plan and I rest assured that, as His Word promises, "He who began a good work in you, will be faithful to complete it" (Philippians 1:6). The patriarch of our family is gone, but Jesus is leading us into a land of promise.

Week Thirty-One: The Intimate Name of God, I AM

May 15, 2014

Thirty-one weeks. Today marks the thirty-first week of my existence on earth without the one for whom I always felt like I was created. God created me to love that precious soul. His birth preceded mine by a little more than four years, and I feel that those were the only days Del walked on the earth that there wasn't someone breathing the same air and living under the same heavens who was meant to be his mate. Even before we met, we were in the same elementary school, just steps away from one another for the first two years of my schooling. I often wonder if we might have bumped into one another in the hallways or have seen each other across the playground.

My heart was his for the taking from the moment I met him at the age of nine. I admired him, respected him, and wanted to always make him proud of the woman I was becoming. Much of who I am is because of the love and wisdom he poured into me throughout our journey together. The source of that wisdom was not of this earth. God was the grantor of that resource and the grantor of the love we shared. Del walked in a humility and dignity that I have never witnessed in another. Pastor Mark Appleyard said of him, "When he walked into a room the spiritual climate changed because of his presence." Del was a carrier and courier of the presence of God. He was a lover of God. He was one who sought to understand God and to be sensitive to the leading of God's precious Holy Spirit. The spiritual climate could not help but change when he entered!

One of the Hebrew names of God is El, this is composed of the Hebrew letters Lamed (which represents thirty) and Aleph (which represents one). Combined these two numbers equal the number thirty-one.

God gives us a number of names by which to call upon Him. One of my favorites is El Shaddai, meaning "The God Who is More Than Enough!" or "The All Sufficient One," or "The Breasty One." Another one of His names is El Roi, "The God Who Sees." He is El Elyon, "The Most High God." He has carried me and been my sufficiency through my sorrow. I know that He sees me, and He is More Than Enough for me. He is high in the Heavens and He sees, and He knows, and He loves. Although I can't see what the days ahead hold for me, I know just as certainly as I knew that I was formed to be Del's mate, that God has a plan for the rest of my days. He doesn't waste anything. He uses all of life's challenges to help craft us into the beautiful creatures we were meant to become.

There is a popular song right now that is entitled, "All of Me" and I smile when I hear the lyrics, "All of me loves all of you, all your curves and all your edges; all your perfect imperfections..." (John Legend, writer). That is how God sees us. We are still becoming what we are meant to be. We haven't arrived. I have lots of "perfect imperfections" that need to be chiseled away, leaving only what He has in mind. Del loved me with all of my imperfections, and I loved him with all of his. There were times when we were not pleased with one another and we had disagreements, but we still always knew that we were meant for each other and we worked through those disagreements and found peace with our differences. Father God may not always be pleased with our imperfections, but He sees from a higher perspective and He is committed to us no matter our shortcomings. His perfect love trumps all of our shortcomings. He meets me, daily, with Divine hugs and kisses and signs and wonders. He occasionally lets me hear or see something that lets me know that Del is still up there pulling strings and cheering me on. God meets me with grace sufficient each day to make it through the pain of loss and look for a brighter tomorrow because, ultimately, He is preparing a Bride for Himself without spot or wrinkle and I want to be in that number.

Week Thirty-Two: Covenant, Fellowship

May 21, 2014

Thirty-two weeks. I find it hard to believe it has been thirty-two weeks since I poured my heart out to the one who always knew what to say (or what not to say). The number thirty-two is symbolic in the Bible of both "covenant" and "fellowship."

If you study the works of Dr. Gary Chapman, the author of The Five Love Languages series, you learn that most of us speak one of five love languages. If your mate learns to understand what language you speak and fills your "love tank" by speaking your language, you have a fighting chance at a great relationship. The five love languages are physical touch, quality time, gifts, acts of service, and words of affirmation.

My husband and I had exactly the same love language and it made it so easy to fill each other's love tanks. We both had physical touch as a primary love language and quality time as a second. We were in covenant together and we had sweet fellowship. I miss his counsel and his sweet presence. In this thirty-second week, I have found the courage to go back and read the sympathy cards that came pouring in after his sudden death. Going back and reading the words and reflections from so many who expressed their condolences and sympathy was bittersweet. In the fallout immediately following his loss, I tried to process all of the sentiments being expressed but could not. I was too busy coping with my own grief to allow room for the full impact of the grieving or the concerns of others to fully find a voice in my heart. Reading the words that so many folks wrote to honor Del and reflect on his influence in their lives was so precious to me. One of the things that struck me is that so many of the cards and letters were from folks who had never physically met Del.

He telecommuted for about thirteen years to both IBM and Dassault Systems. Many of his colleagues in Dassault were in France, and he had never traveled there to meet them. He would usually make it to Boston or New York to meet with his coworkers who were stateside once a year, but he didn't want to go to Paris (although they wanted him to come). In spite of the fact that he didn't get to see his coworkers in person, his personality and character were communicated (during phone calls and emails and webcasts) in such a way that these folks really had a sense of who he was. Some commented on what a gentle person he was, others on how generous he was, and one talked about how he knew that Del's family would be okay because Del was always planning ahead and coming up with a strategy for the future. Although they never saw him face to face, they knew him.

I was reflecting upon Father God's love for us and how He communicates it to us. Even though we don't get to see Him face to face yet, He is in covenant with us. He loves our fellowship and He loves to speak to us through so many different means. He isn't limited to language. He speaks to us through kindnesses expressed by others, through birds singing high up in the trees, through sunsets and sunrises that are painted in splendorous colors, no two ever precisely the same. He communicates His love through the hugs and affection of those with whom He has joined us. He speaks to us through His written Word. Truly it is a love letter, filled with raw emotion and broad strokes that paint a picture of a Father Who loves us dearly and longs for our fellowship. I am so thankful for the marriage covenant that I enjoyed with Del and for the family that is the fruit of that covenant. I am even more thankful for the God Who created covenants and patterned what it means to be in a covenant relationship. He loved the world, His creation, so much that HE GAVE HIS ONLY SON to die for us to restore us back into relationship with Him after mankind had fallen. I am privileged to walk out each day under the grace that His covenant provides. Although I am a widow, I am His Bride and His banner over me is LOVE! He speaks all of the love languages fluently and fills my cup to overflowing!

Week Thirty-Three: Amen! So be it! A Promise Fulfilled

May 28, 2014

Thirty-three weeks. Today we observe the passing of thirty-three weeks since Del went Home and left us here to figure out how to manage without his voice of wisdom and sanity. His voice is still in our heads and his good wisdom still guides our hearts, for the Source of that wisdom has never left us and never will.

Biblically, the number thirty-three represents the promises of God. When you look over the canvas of God's love letter to us, His Holy Word, you see many times that the number thirty-three correlates with the fulfillment of a promise. The thirty-third time Noah's name is used in His Word, God makes a promise to not destroy the entire world again with a flood. He puts a rainbow in the sky as a sign that He is pledging to never extinguish the earth again in the same way. When we see the rainbow today, we are reminded of His promise. The thirty-third time we see Abraham's name used in the Bible is when the child of promise, Isaac, is born to him. He was ninety-nine years old (3 x 33)! The most significant time that we see the number thirty-three in His Word is when the Promise of Redemption lays down His life for us. Jesus was thirty-three years old when He suffered the crucifixion and thirty-three years old when He triumphed over death, hell, the grave, and sin! God's Word tells us that this Lamb was "...slain from the foundations of the world" (Revelation 13:8). What an amazing concept! God already knew that we were going to mess up and He already had a plan to set things back in order.

My life has been through great upheaval in the past thirty-three weeks, but God has a promise for me and I am holding onto it. Though Abraham had to wait for it for ninety-nine years, the promised seed was born in the person of Isaac. Although the world had to wait for the Messiah for four thousand years, the promised seed of

God's only Son did come into the world to redeem us. Compared to the seed that God brought forth in these two sons of promise, my hope seems trivial, but not to Him. Del always told me that God was into the details of our lives and that He wanted to be invited into the minutiae of our daily grind. Father God has promised me that He has a hope and a future for me. He is the God of multiplication and not division.

I am believing that He will bring a new love into my life to share the rest of my days. Del and I always spoke about how we would cope without one another should God take one of us before the other. I felt that it would be years before I would be ready to consider the potential of a new companion, but God has been moving on my heart and showing me signs and wonders to prepare me for this possibility. I am in no hurry and if a new relationship unfolds, I will embrace it as His merciful gift and provision. He has afforded everything that I have ever had need of and if He has decided I have need of a new mate to share the balance of my days, I have no doubt that He will supply that need as well. I have learned that thirty-three is also the numeric equivalent of the word "AMEN," which means, "So Be It!" God has ordered and paid for many things for me over the past months in a supernatural way. If He should order a new companion then, "So Be It!" I will trust in His always-good love to bring me what I need when I need it. I will always love Del. He was my first love and my only love. If my life is a book, Del was the first half of the book, but God still has many more chapters to be written, and I am looking forward to all of the characters He will introduce to me in the second half of this saga.

(Thanks to all of you who have been following these ramblings and encouraging me in my journaling. I had thought about keeping this phase of my process to myself but thought it would not be honest to withhold this very sensitive and tender part of my journey from those who are walking with me through each step. Please keep me and my family in your prayers. I have felt those prayers sustaining me and there are many days that it is the glue that is holding me together. Blessings upon you...)

Week Thirty-Four: Identity, the Naming of a Child

June 5, 2014

Thirty-four weeks. The time passes, and I find that Father God still remains as near and tender-hearted to me as He was in those first moments when Del's life ceased on this side of eternity. He shows me through signs and wonders just how much He cares for me. He is aware of how deeply I feel the loss of the one whose life was so intertwined with mine. Thirty-four. Biblically, the number represents "identity" and is connected to the naming of a child. Thirty-four is also the product of seventeen times two (17 x 2). At week seventeen, I discovered, through researching several scholars who have made it their life pursuit to uncover the mysteries of how God speaks through numbers in His Word, that this was the number associated with the Love of God. My identity is tied to understanding just how greatly He loves me. I did nothing to deserve His great love. I am amazed by the favor under which I operate. Del would remind me of that great favor frequently. He would escort me to a front-row seat at a crowded event or a front-row parking place and say, "See how much Father cares for you? He is into the details of your life and He is just showing off for you." As Del would point out these small tokens of affection from Father God, I began to search for them myself and come to believe in the identity that He was revealing to me. He was saying, "Do not fear, for I have redeemed you; I have summoned you by name; you are mine" (Isaiah 43:1).

When Del was in tenth grade and I was in sixth grade our two choir teachers decided it would be fun to put the two choirs together for a Christmas production. During rehearsals at the high school, the other sixth graders were running around the gym making lots of noise in the wide-open spaces as I stood on the sidelines talking to Del (even then my main heartthrob, though he didn't know it yet). I was so pleased to be with him and to be treated like a "grown-up." When the older teenagers decided to corral the youngsters, they came over to gather me with the rest, and I was feeling a bit deflated when Del said to his upperclassman, "She's with me!" The upperclassman was satisfied that I was being accounted for and walked away. I instantly felt like I had grown ten feet tall. Del covered me and placed me in a position of favor that allowed me special privileges granted only to the students who were much older than I was.

At the age of seventeen, just after graduating from high school, Del gave me his name. I have always loved the name we shared and loved the identity that I wore as the bride of Delbert Lewis Teel II. As my life goes on, I don't know what my future holds, but I know that the identity that I carry as the Bride of Christ is enduring. He has called me by my name. I am His. He has redeemed me and loved me with an everlasting love. In a few days we will cross over the mark of the eighth month since Del's death. Biblically, the number eight represents new beginnings. In just a few days, I will be embarking on a trip to Ireland. This will be the first time I use my passport, as I have never traveled abroad. I don't know what Father God has for me on the Emerald Isle, but I know that there will be front-row seats and front-row parking spots and places of intimate encounter with Him there as I begin anew to discover who I am without my childhood sweetheart. Del's wisdom and counsel are forever emblazoned upon my heart, but my life has to find new purpose and meaning in this great unfolding of the journey Father God has for me. I am discovering who I am because I know Whose I am.

Week Thirty-Five: Hope

June 12, 2014

Thirty-five weeks. This is the Biblical number that represents "hope." In its use in the New Testament, the Greek word for hope means "a confident expectation." For thirty-five weeks I have awakened each day without Del beside me, but I rest assured in my confident expectation that I will one day gaze upon his face again, and we will continue to share our heart connection on the other side of the veil.

When Del and I were planning our family, he was desperate for a little girl. We had two amazing sons who had set the standard pretty high for being spectacular and accommodating, but he longed to be a daddy to someone whom he had imagined for years. He described her to me. He said she would have huge brown eyes and long dark hair. I knew how to parent little boys at that time, but I wasn't so sure how I would do with a little girl (having been one and knowing the fits I dealt my own mom). Lol! Del began to speak life over his dream. He said, "You will be best friends with our daughter. Your relationship will not be like any other that has ever been. It will be sweet and intimate and precious and legendary. You will 'get' each other and respect each other." He had "hope" and, a few months after he began making his declarations, I gave birth to Bethany Hope Teel. Her first name was in honor of the town in Israel where Jesus would go to find rest with his friends, Mary, Martha, and Lazarus. Del wanted her to be a friend of God and a habitation where He could go and be refreshed. Her middle name was for the "confident expectation" that he had that she would be brought forth to be a friend to her mother and a friend to God. She has been both. She is also fierce in her love and devotion to her friends. She is particularly tender during this season that she is observing the loss of the dearest friend God ever gave her besides His Own Son.

As we approach this first Father's Day without his sweet presence in our home, it is especially challenging for our family. Del's birthday and Father's Day often coincided. His birthday is June 18th and often fell on the weekend of, or the day of, Father's Day. We always tried to make a big event to mark that special day because he was so worth it. He would tell us not to make a fuss, but we always delighted in any excuse to honor him. He was such a godly example to me of how Father God loves us. You see, Father God has always had a plan for each of our lives. He has called us forth and given us a special name, known only to Him. He imagined us, and He spoke throughout the ages and called us forth.

Tomorrow I am taking two of my sons and one of my daughters-by-love (along with her sister) to Ireland. I have HOPE that during this Divinely appointed trip, I will see glimpses of Heaven there, through signs and wonders and favor that rests above me like the dew on the morning grass. I long to hear my Father's Voice speak to me of His future plans and direction for me and my family. I have a "confident expectation" that He will meet us there in a tangible way. I am also believing that my beloved Del is pulling on Father's heart to assure that Bethany and Joel (who will not be accompanying us this time) will be met in tangible ways with heaps of comfort and precious memories that warm their hearts and make their souls rejoice. Tomorrow, on week thirty-five plus one, I am stepping into the wondrous unfolding of my destiny. "For I know the plans I have for you, declares the Lord, plans to prosper you, and not to harm you, plans to give you a hope and a future" (Jeremiah 29:11).

Week Thirty-Six: The Wonder of Creation

June 18, 2014

Thirty-six weeks. Biblically, this number is linked to the wonder of creation. The eighteenth day of the sixth month (both based in the number six) is Del's birthday. My conviction is that God was having an especially brilliant moment when He created Del.

Today I am celebrating the amazing creation God made when he formed Del. I am marking the passing of thirty-six weeks since his departure. I am celebrating Our Father who created Del as one who truly carried His presence. He is now enjoying a portion of creation preserved for those who have fought a good fight and kept the faith. Some of my family (and extended family) have joined me in Ireland to mark this day. We have been overwhelmed by the beauty of His creation on this Emerald Isle. Father God has blessed us with supernatural weather. He promised me, a few weeks ago, that He would be smiling on Ireland while we were here. He has more than smiled. He has been dancing over us with singing. I have felt His warm embrace on many occasions. I have heard His sweet Voice (often with an Irish lilt, but unmistakably Him). I have witnessed profoundly moving landscapes and been more aware than ever of the value of LEGACY.

Our tour guide came out of retirement to lead this tour. I feel as though God plucked her out of repose because she was the best and He wanted us to have only His best. The lilt of her voice and her passion for Ireland along with its history are the perfect soundtracks for our experience. This morning she was sharing, with great pride, some of the works of Ireland's most renowned poets. She shared a poem that was so perfect for week thirty-six, which marks the wonder of creation. I am sure many of you have heard it in a hymn or read it before. It is entitled, "All Things Bright and Beautiful," by Cecil Frances Alexander. I encourage you to look it up and soak in the beauty of its words.

Week Thirty-Seven: The Word of God

June 25, 2014

Thirty-seven weeks. The number thirty-seven has been linked by Bible scholars to the Word of God. Delbert loved God's Word and made it a habit to consume it from an early age. Our youth pastor gave out special awards to anyone who would take the time to read the Bible from the beginning to the end and keep notes. As a teenager, Del completed that assignment at least twice. He told me that as he grew older, it was hard to get past the book of Genesis. He would find so many fascinating things to study in the book of beginnings, that it was hard to press past it. He once did a study on the men of Genesis and their ages at the time of their deaths. As he studied and did a graph of their ages, he discovered that it was altogether possible that Adam was still on the earth and in relationships with his descendants in such a way that the stories of creation would have easily been passed on from generation to generation. He was fascinated by the friendship that God had with Enoch. God's Word says that Enoch walked with God and that, one day, God took him. He never died. The friendship God had with Abraham also fascinated Del. It was always Del's desire to be a friend to God. When he would pray, he would often ask God, "How are you doing, Father?" He would align himself in such a way that he could hear what was on the Father's heart and pray according to what he was sensing in his spirit. This simple practice made him one of the most powerful intercessors I have ever known.

Many amazing men of God have been taken from us in the past few months and I have often wondered if they are up there talking to Enoch about what it was like the day God just walked home to Heaven with him. Del always said he wanted to ask Father God to show him the video feed of some of those amazing moments in the history of the earth and the lives of our fathers and mothers of the faith. If he has been able to tear himself away from the presence of God, I am sure that engineering mind of his has had delight in viewing those moments throughout the Word of God that provoked more questions than answers.

Week Thirty-Eight: The Glory of God

July 3, 2014

Thirty-eight weeks. Today we observe the passing of thirty-eight weeks since the physical departure of my beloved. Thirty-eight. It is the numeric value of the Hebrew word *kavoto*, which means *His glory.*

As the weeks have passed since Del has left us I have expressed multiple occurrences of a strange phenomenon. I find myself thinking, "I can't wait to share this with Del!" or "I will ask Del what he thinks," and then I remember, much like someone who has an appendage amputated and still feels phantom pains or itches in a toe, or leg, or finger that is no longer there, I can no longer tell Del anything on this side of eternity. My mind betrays me and makes me feel the pain of his loss once again. Then I remind myself that Del is in Heaven and basking in "His glory." Del is in God's presence. Our Father sees all and knows all and Del is hidden in Him. Therefore, I believe that Del already sees what I am seeing and knows what I am experiencing. I know that He would want to say to me, "In the presence of His glory, there is no darkness or sadness or betrayal. There is only love, joy, peace, and abundant provision."

Before I left for Ireland, my former pastor, Barry Taylor, said to me, "Be sure you take both sets of eyes with you, both your natural and your spiritual." He told me, "You will see glimpses of Heaven." He couldn't have been more accurate. As we moved throughout a Divinely orchestrated pilgrimage, Father kept showing me His glory. The whole adventure could be summed up in one word: love. He manifested His unmerited, extravagant favor and love at every turn. He spoke to me through the beauty of His creation, through the ancient stories of that land, through the mournful sounds of the pipes, the jubilant sounds of drums and reels, and through the lilt in the voices of the folks who call Ireland home. His glory surrounded us. As we continue to adapt to a life that is absent the fellowship of our dear patriarch, we revel in the presence of The One who will never leave us, never forsake us, and whose heart can be trusted with all of our tomorrows. We cry out, "Show us your glory, Father!" Not only will we find everything we need there, we will also find Del there, abiding in His presence.

Week Thirty-Nine: Morning Dew and Excellent Things

July 10, 2014

Thirty-nine weeks. Thirty-nine weeks have passed since we lost the gentle soul that was Delbert Lewis Teel. The pain is less acute than in the first days after his passing, but the knowledge that we will not hear his most excellent wisdom or feel his touch on this side of eternity is more real than ever and often leaves us feeling completely hollow. Life has thrown us a few curve balls and our first thought has always been to run to Del with our troubles, listening for his wise counsel and leaning on his understanding that often exceeded our own. We would talk to him about our challenges until he had either helped us find a solution or had given us the encouragement we

Grieving by the Numbers

needed until a solution developed. Del excelled as a father and a provider because he always had his eyes on the pattern of his Heavenly Father and Provider.

When I see the number thirty-nine, I immediately see a combination of threes and hear the scripture "Have not I written to thee excellent things in counsels and knowledge..." (Proverbs 22:20). (The word "excellent" in this place of scripture is rightly divided as "three-fold things.") The number thirty-nine also has the "value" of the Hebrew word *tal*, which means *morning dew*. Making decisions and plans without Del has made us drawn even nearer to The One Who wants to teach us "excellent things." Father God is The One Who is the source of all wisdom, understanding, and counsel. His Word encourages us, "If any of you lacks wisdom, you should ask God, who gives generously to all without finding fault, and it will be given to you" (James 1:5).

This morning, in preparation for my parent's departure as they started their journey back to St. Louis, I walked out to the garden to see all that my father had been fussing over the weeks that he has been here. (Jeremy and my dad had planted a garden a few days after Dad's arrival, and it is already producing fruit.) The morning dew was still embracing the grass as I made my way to the garden, causing me to reflect upon how Father God once walked the earth and had communion with mankind. The earth, before the fall of man, was watered by the morning dew and that is all that the Garden of Eden required. I long for the day when we will be restored to fellowship with Father God in such a way that we can walk in His garden, once more, and hear His gentle voice and enjoy His fellowship in

137

a tangible way. For now, He invites each of us to seek Him and His good counsel and kind heart. Although we may not be able to hear His audible voice, He is still speaking to us. Sometimes we hear Him through the voice of our pastor on a Sunday morning. Sometimes it is through the sweet fellowship of His Spirit as He makes a scripture come to life for us and speaks exactly the right word we needed to hear for that day. (It is our daily bread.) There are times He speaks to me through nature, and times He speaks to me through the kind act of a stranger. I am confident in this one thing, He is GOOD, and His mercy endures FOREVER. I know that He has an "Act Two" for the unfolding of my life and the lives of my children. I know that He will raise up saints who will help to fill the empty places in the chambers of our hearts. He will teach us excellent things and we will dwell in the house of The Lord forever, where Del is dwelling now, looking through Heaven's portals and cheering us on from a much higher elevation.

Week Forty: The Test, Trusting in God

July 17, 2014

Forty weeks. Today we observe the significant mark of forty weeks since Del drew his last breath on earth and began breathing the air of Heaven. He has been enjoying that wondrous atmosphere now for 280 days! Forty is the Biblical number for testing. Del used to say, regarding the forty days Jesus was in the wilderness facing His test, "It took the children of Israel forty years to pass their test in the wilderness. It took Jesus only forty days." As I have reflected on Del's early departure, I have often thought of his statement and said, "Del passed all of his tests and got to go home early."

My forty weeks have certainly been a time of testing and stretching. Father God's always-good love has been demonstrated to me extravagantly. Whenever I waver in my steadfast hope in Him and doubt myself, I hear His voice asking, "Do you trust me? Have I not proven over and over that I have covered you with my wings and hidden you in the cleft of the Rock? Have I not poured out my favor and love over you in full measure?" And I answer, "Yes, Father. My cup is overflowing with Your great love."

My businesses have prospered supernaturally. His provision throughout this tender season has been nothing short of miraculous and breathtaking. While in Ireland a few weeks ago, I described the experience as "Awe Overload" because of the beauty and wonder my soul was experiencing around every corner. My walk with Father in all matters concerning my provision has been the same. I have been in awe at His goodness and bountiful provision. He has shown me hidden things to supply my every need.

Del went home just two months shy of our fortieth wedding anniversary. I had never been on a date with anyone but Del, until this week. This week I went on my first date, and it was terrifying. I felt as if it were a test. I felt the peace from God to go (although the butterflies in my stomach were not giving me peace). I felt Del cheering me on. I had all of my children encouraging me. (They even had a slumber party they let me crash afterward to "dish" on how it went.) I tried to just treat this launch as a test. I must confess that I walked away feeling more insecure and questioning myself further. I heard the Voice of my Father asking me again, "Do you trust me? Have I not proven my extravagant love and provision for you? Do you think I have forgotten to supply ALL OF YOUR NEEDS?" You see, it was a test. For, although I can put on a piece of paper what I think I must have in a mate (and believe me, I have written a "Manifesto" about act two that articulates those things), only He knows exactly whom He has hidden for me to share the second act of my life with. He knows, and He is watching over me and Mr. Act Two and assuring that everything will be aligned in perfect orchestration. He has so beautifully conducted all of the music of my life thus far. How can I doubt Him?

Del passed all of his tests early. When he was in school and classmates saw him walk in they would groan and say, "Oh, no! Teel is going to ruin the grading curve for all of us!" because he excelled in his studies and typically aced all of his tests. If anyone deserved to get a jump start on fellowshipping and drinking in the joys of Heaven early, it was Del. I am still here, muddling through, but I think I passed this latest test. Every time I find myself fretting, I just remember Father asking, "Do you trust me?" I take a deep breath, step into His abiding presence, and say, "Yes, Abba, I do!"

Week Forty-One: Separation and the Flowing Waters

July 24, 2014

Forty-one weeks. Today marks the passing of forty-one weeks that Del has been separated from us here on the earth. Del ran the race and finished his course. He crossed over the waters of the spiritual Jordan and stands on the Promised Land on the other shore. Biblically, the number forty-one is symbolic of both separation and the flow of water.

As I reflect on these two things, I think about what has developed with me this past week. After visiting with a very dear friend on Sunday, I took a drive into Wilmington. While on my way there, my vision suddenly became blurred and I was seeing double at a distance, which was a disconcerting feeling. The headlights coming toward me seemed disconnected from the cars. I was disoriented. My eyes had been perfectly focused earlier in the day. I grabbed my prescription sunglasses and put them on. Suddenly, things came back into focus, but only as long as those glasses were in place. (As it is an extremely mild prescription, I don't normally wear them for any other reason than for the lower portion that acts as a magnifier; my arms just aren't long enough anymore to focus on the tiny print. LOL!) When I went to see a local eye doctor I was informed that I had two issues. One issue was eye strain (thank you, goofy smartphone) and the other was that I was "not producing enough tears." The irony of having a recently widowed woman be told that she wasn't producing enough tears almost brought on a floodgate of tears all by itself.

This paradox made me think about the scripture in 1 Corinthians 13:12: "For now we see through a glass, darkly; but then face to face: now I know in part; but then shall I know even as also I am known."

The Message translation reads, "We don't yet see things clearly. We're squinting in a fog, peering through a mist. But it won't be long before the weather clears and the sun shines bright! We'll see it all then, see it all as clearly as

God sees us, knowing him directly just as he knows us!" (1 Corinthians 13:12).

As long as I had my prescription glasses on, I could focus on the lines in the road and see the outline of the headlights coming toward me, but when the glasses were removed, I was not seeing a true picture of what was coming at me.

Father God has a set of glasses He wants us to put on. His filter allows us to see the world, and our lives, through His perspective. With His lenses, we can see that those who have been separated from us are only a short distance ahead of us up the stream and around the bend. Our loved ones who have gone before us are totally aware of their true identity. Some may have been aware of it before they parted this earth. Most, I imagine, didn't find out until they crossed over that vast expanse and saw themselves as Heaven has always seen them. I want to know now what my true identity is, as defined by my Heavenly Father. I want a clear focus so that I can see what lies ahead and I can run the race set before me as brilliantly as Del ran his race. I want to run my race the way Jesus ran His race. He always knew His true identity. He was His Father's Son and, because of the atonement paid for by His precious blood, I am my Father's daughter. I am contending for clear vision so that I may finish all He has for me to do before He bids me to come to the other side of those waters. Del was my first love but The Lord Most High is my Everlasting Love. I will not be satisfied until I have fulfilled the destiny He has for me. "Father God, let the waters of revelation flow from your throne of grace and separate me from the tyranny of the temporal so that I am living from Heaven to earth!"

Week Forty-Two: Laboring to Enter into Rest

July 31, 2014

Forty-two weeks. We have made our sojourn without the precious voice of our family's patriarch for forty-two weeks now. We are each processing it in our own way. Tonight, I watched the video that Bryon Bench (Bench Studios) put together to honor Del after his passing, a compilation of pictures and some of Del's favorite music compositions. I hadn't watched it in several months. Del loved well-written music. He would play the same piece over and over again and try to figure out each and every piece. "What was that instrument?" or "What chord progression did they use there?" Where I once wept when I reviewed it, a warm smile now crosses my face as I reflect, once more, on how truly special he was on this earth, and how blessed we were to be part of his tribe.

In God's Word, we read that the tribes of Israel had forty-two sojourns (wanderings) in the desert until they finally found rest. I have felt the voice of God telling me that I need to go and rest and reflect. I went to the North Carolina Mountains last week and had a time of reflection. Father arranged for a spiritual brother to take me on a tour of some wondrous sites I didn't know existed in this state, including a magnificent waterfall that roared and reminded me of the voice of God. "And His voice was like the sound of many waters, and the earth shone with His glory" (Ezekiel 43:2). The rest was precious (and far too brief). I felt like He was showing me hidden things. They were not hidden to my guide, but I knew nothing about them. God revealed them to me in His time, with the help of a kingdom-minded brother who had been there before.

The number forty-two is the product of six times seven (6 x 7). The number six is the number of man. We know that God created man on the sixth day. We know that He rested from His work of creation on the seventh day. Seven is the number for perfection. Notice that perfection doesn't come without rest.

I have felt driven to perform, to succeed, to overcome since Del passed. I have a "to do" list that never ends. I keep hearing this voice that reminds me that I must "Labor to enter into God's rest. For anyone who enters God's rest also rests from their works, just as God did from His. Let us, therefore, make every effort to enter that rest" (Hebrews 4:10-11).

To have to "labor" to enter into rest seems like an oxymoron. The struggle I face is constant. Father has provided for us in extravagant measure since Del's passing. He has miraculously anointed my business and given me favor at every turn. Last week, as I contemplated whether I should spend the money on a little getaway and some "me" time, He reminded me of just how generously He has blessed all of my labors. I have very clearly been given a gift of a season of supernatural favor and Divine provision, and yet I struggle to give myself permission to just rest. I know that I am walking in a grace bubble and I am tempted to let the enemy drive me out of it. When he rages against me and causes me to fear, I run into the arms of Abba and find rest there. His perfect love casts out all fear. His blessed assurance quiets my soul and helps me to get up and face another day with the knowledge that I am one step closer to being reconciled to Him and to Del. He also reminds me that I have only finished act one and I still have at least one more act in this play that is unfolding.

Just a couple of weeks after Del's passing, in the early morning hours between waking and sleeping, Del came into our bedroom. I saw him walk through the closed door. I saw only his profile. He never faced me. I lay on the bed, looking at his silhouette as he said, "You are so loved and so covered in prayer." I smiled and said, "I know." He then vanished, and I awakened. When Del was on this earth he was devoted to prayer. I feel that we are abundantly blessed with the harvest of the seeds that he planted while he was here, along with the prayers of our precious family members who have preceded him into Glory. Our wanderings continue until we reach our Promised Land. In the meantime, we remember that the children of Israel had manna rain down from Heaven to meet their daily needs. Their shoes never wore out and there was not one feeble among them. As I learn to live from Heaven to earth, I hope to become far more skilled at the discipline of resting in Him. He is worthy of my trust. He is worthy of my faith. He is worthy of all my devotion. "Thank you, Father, for teaching me to rest!"

Week Forty-Three: Contending

August 6, 2014

Forty-three weeks. This Thursday marks the forty-third week that has passed since our contending for Del to remain on earth ended. The number forty-three in God's

Word is the number for contending. During the first moments of that fateful event, the attending physician came out of the emergency room where they had been working on Del (after he had collapsed in the floor with a massive heart attack as we were having him admitted) and said, "Your husband is clinically dead. We can't get a consistent rhythm and hold it steady." I looked her in the eye and said, "The Lord is going to give you wisdom so that you will know what to do to get his heart going again." (My gift of faith was on automatic pilot.) She took a deep breath and said, "Thank you for that!" Then she turned and went back into the room and continued trying other methods and soon I heard the rhythm of his heart. That blessed sound gave me a moment of hope. As a floodgate of emotions assaulted my soul, my spirit was in another place, contending for the life of my beloved to return to me every bit whole. Reinforcements began to arrive to assist me in my contending, as forces from around the globe got word that Del was fighting for his life and joined their faith to ours for a happy outcome. As they transported Del to another facility where he could receive even more excellent care, we continued to contend. We had more folks join us in our battle at the new facility. Still more believers were awakened to the news and added their prayers to ours as the army of contenders grew. Surely God would hear our prayers and answer them, we thought. But, twenty-eight hours later, Del stepped into his Heavenly Father's arms and out of mine.

This past week has been an especially difficult one for me as I process his loss in new ways. Things seem fractured, disjointed, and chaotic without him. Del was the one who brought sanity to my crazy life. He was the safe harbor I always returned home to after a stormy day. I miss having him walk up behind me and just wrap his arms around my waist and hold me. I miss the long conversations as we would lie in bed in the darkness, reflecting on our day or sharing our hopes and dreams for our future. A million tiny little things I miss, and I cherish the memories that are so dear.

When we first lost him, we would take turns going into his office to feel like we could still absorb some of his wisdom and sense his presence. That feeling of proximity related to his physical possessions has long since faded. I am faced with a closetful of clothes that need to find a new home and an office filled with remnants of an industrious genius whose projects I can't begin to wrap my head around. He was always researching, scheming, inventing, and strategizing. The accolades from his successful career are on the bookshelves and his desk.

There is a model of the F-15 fighter he helped to design for McDonnell Douglas in his early career, a project of which he was particularly proud. A letter of thanks for his contributions to the advancement of blood processing machines as he worked in the biomedical division of IBM is among his possessions. Books about the French culture and software for learning the French language so that he could more effectively communicate with his French counterparts in Dassault Systems line the shelves.

Del's greatest achievements, however, cannot be found within the walls of his office or the files of the corporations he so faithfully served. For, you see, Del was a contender. Del would contend, in prayer, for those who the Holy Spirit laid upon his heart to carry before the

Throne of Grace for answers in their hour of need. He was the one who first taught me how to contend for the promises of God. He discipled me in the Word of God and taught me how to bring my petitions before Father God and expect Him to hear me and bring about answers that were for my good. Those answers were not always what we had hoped for, but we didn't stop contending. One of the most important lessons Del taught me was that "Without faith, it is impossible to please God" (Hebrews 11:6), and "The trial of your faith, being more precious than of gold (to God) ..." (1 Peter 1:7). Del would say, "Your absolute faith in God, whether His response is what you had hoped for or not, is one of the only gifts you can give to Him. You have no possessions in life that did not come from Him. The one thing you can give to Him is your trusting heart." Just as the currency of Heaven is love, the currency of our earthly devotion to Him is our faith in His always-good love.

And so, I give to God this heart of mine, with all the trust that He so rightly deserves. I trust that He knows my longings and my heartache and that He sees my loneliness and He collects these tears, which lie in puddles at His feet. I trust that He knows my insecurities and my weaknesses and loves me in spite of them. And, I trust that I have, in His Beloved Son, a Contender who is seated at His right hand, ever interceding for me. "Comfort me, Holy Spirit, that I may comfort others with the same comfort by which you comfort me! Contend for me, Jesus, until I feel Your loving arms surround me and hear Your whispers speak to my soul in the lonely hours of the night. Dream with me, Father God. Bring to me the dreams of Heaven and the future that will unfold brightly and full of the fulfillment of Your promises. My hope is in You!"

Week Forty-Four: A Chosen People, the Sons of Light in Double Portion

August 14, 2014

Forty-four weeks. Today we mark the passing of forty-four weeks since we last heard the quiet shuffle of feet across the floor or the gentle sound of Del's comings and goings from a room. He was so quiet in his manners that he would clear his throat or give a short cough as he was coming into a room so that he would not startle you. Years of realizing that he startled people because of his soft approach had taught him to announce himself, in some small way, to avoid feeling badly about the unintended effect his ninja movements would have on his fellow man. If he engaged my eyes before approaching me, he did not have a need to make those quiet sounds. If he didn't have my eyes upon him, he knew to make certain that he had given warning to me. This consideration was just one of the endearing qualities that I adored about this man. There were so many thoughtful and extraordinary things that he would do as a part of just being "Del" that would never have crossed my mind to do because I am not bent the same way. No wonder my heart chose him when I was only nine years old—or did it?

Biblically, the number forty-four correlates with a "chosen people" and is double the number twenty-two which is the number for "sons of light." Del was definitely a son of light. He brought wisdom and calm to any room he entered. At his homegoing service, Pastor Mark Appleyard had observed, "Del walked into the room and instantly the spiritual temperature was changed by his presence." The number forty-four is also two fours side by side, which points to the creation. (On the fourth day God created the sun, the moon, and the stars.) I have always been astounded that God's Word says in the Gospel of John, "You did not choose Me, but I chose you..." Can you imagine the significance of being told that the God of all creation chose you? What an astonishingly wonderful thought! God chose me! The passage goes further to say: "I chose you...that you should go and bear fruit, and that your fruit should remain..." (John 15:16). So, He chose me to make a difference in His creation. Del's fruit remains. His words of wisdom still echo in our ears. His prayers are still being answered every day. His children carry the bearing of his dignity and grace. His grandchildren will be taught their grandfather's wise sayings and carry that mantle with them into the generations to come.

God's Word says that He gives us the desires of our hearts. That doesn't mean that He gives us what we want; it means that He places certain desires inside of us that He chooses for us to contend for, and to realize as His best and brightest hope for us. I think that, because I was a child when I first met Del, I was still moldable to the moving of His Spirit in me to see that my future was intended to be linked to Del's. As driven or task-oriented as I may be, there was a quietness in me that resonated when Del was near, whether occupying my thoughts or engaging my eyes. He was my chosen one. God placed the desire in my heart for him and He was faithful to fulfill that desire.

In this forty-fourth week, I reflect on the longings and stirrings in my heart to have that kind of connection again. Not because my love for Del was so shallow that I am ready to move on to my next heart connection. Rather, it is the certainty that Father God has already chosen another heart to share my act two, and I want to know that kind of fellowship and friendship again. I remind myself that I had to wait a lot of years for my body to mature to a point that Del would see me as anything other than his "little sister."

Perhaps God is preparing my spirit to mature to a place that I am ready to be the helpmate to the one He has chosen for me. I have cried out to Him and asked Him to just take this part of me out so that I can go on without ever having to connect with another love again. Del loved me so well and made me feel desirable, no matter what I looked like. On good days and bad days, he always made me feel loved and wanted. When I look in the mirror, I don't see what Del saw. He looked at me through the love Father God had placed in his heart for me and loved me in spite of my flaws, just as I loved him. That is how Father loves me. He sees me through a lens of love. He sees me through the covering of His perfect Son, Jesus.

And so, I wait. I take all of my hopes and desires to His feet and try to leave them there. I remind Him that He created me with all the attributes I possess, and I give Him permission to write new instructions across the tables of my heart. Recently, Jason Clark spoke in our church and encouraged us not to settle for a bathtub full of water when God has an ocean filled with promises awaiting us. Those words resonated with me, and I was encouraged to contend for all His promises, including the promise of another love to share my life and my longings. I am His chosen one. I am a daughter of light, created in His image, and destined to bring forth much fruit that will last. I am destined to keep creating a legacy on the earth for the glory of Father God and to honor the memory of the one Father joined me to for what feels like only a fleeting moment on this side of the forty-fourth week.

Week Forty-Five: Preservation of the Priceless

August 21, 2014

Forty-five weeks. Today marks the passing of 315 days without my spiritual mentor, my best friend, my lover, the father of my children, my anchor, my most treasured and undeserved gift. Biblically, the number forty-five deals with maintaining, protecting, or preserving the things that are the most precious to you. As we march further and further away from that life-altering date, we are forced to deal with what is left of Del's treasures. We have marched up that mountain before and slain a few giants, only to return, weary from the effort. What stays? What goes? Who might enjoy this memento or this trinket? Who would truly understand the history behind this little piece of nostalgia? Then we walk away, too frustrated with more questions than answers and unwilling to mentally sort through one more drawer or one more notebook filled with his reflective musings. Del journaled everything. We have stacks of books that contain his notes from various projects he was involved in but, there in the margins, are notes such as, "Joel took his driver's test," or "Jan returns from St. Louis today," "Jeremy asked Elizabeth to be his wife," "Nathan conquered next level," "Joel and Laura are going to have a little one," "Bethany in Israel at Embassy," "A.J. asked me for Bethany's hand in marriage." As Joel was thumbing through the journals shortly after his father's death, he said, "Dad lived his life in the margins." Del preserved for us the history of our family from his perspective.

We never realized just how much of our family's history and moments Del was preserving because his journals were sacred. We didn't dare touch them for fear of disrespecting things he treasured and counted on every day. When I couldn't remember a date that something happened, I would go see Del and say, "Do you remember when we had the fence put up?" or "Do you remember who the guy was who said he would come back next year and trim the trees again?" And Del would thumb through one of his engineering notebooks and find the answer almost every time. In the days following his death, we would take turns sitting in the chair in his office and scouring through the pages of his sacred scribbling, reading journal after journal in chronological order, trying to draw out a snippet of connection to this dear one who would never return. We would look with hungry eyes for some new revelation that had been hidden from us. I always knew he had a brilliant mind, but the compressed pages filled with his thoughts revealed even more of his genius and his tender heart.

Among all of the earthly treasures that Del left for us, these journals are the most valued. Time will pass, and other items may lose their perceived value, but those words represent an investment of time and energy that cannot be duplicated. No one else has the same history as this family. No other family would treat these words as sacred treasures because this family knows the author of these words. They have felt the beating of his heart as he held them near. They have known his gentle touch and quiet ways. They have known that his love for them was fierce and generous and he was proud of their accomplishments and shared in the grief of their sorrows.

Father God has left us His journal. He has left it in His Holy Word. He has left it in His creation. He has left it in the imprint of His influence on the lives of those who have demonstrated His love toward us in friendship and fellowship. He has left it in the deposit He makes within us when we receive Him into our hearts. His Word says, "But we have this treasure in earthen vessels (jars of clay) . . . We are hard pressed on every side, but not crushed: we are perplexed, but not in despair; persecuted, but not forsaken; struck down, but not destroyed" (1 Corinthians 4:7-9).

Those who know Father God appreciate these treasures more than those who do not know the Author, just as Del's family reveres his journals because they know the author. God is preserving, maintaining, and protecting us. We are His greatest treasure. We are His greatest work of art, work of literature, and work of creation, still being formed. As we face these tender seasons of transition and we awkwardly try to figure out how to do life, He is still writing instructions on the tablets of our hearts. My conviction is that Del is with Father in Heaven now and he occasionally asks for permission to intervene to assure that his family is heading in the right direction. We are still trying to achieve things that would make Del proud and, more importantly, things that make Abba Father proud, just as Del taught us to do. "Father God, help us to treasure the things that you treasure. Help us to sort through the stuff of earth and find the gems in this life. Help us to preserve those things that money cannot buy and pass along this unspeakable treasure to other hearts so that they may be changed by truly knowing the Author and Finisher of their faith."

Week Forty-Six: Reconstructed Life and Resurrection

August 28, 2014

Forty-six weeks. Today we observe the forty-sixth week of trying to figure out how to do life without the gentle voice of wisdom who walked among us far too briefly. Oh, how we have longed for his sage counsel over the past ten months, and especially so in the past few weeks. In an effort to be totally transparent with those of you who have been following these weekly posts for the past ten months, I must tell you that this past week brought me some of my highest highs since Del's departure and some of my lowest lows.

Biblically, the number forty-six represents reconstructed life and resurrection. In order to have my life reconstructed, elements of the old life must change. This transformation is painful to me and my family. We are forced to, once again, release Del and all that he was to us on this side of eternity. For there to be a resurrection, there must first be a loss. Change is uncomfortable, and our loss is profound.

In this forty-sixth week, I introduced a new person Father brought into my life to my family. He and his children have suffered the same kind of loss as this clan. In many ways, I believe their loss to be even more profound as the very heartbeat of their home, their mother, was taken from them far too soon. I have found in this precious soul a heart that understands my loss and knows that I will never "get over it" and nor will he. We have an opportunity to partner with Father to build a new life and to experience a new love. Reconstruction. Resurrection. Father is in the business of redemption. His Word says, "Behold! I make all things new" (Revelation 21:5). This renewal is both a marvelous thing and a tender thing. I was simply looking for a companion to share my sorrow and lift my heart's load. What I found in him was a lovely and unexpected gift. He took my heart by surprise because that is what Father ordered and I don't say "No!" to Father's gifts.

My family, although expressing their desire to see me happy again, were not prepared for the reality of seeing someone (other than their precious daddy) standing beside their mom and declaring his affection. One of my sons even told me that he knew, mentally, this was okay. His heart, however, kept screaming, "Are you two crazy? What is Dad going to say when he comes around the corner, offering everyone a cold Starbucks Mocha and another man is taking his position?" The stark reminder that Dad is not coming back was standing before them, holding Mom's hand and proposing a new future that included a stranger. They didn't take the prospect easily.

As the days since the initial shock have worn off that, yes, Mom is moving on with her life and believing Father's promise that He will make all things new, hearts are beginning to open. This beloved "interloper" has three lovely daughters and a handsome son, and I have one lovely daughter and three handsome sons. Facebook has provided a vehicle by which these eight souls can initiate getting insight into one another's family dynamics and begin to carefully reach out and request an opportunity to get to know one another. It is a tender season for everyone, and, only as we lean into the One who promises that He will guide our every step, do we find peace.

Delbert Teel was a legend. His wisdom, compassion, and generosity cannot be matched because he reflected his Heavenly Father with excellence. He loved us well and he was well-loved. He would be the first person to applaud this new beginning and to cheer us on and encourage us to listen to the Voice of God's Spirit, believing the best and hoping the best. Del once told me, when we were embarking on a scary new chapter of our lives and leaving behind what was familiar and comfortable, "New beginnings are so exciting! Who knows? Perhaps the Lord has brought you here for such a time as this?" I feel like this is one of those moments.

So, my faithful friends, family, and curious followers, please continue to carry this Teel Clan before Father's throne of grace and request His continued favor and wisdom. While there in His presence, please add the Nealis Clan to your petition. We are all believing for Father's gift of a reconstructed future and resurrected hearts. We covet your prayers and treasure your friendship.

Week Forty-Seven: High Calling, Humility

September 3, 2014

Forty-seven weeks. This Thursday marks the forty-seventh week since Del drew his last breath on this side of eternity. Every Wednesday since that life-altering date, I look at the clock and think about what I was doing during those hours after he suffered the heart attack that would prove to be fatal. Every Thursday I consider what it was like to have the doctor state, "We have done all that we can for him. Your husband will not survive this event. You must prepare to let him go." The doctor's words were spoken as if he didn't realize that he had just told me that the person I loved the most dearly in all the world was going to be leaving me, and there was nothing that I could do to pull him back. No amount of crying out, bargaining, or pleading with God would bring his broken body back to life. No heart-wrenching screams of disbelief (and there were plenty of those as my family gathered to hear the news) would alter God's decision to take Del home. He had a higher calling awaiting him that I still don't understand. (One of the meanings of the number forty-seven is a "high calling.") I watched as God called home several of His special generals during that season and I contemplated what might be happening in a realm beyond what we could see on this side of the veil.

One of the meanings of the number forty-seven is humility. Del was one of the humblest souls I had ever encountered. He would have been amazed at the impact of his passing on so many hearts. He never boasted of his accomplishments and never thought more highly of himself than he should. He was always thankful for the opportunities he had been given and the wisdom God had granted him in answer to his heartfelt prayers spanning a lifetime. He also knew that he was standing on the shoulders of spiritual giants, such as Harvey Dunn (his grandfather) and Delbert Teel Sr. (his dad). He was mindful of the impact of their prayers and knew that the favor of The Lord rested on his life because of their spiritual legacy. God's Word says that "humility comes before honor." In order to walk in the high calling of God, one must first learn to walk in humility and gratitude. Del passed that test with flying colors.

As I have found myself experiencing joy again in recent days at the thought of a future that includes another love, I am reminded of a reading that my daughter-by-love, Laura Teel, shared with me after our grandson died. She said that the words helped her to heal and to open her heart again to receive the life and love of a new child in the person of Cadie (our two-year-old granddaughter who was born after Marcus went to Heaven). The reading was entitled, "On Joy and Sorrow," by Khalil Gibran Knopf. One of the excerpts from his writings states, "...Your joy is your sorrow unmasked. And the selfsame well from which your laughter rises was oftentimes filled with your tears." I encourage you to look up his writing and reflect upon its wisdom.

God's Word says that, "Weeping may endure for a night, but joy comes in the morning" (Psalm 30:5). I know that our lives are on a scale that is tempered by what challenges we face. Our greatest challenge is to walk in humility and answer the high calling of God when He bids us to come, to move, to change, and to believe in His steadfast, always-good love. "I would have despaired unless I had believed that I would see the goodness of The Lord in the land of the living. Wait for the Lord; be strong and let your heart take courage; Yes, wait for the Lord" (Psalm 27:13-14). I am standing in the land of the living and I am seeing the goodness of The Lord. I am humbled by His precious gifts and I will answer Him when He calls to me.

Week Forty-Eight: Father's Blessing, Majesty and Greatness, Dwelling Place

September 12, 2014

Forty-eight weeks. Today we observe another week without Del's tangible presence to speak comfort and wisdom into our lives. Each week since he crossed over into the place where we all long to follow, we have been met with challenges. We have also been met with amazing grace and a demonstration of the greatness of Father God's love for us that we may never have known had we not experienced such heartbreak. God's Word says that He is near to the brokenhearted. We have had periods of great peace only to be overrun with inexplicable sorrow at such a devastating loss. There are events that have unfolded in recent weeks that have made us even more acutely aware than ever that he will not be quietly coming around a corner, in his stealthy ninja mode, and offering us a Starbucks mocha. He will not look across a room with compassion in his eyes and ask me, "Are you alright?" He will not grab my hand in the darkness of the night and speak tender words of love or offer a prayer on my behalf when my heart is overwhelmed. I will forever be thankful for the love of this precious man and amazed that Father allowed me to walk beside him as his bride for so many wondrous years. Through the hard days and the days of laughter, we had this assurance that we were just passing through this life while aiming for a destination that Del reached before us.

Biblically, the number forty-eight represents many things on its own. Forty-eight can mean "dwelling place," or "Father's blessing," or "majesty and greatness." As the sum of forty and eight, it represents both a time of testing (40) and a new beginning (8). This past year has definitely been a time of testing. As Father has been graciously opening my heart to embrace a new beginning, it has also been a time of testing for relationships that have been in place for a lifetime. I tenderly stretch forth my faith and believe His promises. I ask my children and the family of my new love to stretch their faith with me and believe that He is the God of majesty and greatness and that He is well able to do exceedingly and abundantly above all that we may ask or think. He is the God of multiplication. He is my dwelling place. When my heart is overwhelmed, I find my rest in Him.

Del was fond of living his life vicariously through his children and me. He loved to wind us up and send us out into the world to have new adventures. As long as we came back and told him all of the details of what we had discovered, he felt a part of it all. I know that he is seated with Christ in Heavenly places and that his intercessory prayers have not ceased to be active in the earth. My absolute conviction is that Del's prayers are a part of the reason that I am now embarking on this new journey of discovery and having the adventure that he always told me that I would have if he departed this earth before me. One of the most difficult things about not having him here is that he was always the one to whom we turned with our joyful news and our sadness. I am having a joyful quest now and can't tell him all about it and see his face beaming with delight as I share with him how much peace this new love has brought to me. I can't tell him how my heart is being mended in the company of one who has also suffered such immeasurable loss.

While my new love and I try to navigate these uncharted waters, we are also mindful that our spouses left us with priceless legacies in the persons of our children, both those born to us and those joined to us by their love for our children. Between my new love and me, we have twelve children, some by birth and some by love. We know that twelve is the number for Divine order and the family of God. We earnestly seek wisdom from above to blend these hearts and blend our homes in a manner that brings glory and honor to the One in whom we live and breathe and have our being.

As those of you who have followed my journey through these months have already done, I beseech you to continue steadfast in lifting up the Teel clan (and now the Nealis clan) before the courts of the Lord and asking for His wisdom and favor to cover us. We need His Divine order in our lives. Although my Del walked in a wisdom that was not of this earth, we know that the Source of his wisdom was from above. Del was not the standard. Father God is the standard and, by His Spirit, we will continue to advance His Kingdom and bring Him the glory and honor due His wondrous name. From the bottom of my heart, I thank you for your kind words and the demonstration of your support and kindness toward me and my family. We are humbled by your friendship and overwhelmed by your love.

Week Forty-Nine: The End of Slavery, Complete Perfection, The Father's Love

September 18, 2014

Forty-nine weeks. Today marks the forty-ninth week since Del attained complete perfection by leaving this earth and rejoining his Heavenly Father. The number forty-nine, as I have discovered with many of the numbers I have researched over the past year, has multiple meanings. The product of seven times seven is forty-nine (7 x 7 = 49) representing complete perfection. Nothing could be more perfect than running a good race and finishing by enjoying the always-good love of Father God in the place that Jesus promised He was preparing for us to abide with Him for eternity.

For those of you who knew my beloved Del, you know that he was a perfectionist. He would avoid participating in any activity that he felt he couldn't execute with excellence. Because of his propensity for perfection, he often missed opportunities to cut loose in wild abandon and just enjoy life. He would make fun of himself and say he was experiencing "paralysis by analysis" when he just couldn't move forward with a project or activity because he was so busy examining it from every angle. I sometimes think of him in Heaven dancing and laughing and just being free to express himself without the care of looking foolish or not getting it quite right and it makes me chuckle.

The number forty-nine is associated with the Jewish observation of a wonderful and freeing year called "The year of Jubilee." This year of "Jubilee" marked the end of a cycle of seven Sabbath years. Every seventh Sabbath year, if you or your children had been sold into slavery, you were freed. If you had sold your land because you fell on hard times, you got your land back, your freedom back, and you had a fresh start with no debt. Imagine an eternal Jubilee. There is no slavery or debt. You have been redeemed and you have a fresh start without the cares of this life. Del is enjoying that eternal Jubilee.

The final meaning that I discovered for forty-nine is Father's love. What a matchless Heavenly Father we have Who has made a way to redeem us from our mistakes. His always-good love has brought us out of the pits of sorrow and set our feet on a higher place. He says in His Word that He has raised us up and, "...made us sit together in heavenly place in Christ Jesus" (Ephesians 2:6-7). What a wondrous thought and a precious promise. We don't have to wait to experience this joy. As we learn to live from a perspective of Heaven to earth, we will manifest the joy of The Lord in a way that causes us to rise above our circumstances and embrace every moment that we are granted on this side of eternity.

Father God, please teach us to live in the freedom that You have already granted us. Help us to walk as little children in our pursuit of Your Kingdom, with wild abandon and hearts filled with love that is overflowing. Help us to dance without fear of looking foolish and sing without fear of being out of tune. Let us so reflect Your glory and Your nature that the hearts of those who do not yet know You will be drawn to the light of Your presence and Your sweet embrace.

Week Fifty: The Fullness of Time

September 25, 2014

Fifty weeks. I still find it hard to fathom that Del has been away from us for fifty weeks now. In the beginning of my journey away from the date of his death, I could feel him hovering near me. Perhaps it was just the Lord's presence giving me comfort that made it feel like Del was still near. There were signs in the Heavens that pointed to his nearness. There were little messages left behind that seemed to still connect him to the things of this life. Those little, seemingly insignificant, signs and wonders helped me to make it through some of the darkest days of my existence on planet earth. In recent months, however, I have not sensed his nearness nor seen any signs that indicate he is still hovering or fretting over the welfare of his family. The fullness of the time of our connection on this side of the veil has been completed and he loved us so well and provided for us so thoughtfully, we are equipped to move on to the next adventure Father has for those of us who have been left behind.

The Biblical significance of the number fifty is vast. Fifty is the number for fullness, or the "fullness of time." After the Hebrew nation had celebrated the seven cycles of seven Sabbath years, they observed the Jubilee. As I shared in my last entry, Jubilee was an opportunity for Divine reversal in the lives of those who had been sold into slavery or who had acquired debt. Jubilee represented a brand-new start in the fullness of time.

This past week I went back to my hometown of St. Louis with my youngest son, Jeremy Luke, and my new love, Dale Nealis. We were there to celebrate my birthday. I knew that this one was going to be especially hard because Del had always made celebrating my birthday a priority and had taught my children to honor me on that day. In his absence, I was sure this day was going to be one of the hardest days I had observed since losing him. Instead, my extended family kept me so occupied and made me feel so cherished that the sting of Del's absence was overshadowed by the promise of a new beginning and a demonstration of love and support that was humbling and sweet.

While visiting my dad in his home, Dale asked him for his blessing over our union. My dad took both Dale and me into his arms as we all three wept in a mixture of sorrow and delight. We were all three saying goodbye to the past and embracing what was before us. He gave us his patriarchal blessing as he prayed over us and all our children. His blessing was the greatest birthday gift I have ever received, and I will cherish it forever. Father God has turned my mourning into dancing. He has lifted my sorrow. In the fullness of time, His redemption has unfolded over me like a banner unfurling.

The number fifty also represents the coming of the Holy Spirit. It was fifty days after Jesus left the earth for Heaven that His followers were assembled in the Upper Room, awaiting the Promised One. On the Day of Pentecost, at the fiftieth day after Jesus ascended into Heaven to be seated at Father's right hand, the Holy Spirit was poured out upon those believers in that place of unified assembly.

Jesus referred to the Holy Spirit as "The Comforter." I have walked with this Comforter in a more intimate way than I could have ever imagined in the past fifty weeks. I have been comforted in a way that has expanded my heart and my hope for tomorrow. God's Word says that we will comfort others in the same way that we have been comforted. My hope for my children who have lost their earthly father and the children of my new love who have lost their earthly mother is that they will be comforted by the only source of comfort that is lasting, His Holy Spirit. He gives us beauty for ashes and the oil of joy for mourning. Selah!

Week Fifty-One: Divine Revelation, Praise

October 2, 2014

Fifty-one weeks. 358 days. As we stop and reflect on this last week before the one-year mark of a life without the quiet and steady presence of my first love, there are many things to ponder. I have discovered that the number fifty-one relates to Divine revelation and praise. What amazing and Divine revelations Father has brought to us in this journey on a path we would never have chosen if He had given us a say in the matter! What praise has filled my heart, even in the midst of my sadness, as I count my blessings and live in the assurance that God is for me. His always-good love is my constant guide and anchor.

We set a monument stone and a bench on the place where Del's earth suit was laid to rest several months ago. Only in this past week, however, were the final proofs sent to me to show me what the etchings on his monument would look like. I decided that the earth did not contain enough granite to properly write an epitaph for this dear soul. How do you properly sum up a life in just a few letters? How will others know, when they happen to come across his marker in years to come, that they are approaching the final resting place of a humble, gentle, spiritual giant?

Del lived a life of quiet reflection. He loved his family and he loved Father God. He waited on The Lord for Divine revelations and reveled in sharing what Father had shown him. He once shared the story of Enoch with our children. God's Word says in Genesis 5 that "Enoch walked with God; and was not; for God took him," (Genesis 5:24). Enoch never saw death. Del told us that, "Enoch walked with God continuously. One day, while they were enjoying one another's company, Father God said to Enoch, 'We have walked so far today that we are closer to my house than to yours. Why don't you just come home with me?'" Del had purposed in his heart, for a season, to lead our family in a time of devotion on Sunday nights. We called it the family altar. The theme of Del's family altar and his life mission was to learn to be a friend of God. He didn't always walk it out perfectly, but he did always have a passion for trying. I decided that his epitaph should reflect that passion. The script on Del's monument reads, "He walked with Love and was not because Love took him." God is Love. Father God doesn't just love. He is the embodiment of love. Del walked with God. He walked with Love.

I pray that Del's passion for being a friend of God's will ever be an inspiration to his children and grandchildren. May all of Father God's children ever press into his presence and learn to be His faithful friends. "Help us, Father, to not settle for mediocre relationships with You. Help us to seek and find that Divine revelation that transforms us as we see Who You truly are. Grant us the grace to walk with You continuously until the day that we are closer to Your house than to ours and You just take us home as You took Del home, where he happily abides with You." God's Word tells us, "We are confident, I say, and willing rather to be absent from the body, and to be present with the Lord" (2 Corinthians 5:8).

Week Fifty-Two: Messiah, Word, Light

October 9, 2014

Fifty-two weeks. I have come to a paradox in my marking of the weeks since the most precious and influential person in my life entered Glory, leaving behind a broken-hearted family and a void that can never be filled. Delbert entered the hospital on Wednesday morning, October 9th. We contended with Heaven for a miraculous turnaround, but Heaven held him steadfast in its grip and we released him from his earth suit and into Heaven's embrace on Thursday, October 10th. As the weeks since that life-altering event unfolded for us, I have observed each Thursday with what I felt Father was revealing to me in the numbers that marked the passing of time with a post about my reflections. At this time, I have two dates contending to be recognized as the one-year mark. One is the passing of weeks, the other is the passing of an entire year.

As I sort through the numbers to determine which should be my focus, I am met with another paradox. Do you truly believe that God uses everything in life to help to shape you into who He is making you to be, sons and daughters of God who are made in the image of His pattern, His Son, Jesus? The number fifty-two symbolizes that Beloved Son, Messiah, Word, and Light. On this side of eternity, I have never known anyone who sought to understand what it meant to be like Jesus more than Delbert. His favorite book of the Bible was the Gospel of John. His favorite chapter of that book was John 17. Delbert would say, "We get to eavesdrop on a conversation between the Son and His Father. We get to see how two hearts beat as one." Del would also remind us of Jesus' words to His followers, "The Son can do nothing of Himself, but what He sees the Father do; for whatever He does, the Son also does in like manner" (John 5:19).

When I was a little girl, Del's intimate prayers to Father God always amazed me. When we would have prayer services in our small church, I would try to sneak over and kneel in a pew that was close to where Del was kneeling because I could eavesdrop on his prayers. I know, "Shame on you, Janet Lynn!" I couldn't help myself. Whatever intimacy he had with Father God, I wanted to have it too. He inspired me to consider that Father wasn't far off. He was a beloved friend and confidant who was interested in being invited into all of the minutia of my life. I will forever be thankful for the pattern Delbert set for me and the inspiration that he provided for me to want to know the Father and the Son more intimately. I will be eternally in his debt for choosing me to be his life partner and the mother to his four amazing children, who are all hurting and so tender as they mark the end of this fifty-two-week cycle.

A few short months ago, I met another godly man, Dale Nealis. He was completely different in temperament to my Delbert. In my careful planning and strategy for my future, Dale Nealis was not a fit. I thought I knew what I needed and what my future would hold. Dale was unlike anyone I would have ever imagined Father would Divinely connect me with for a life partner, but he was a gift and a part of the unfolding of a new hope in my life for a Kingdom future. I have been profoundly humbled by the supernatural connection God has blessed us with. Amazingly, Dale's birthday is October 9th. (The number nine is the number for Divine completion.) This year, that birthday falls on the fifty-second week of the passing of Delbert. My family will observe the date of Delbert's entrance into Glory on Friday, October 10th, the one-year mark. I have had a choice to make about how to mark these tender days. Do I focus on the eternal or the temporal? Do I focus on the fact that Delbert has been in the presence of the Lord now for a year, or the fact that I have been without his sweet embrace, his laughter, his wisdom, his compassion, and all that his physical presence provided for me in my life? So, this Thursday I will celebrate the life of Dale Nealis and the gift that he has been to me in this transitional season. I will focus on Delbert's answered prayers throughout my journey (for I have no doubt that my beloved Delbert prayed about all the needs his family might have in a future without him). I will hold a heart of gratitude for Father God's Divine provision, not only for my physical needs but also for my emotional ones.

Every day of our lives we are faced with a decision about where to set our focus. God's Word says, "Set your mind on things above, not on things on the earth" (Colossians 3:2). When we step up into the higher elevations, we see the landscape of our lives and His Kingdom differently. We are delivered from the tyranny of the temporal and into the everlasting peace of the knowledge that He is coming for all of us one day. We will all be changed in one moment, in the twinkling of an eye. Delbert has already embraced that change and is living in the provision of a new body and a new life without sorrow or suffering.

Only the guidance of God's Holy Spirit, our Comforter and Guide, has carried me through this past year. His Word says, "Weeping may endure for a night, but joy comes in the morning" (Psalm 30:5). I am learning to treat each new day as a gift. We are not promised tomorrow or next week. If it weren't for the certain knowledge that I will see Delbert again one day, I would not have had the strength to carry the burden of my sorrow. I don't know how anyone can survive the loss of someone so dear without the absolute conviction that we will all be reunited for eternity with the ones we love who have died in Christ. The loss of Father God's beloved Son, Jesus, paid the price for that sweet assurance. How can I ever repay that debt? I can't. I can only embrace it and live my life in such a way that I can be as inspirational as the man that was, and shall always be, my first love, Delbert Lewis Teel II.

Chapter Eight: Ireland's Promise

As I shared in Chapter Five, from the conception of the journey to Ireland, I was wrapped in assurance that this trip was a part of my destiny. Having never traveled outside of the United States other than a brief foray to a remote island in the Bahamas for a youth mission trip when I was a teenager, I had some trepidation about the long flight and my family's acceptance on foreign soil. There was never a burning desire within me to go outside of my country of origin because I knew that there was still so much untapped beauty I had yet to see within this continent, I could never view it in my lifetime. Father God, however, had other plans for me.

Once I had made the outrageous declaration that I was going to take my family to Ireland and I had convinced Nathan, Jeremy, and Elizabeth and her sister Rachel to travel with me, we went to see our local travel agent at AAA. Her name was Hope. (Yes, that "confident expectation" thing just kept showing up.) We told her the story of how Del had left us. I even told her about how my out-of-the-mouth-without-processing-through-the-brain declaration had brought about our coming to see her and solicit her services. I told her of Father's supernatural provision with the check for $25,000 we had not expected. She was inspired by all of it and threw herself into the task of helping us maximize our viewing pleasure of a country she assured us was well worth the investment. We chose a tour entitled, "Irish Elegance: A Country Roads Itinerary."

In the months that led up to our departing for the Emerald Isle, I friend-requested a prophetess on Facebook. Her name is Kathy Walters. She had posted excerpts from her books, *The Celtic Flames* and *St. Patrick: The Celtic Lion*, on Facebook. Someone had sent them to me and I had been stirred, in my spirit, to explore more about these Irish moves of God's Spirit. I was preparing for an opportunity to meet God. I felt He had ordered and paid for this trip and He was going to meet me in Ireland in an extraordinary way.

A few days before my departure, a dear friend of mine, Reverend Barry Taylor, texted me. He told me that he had a prophetic word for me about Ireland. He said, "This will be your first trip to Eden, but it won't be your last. Take both sets of eyes with you, both your spiritual and your natural eyes. You are going to see glimpses of Heaven there. God is going to show you wonders about people and certain other things. I just keep hearing, 'people and certain other things.' I don't know what this means, but He assures me, you will know when you see these things." My anticipation was heightened by this prophetic declaration, and my anxiety was quieted by the assurance that Father was even speaking to others about the significance of this adventure.

We decided to take an afternoon direct flight from Charlotte, allowing for an early morning arrival in Dublin. We had booked an extra day outside of the constraints of the tour Hope had booked us on with AAA. We felt we could use that extra day to explore and get over the ill effects of the jet lag. We were told that the best thing we could do was try to nap on the plane but not to nap when we arrived in Ireland. It would be best to stay up as long as possible and then go to bed early to try to adjust to the time difference as well as we could.

The trip over was smooth and uneventful. Having never flown to Europe, I was surprised that we remained within sight of land for almost the entire trip, as we traveled north, before heading east toward Ireland. We arrived and passed through the security measures at the Dublin airport with no problems.

We decided that we would take a cab to the hotel where we had reservations for our first night, and drop off all our luggage for safe keeping, giving us the freedom to explore Dublin without the care of hauling our luggage with us at every turn. As we hailed our first cab driver, we were delighted to find a friendly and helpful soul who made us feel welcomed from the start. He seemed genuinely happy to have us visit his country.

Along the route to our hotel, the cabbie slowed down and called out from his open window to a young couple walking along the sidewalk, "Are you lost? What are you looking for?" We wondered what had attracted him to the young couple and made him feel compelled to ask if they needed his help. This practice certainly didn't exist within the cabbie community I had ever been exposed to in the states. The young couple waved him off.

"We are fine!" they insisted.

"You just looked as though you were searching for something," he explained in his warm, Irish lilt. "I am happy to direct you if you need it," he offered.

The young couple dropped their guard, warmed by his sincerity, and told him what they were trying to find. "Oh, you just missed it!" he said. "Go back to the last street you passed and make a right. You will find the street about a block back down that direction." They thanked him and turned back around.

We were all delighted by our cabbie's friendliness and his pride in this city. We commented to him that it was certainly kind of him to stop and help the young couple, even when they insisted they didn't need his assistance. He waved off our compliments in an "Aw, shucks" manner and continued sharing information he felt we might find useful in our adventures in the city. He delivered us to our hotel and gave us his card and number in case we needed him later. He also offered to pick us up for our return to the airport the following week. What a delightful and warm introduction we were granted by this angel of a cabbie.

The concierge at the front desk graciously took our luggage and assured us it would be awaiting us in our rooms upon our check-in later that afternoon. Although we were tired, the adrenaline from this lovely land propelled us forward to explore its secrets and hidden treasures.

Our first stop was to find a nice cup of coffee and breakfast. We were directed to a little place up the street from the hotel where we were staying that night. We had our first Irish breakfast and the best cup of coffee I have ever had in my entire life. (This, coming from a coffee addict, is high praise!) We had the barista make us a café mocha. Perhaps it was the rich Irish cream that made the difference, or the source of their chocolate. Whatever the reason for the experience heightening our senses, the beverage was like a magic elixir to our palates. We were all so captivated by the coffee and the meal that we tried to make a point to add this cafe to our agenda for a return visit later in the week when we would be back in Dublin at the end of our tour.

After breakfast, we toured the Guinness Factory in Dublin. We also strolled the city streets and began to understand how different the pace of life is in this place. Although a thriving metropolis, Dublin has kept its rich roots and preserved its history in such a way that modern conveniences stand alongside ancient paths. The River Liffey runs along the pathways and made me wish it could speak and share its ancient secrets with us.

We went back to our room that afternoon and refreshed ourselves. We then decided to go to a pub outside of the local tourist attractions because my son Nathan longed to hear a local musician play traditional Irish instruments, including the Uilleann Bagpipes. Elizabeth did a Google search and found an out-of-the-way pub where local musicians were regularly known to play. We arranged for a cab and went across the city to this locale, where Nathan was greeted by a skilled musician with his pipes playing hauntingly beautiful melodies. The piper was joined by a violinist and a few others who added to the wonder of our first sounds of Ireland washing over our souls. Nathan was enthralled by the performance and the casual way each of the musicians handled their instruments. He was grinning so hard, I thought his face might break. He reminded me, in those moments, of his dad. Del would physically lean in when something was captivating him, and I saw his spirit in Nathan that night.

We sampled some of the local pub fairs and enjoyed a relaxed evening, leaving earlier than Nathan may have liked, to assure we got our rest before joining our tour group the next morning.

Listening to the nostalgic melodies of the Irish music made this pub visit a cherished memory of our first night in this wondrous land.

We awakened the next day to a traditional Irish breakfast that was included in the cost of our accommodations at the hotel. We had all rested well after having not slept for so many consecutive hours. We gathered our belongings and took another cab across the city to join our official tour.

The first day, we toured Trinity College and St. Patrick's Cathedral. We met our tour guide. Liz was passionate about the history of Dublin and these great institutions. The artistry of the ancient Book of Kells is housed at Trinity College and it was a fascinating tour for its content, as well as the splendid architecture we viewed within these walls. The artisans who worked on many of the cathedrals in Ireland knew that they might never see the completion of their work because the kind of craftsmanship required to achieve this level of splendor could take generations to achieve.

The following day, we headed away from Dublin in a large coach with about thirty-five other tourists to view the countryside. The landscape seemed rugged and untamed, dotted with remnants of old stone structures that the locals refer to as "famine cottages" that mark a dark period in the history of this nation. When the famine hit Ireland, 38 percent of its population was destroyed because of hunger and disease. The famine cottages are now designated as historic places and people are forbidden to disturb them.

Our first major stop of the day was at the Cashel Rock. This is a place where I had my first overwhelming encounter with the land. The Rock of Cashel can be seen from far away and was once a fortress from which kings ruled. At the top of its peak, remnants of what was once a great cathedral and a cemetery remain. Some of those buried there are people who lost their lives defending this sacred ground from threats throughout the ages. As we walked among the remnants of what was once a glorious work of architectural splendor, we were told about its history and why it now was in ruins. As I heard the story, I was brought to tears. I felt connected to those whose bones were beneath this turf. The site was donated to the church by the ruling king in 1101 A.D., and the lovely cathedral was built over the course of decades. The Archbishop of Cashel, Arthur Price, enjoyed the benefit of a new cathedral built down in the village in the 1740s. It was far more convenient for him to avoid having to take the long hike up the steep hill to serve the people in his parish. The people, however, continued to make the pilgrimage up the ancient path to pay homage to their ancestors and the old cathedral. Archbishop Price decided to have the roof taken off of the cathedral in 1749 and let nature have its way, an act that ultimately caused the formerly magnificent edifice to fall into ruin.

As I contemplated this historic unfolding, Father God began to speak to me about what happens when one is not under the proper cover. When you defiantly uncover yourself, removing the provision He has made for you to be protected, your life will fall into ruin. The short-sightedness of this Archbishop of Cashel brought to ruin the legacy of generations. Just as Delbert and I have ancestors who have paid dearly in their prayers, their physical labors, and their giving to provide us with an inheritance, we now are carriers of this burden for future generations. We must remain under the cover of His love and His favor in order to preserve an inheritance for those who will follow us and leave a lasting legacy. We must not allow selfish pride to tear down what others have built up as a gift to be passed on to others.

At the base of the Rock of Cashel, there is a little village where we were introduced to Irish scones and cream. I must tell you that the scones in Ireland are not at all what I have ever had here in the states. The gentleman who ran the establishment boasted, "If you find a better scone in all of Ireland, let me know and I will refund your money." He was filled with Irish pride and confidence. He was justified in his boasting. The rich taste of his scones was a delicious discovery and we were all happy to try to meet the challenge.

Our days were filled with wonder. As I went to bed each night, I so wanted to tell Del all about what had transpired. I often went to sleep with tears on my pillow as I realized he wouldn't be on the other side of the pond to share my stories. He had crossed over an expanse that was too great for me to ford at this point in my story. I longed for Father to fill my empty arms again so that these magical moments could be shared more fully. My heart was so thankful for the traveling companions I had with me and I delighted in how they were drinking in the experience.

We went to the Blarney Castle and took the steep climb to the top so that we could kiss the Blarney Stone. We were told that there was a great legend surrounding this magical place. The owners of the castle had a son who went swimming in the water near the castle and almost drowned. A servant girl with a speech impediment jumped into the water and saved him. His parents were so thankful that they asked her what they could gift to her to express their gratitude for saving their son's life. She told them, in her halting tongue, that the only gift she wanted was the gift of eloquence. Her benefactors told her that if she climbed to the top of the castle and kissed the stone, her wish would be granted. According to folklore, she kissed the stone and came back with fluid speech and later married the young man whose life she saved. While the story may not be true, it is certainly captivating.

One morning we were given the option of sleeping in or going to view the Torq waterfall in a National Forest at the base of Torq Mountain. As tired as we were from the ambitious schedule we had signed up to keep, I didn't want to miss a thing. Elizabeth and Rachel decided to stay and get some rest, but Nathan, Jeremy, and I embarked on an adventure with a few of the other tourists. We were rewarded with one of the most captivating sights I have ever beheld. The tour guide had given us headphones to listen to her in case we couldn't keep up. As we entered the forest, it felt like we had walked onto the set of a Technicolor movie. The vibrancy of the greens seemed to be alive and breathing. The crystal-clear water and smooth stones, worn from the path of the water over millennia, glistened and bid us to come and explore. The fauna on the floor of the forest consisted of tiny wildflowers and budding plants of various colors. The sound of the water falling against the stone drew us into its beauty. Nathan, Jeremy, and I seemed to be in our own little world. Each of us wandered the forest, just basking in its welcoming embrace. Nathan took his camera and zoomed in on the rich colors on the bed of the forest. Jeremy jumped down into the water and climbed upon the rocks, drawing nearer to the roar of the falls. The other tourists took in the sight and then continued on the tour outside of the canopy of this luscious, green paradise. We could hear them off in the distance through our headphones. We listened until they were no longer within range of us.

I joined Jeremy down in the stream as we took pictures to capture our adventure. My heart was swelling with the splendor surrounding us. I began to weep with joy. This moving experience was a part of what Father had planned for us. I could feel it. As I drank deeply of the nectar of this marvelous scene, I felt connected to Del in a new way. I could feel him kissing us from Heaven and coming along for the adventure.

After a time, I knew we needed to join the others. We had been out of range for a long time at that point, and we didn't want to be left behind. I started making my way out of the forest and across the path that led to the other sights we were to take in on this tour. After I had walked about a quarter of a mile, I heard a voice in my spirit say, "Turn around and look behind you." The voice was not audible, but it was very clear. I felt compelled to follow its strong urging. As I turned around, I looked at the mountain behind me. Splashed in a broad spectrum of sunlight illuminating the bright blooms that were covering the mountainside, a brilliant display of purple seemed to sing its praises to the Heavens. I heard the voice again say, "There is your 'purple mountains majesty!'" and I began to laugh out loud.

Delbert had taken me to Colorado many years before. The state of Colorado was beautiful, but I kept telling him how disappointed I was that I wasn't seeing any purple mountains like those we sing about in the song, "America, the Beautiful." He would laugh and say,

"Knock it off with the 'purple mountain majesty' thing!" I would insist that I had expected to see purple mountains and didn't want to go home until he showed them to me. We would laugh about it over the years as he would recall how much he loved the Rocky Mountains, and I would chime in about how let down I was that there hadn't been any purple mountains there. The exchange became a private joke between us, but here I was so many miles away, seeing my purple mountains. I couldn't have been more tickled if God had been poking me in the sides with His fingers.

Around that time, another sight captivated me. A large sparrow hawk came sweeping down out of the mountain and glided alongside me for a few hundred yards. Hawks had come to mean something very significant to my family, and I considered the appearance of this one to be a final kiss from Heaven on that day.

Before Del's death, we had a hawk that was a frequent visitor at Serenity. He would sit outside the window and stare at us, or perch on Del's car or my van and look at us, with his head moving from one side to the other as if trying to communicate. The hawk had seemingly decided to adopt us.

Around the time of the hawk's appearing, I began to do business with a young man named Geoff Hawk who owns Hawk Construction Company in the Carolinas. The Lord began to move on my heart concerning doing business with Hawk and supporting him and his enterprises. Geoff also began sending customers to me.

Delbert always named our computers after birds. We had Sandpiper, Eagle, Songbird, Oh My Dove, Falcon, and other named computers designated within our network at home so that there wouldn't be any confusion. Del had ordered a new laptop for me shortly before his death. He asked me what I wanted to name it. I had never named one before, but immediately I said, "Hawk!"

Del was taken aback by my quick response. He asked, "Why?" in a melancholy way that was inexplicable to me. "Did I see a trace of sadness there?" I wondered.

I quickly explained, "Because of the hawk that has adopted us and because of Geoff Hawk. You can name it whatever you want, though. I was just thinking of those two things, but it really doesn't matter to me." Del named it Hawk.

A few weeks after his death, one of my sons told me why Del was probably a little melancholy about the name I had suggested. He explained to me that, in the online video game that he and his dad frequently played, when a player was killed, they had the option of coming back as a hawk. They could no longer interact with the other players, but they could watch, as a hawk, from up above the field of battle. I was both saddened and touched that Del may have had a premonition of things to come.

In the weeks following his death, the hawk was an even more constant fixture. Del had battled with moles that kept ripping up our yard. Since Del was no longer there to engage in the ongoing battle, the hawk swept in and kept carrying them away. I would frequently see it on my outings around our area as I would be showing houses or working on the home sites my company was flipping.

God's Word tells us that His eye is on the sparrow and that we are of much more worth to Him than a sparrow. Here I was so far from home and, since there were no golden hawks indigenous to Ireland, he sent me a sparrow hawk.

This special moment outside the Torq Waterfall moved me in a profound way, as it would be the last time that I felt Del's spirit near me in the way that it had been hovering for months. I felt as though Father was telling me it was time to let go of the past. Del's memory would always be there with me, but the connection wouldn't be the same any longer. He gave me a great peace in that knowledge that passed my human understanding. I embraced the sweet goodbye and quietly moved on, thankful for a Father Who understands our human weaknesses. I am thankful for the One Who sees me and knows how to bring me kisses from Heaven that touch me in a way nothing else could.

Later, we visited the Connemara Marble Factory and the first thing that I saw was a small figurine shaped into a sparrow hawk. I bought it as a token to remember that day that God had met me in such an intimate way.

As we made our way across the Emerald Isle, we came to Kilarney. There was a castle outside this town with grounds we would tour with a jaunty driver and horses. The owners of the lands had gifted it to Ireland with the specific requirement that it never be toured with anything but a non-motorized vehicle. We were told to each make our way to one of the drivers assembled to take us on the tour. We found a man named Dennis who escorted us to his rig, and we departed for the tour of the castle and the lands surrounding it. Dennis settled in at the right, facing the rear of the horses. A woman, one of our touring companions, sat beside Dennis at the front bench. The rest of us, including the woman's husband, settled into the bench seats that ran perpendicular to the driver's seat and faced one another. I was seated directly behind Dennis.

The jaunty drivers make their biggest money from tips given to them by satisfied tourists. They tell the history of the land, but also share funny stories to keep their passengers entertained. Dennis was no different. He rolled from one silly story to the next. "This next castle you will be seeing is known as the ABC Castle? Do you know why they call it that? Because it is just Another Bloody Castle!" He waited for the laughter and carried on. "They call this next area Priest Wood. They call it that because the nuns wouldn't, but the priest would!" These jokes are just a sampling of his slapstick humor. He knew nothing about us, and we knew nothing about him, except that he was hilarious and very good at his vocation. About twenty minutes into our tour, Dennis suddenly stopped the horses. He turned around 180 degrees and pointed to me, very intently, and declared in the most beautiful Irish accent, "Your second time around is going to be even greater than your first!" He spoke it as if it were a portion of an untold story or the punchline to a joke. He turned back around and continued driving the horses and rehearsing his repertoire of humorous dialogue, as if he were possessed for a moment, then went back to his task at hand without ever missing a beat.

My children just looked at me with raised eyebrows as if to say, "What was that all about?" They had no idea the storm that had been brewing inside of me. They didn't know that I had been asking Father God how I was supposed to go on and find another love. Del was not replaceable. I had never met anyone like him, nor did I expect to do so. Yet, I longed to love and be loved again.

After the jaunty driver's declaration, I had an internal dialogue that went something like, "Okay, if it is going to be 'even greater than the first,' then it has to be different." I don't know how I knew this, but just as the driver had to turn 180 degrees around to face me, I knew that the next love I would enjoy would be 180 degrees different than Delbert. God had used Balaam's donkey to speak to him (in the Bible) and now God was using an Irish jaunty driver, who knew nothing about me, to speak to me. My friend, Barry Taylor, had been accurate. God was showing me glimpses of Heaven and wonders about "people and certain other things."

All of these events kept playing over and over again in my heart as we continued our journey across the beautiful countryside and I wondered what awaited me the rest of our time in this wondrous land.

Before we had traveled to Ireland, I had prepared items I thought I might need. We were told that we needed to take rain gear because it rained daily in Ireland. While I had been making my preparations and meditating one morning, I heard the Spirit of God speak to me, "God has been weeping over Ireland for many years, but while you are there, He will be smiling over her."

I asked, "Does this mean it won't rain while we are there?" I hoped that would be the case, but I didn't get a clear answer. Instead, I decided against bringing heavy rain gear after I heard that quiet voice.

Our tour guide kept commenting on how odd the weather was because it didn't rain on us for the first few days of our tour. I told her what God had spoken to me. She smiled politely, but I am sure she thought I was a little touched in the head. One day, however, it began to sprinkle lightly. She said, "Oh, good! Now you are going to see some real Irish weather."

To which I replied, "It is okay if it lasts for about five minutes. After that, it can stop because we will have seen enough." She looked at me like I had three eyes, but in five minutes it stopped raining and it never rained again for the entire trip. This fact was astonishing to our tour guide.

When we got to the area known as The Wild Atlantic Way, the water on that side of the island was as still as glass. "I have been doing tours for almost forty years!" Liz declared. "I have never seen anything like this. It is never this still. It is called the Wild Atlantic Way for a reason." She seemed a bit perplexed, but I was just reveling in Heaven's embrace as my Father was demonstrating His love to me in signs and wonders.

We toured the Cliffs of Moher which was one of the most breathtaking sights I have ever seen. I was truly on "wonder-overload" at every turn in this beautiful land. I could have stayed there for days, but our pace was too fast to spend much time at this ruggedly beautiful place.

Our next stop was Galway, where we would observe Delbert's birthday and Father's Day. We toured the area and then played among the rocks in Galway Bay, where I collected a few stones that I would write his birthdate on to commemorate this trip of destiny Father had arranged for us.

We didn't realize that we would be treated that evening to a special, private show performed for our group by the original composers of the Riverdance production. We were blown away by the traditional Irish dancers, singers, and musicians. The reigning Irish tenor was also part of the troop of performers we were privileged to enjoy. The evening would have definitely lived up to Del's preference for excellence in musicality. I reveled in the experience of seeing people whose skill I had admired on many PBS specials from only a few feet away.

Before heading back across the land toward Dublin, we had one last stop to make along the west coast of this island to spend the night in a castle located just outside of the village of Cong. We were taken to the Ashford Castle by private boat. As we made our way across the water toward the shores of the castle location, a sweet, old gentleman sang to us as he played a small accordion. He had been featured in the iconic film, *The Quiet Man*, starring John Wayne and Maureen O'Hara. He had been a very young man, but he still took pride in his part in the film that helped people come to love Ireland. He was delightful and helped to set the stage for our arrival.

Just before we reached landfall, everything on the boat went quiet so that we could hear the lone piper playing his bagpipes on the shores to welcome our arrival. As we pulled up and disembarked, the castle staff came outside to greet us in the traditional manner that they once greeted the lord and lady of the castle as they came to take up residence, and it was quite the show. My beautiful daughter-by-love, Elizabeth, went in front of them and curtsied denoting her acceptance of their splendorous display. My heart swelled within me at this lovely memory being created before me. I was, again, so appreciative of the way that each of my traveling companions were savoring each moment and making it more special.

During our brief time in the castle, Elizabeth went to the front desk and asked for a private tour of the room where Pierce Brosnan had stayed during the time of his wedding in 2001. The person at the front desk smiled and said, "You know, I have only been working here a short time and I, too, wanted to see that room. I would be delighted to view it with you." We were allowed to view parts of the castle that were off limits to other guests. It was like having a backstage pass for a special event. Again, we were overwhelmed with the kindness with which we were met. The only thing we didn't like about the wondrous castle was how brief our time there was going to be to enjoy its splendor.

That afternoon, various activities could be enjoyed, including watching falcons be handled by their masters, horseback riding, touring the grounds, or going into the little village of Cong and touring its sites and hearing about its history. Nathan went horseback riding. The others went on tours of the little village, and I stayed near the castle and toured the grounds, imagining all the various activities that had taken place in this glorious place over the centuries.

That evening we were treated to the most elegant dining experience I had ever been privileged to enjoy. We were truly wined and dined like royalty. It was delightful and humbling as I considered how Father God must be preparing a place for us at the Marriage Supper of the Lamb that we are promised to enjoy one day on the other side of eternity. Watching the servers following protocols of decorum, established for centuries, reminded me of the Queen of Sheba going to visit King Solomon and being overwhelmed by all that her eyes beheld at his palace and in his kingdom. How much greater will Heaven be for us? What was Del doing in that wondrous place right now, I wondered?

As we departed Ashford Castle the next morning and made our way back to Dublin, my heart was full of hope and a longing I couldn't describe. I longed for Heaven, but I knew my time and my assignment on this side of eternity were not complete. I longed to enjoy love again and I felt a release to pursue it once more. If my life was like a screenplay and the story of my love and life with Delbert was act one, I was now preparing for what act two would hold. I felt as though my sojourn in this land had prepared me for what Heaven was orchestrating.

Chapter Nine: My Second Act

Sometime in the spring of 2014 my daughter, Bethany, had put together a dating site profile for me on something called Plenty of Fish (POF). I don't know if it was because she was following my posts and sensing that I was ready to take the next step, or if she was just concerned that her mom was lonely. Perhaps she was hoping to find a solution to that involuntary solitude to which I had been assigned. This was a brave new world for me. I timidly began to see how this site functioned and started communicating with other singles who were looking for companionship.

As I scrolled through its pages, I decided that much of what was on that site was too vulgar for my tastes. I asked her to help me form a profile on Christian Mingle as well. I felt that at least the premise of this site was that someone drawn to it might be looking for love with another believer and not just any warm body. I was still only answering messages and trying to navigate this new arena that was so unfamiliar to me. After a time, I decided that I might as well try all of the leading sites. I then signed up for EHarmony.com and Match.com. The incredible thing about one of those sites is that it delivered ten really great matches per day, or so they said. I found myself discouraged and disheartened by what they viewed as perfect matches.

The first Sunday after I returned from Ireland, my pastor and our congregation were hosted by Crossroads Church in Concord, North Carolina. Our congregations were combined for this historic morning, as this was to be our last Sunday affiliated with the church in Concord. The pastor of Crossroads in Concord had been the one to encourage Mark and Julie, four years earlier, to leave Australia and begin the church they were now pastoring south of Charlotte. They asked Pastor Mark Appleyard to share a message in each of the services that Sunday, with the final service being a commissioning ceremony where they would pray over our congregation and send us forth as a separate entity with their blessings.

Pastor Mark shared a message on not settling for less than our Divine destiny. He shared the story of Abraham and Sarah and how they tried to make the promise of God come true with the conception of Ishmael, but that wasn't God's best for them because it wasn't the full promise. Pastor Mark encouraged us to write down our goals and the vision God had given to us and make it plain (Habakkuk 2:2). Then, he told us to run with the vision and not settle for less than God's best for us. This message resonated with me in my desire to find a mate who would help me to fulfill all that God had destined for me in my second act.

The following day, June 30, 2014, I wrote what I called, "The Manifesto for My Second Act." I clearly articulated all the things I was believing in God to provide for me in the man who would share the next portion of my story. I then took a copy of the pages to one of my trusted confidants, Lori Clifton, and gave it to her. I asked her to hold me accountable to not settle for less in my next mate than what was on the pages of this manifesto. She agreed to be my accountability partner in this matter, and she was steadfast in her commitment to me.

After having written my vision and making it plain, whenever one of the men with whom I was corresponding asked for my phone number (so that we could move our communication to the next level), I would email him a copy of the manifesto. I would tell him that the pages reflected all that Father had put into my heart to search for in my next mate. "If the words on those pages resonate with you," I would say, "you will find my phone number at the end. If you feel that this is not for you, I have no hard feelings. I don't want to waste your time or mine." I found it to be a very refreshing way to filter out those who were not sincere seekers of God's Kingdom.

A few weeks after writing the manifesto and sharing it with a few suitors, I had my first date. Ever. Del and I had grown up together. Being courted by him was familiar and safe, as I had known him from childhood. We never had that first "getting-to-know-you" kind of meeting. We knew each other from the start. We had seen each other through childhood, puberty, and young adulthood. Here I was, as the mom of four and the nana of two, going out on my first date.

My daughter-by-love, Elizabeth, came to the house and critiqued my makeup, hair, and clothing choices. She tweaked areas that needed help, assuring me that I was ready for this new beginning. She told me to just think of it as meeting a new client for dinner. I had done that hundreds of times before. Somehow, I knew this was going to be different. The butterflies in my stomach were telling me this encounter was not the same, but her coaching was reassuring.

Out of an abundance of caution, the first date was at an agreed upon location in a lovely restaurant in Ballantyne on the south end of Charlotte not too close to my home. I wasn't ready to have anyone picking me up from my house yet. I wanted some safe, neutral territory to meet. Although I felt I had thoroughly vetted the suitor, I felt more comfortable with this arrangement.

I was met that evening by a tall, distinguished-looking gentleman. His demeanor was cautious but kind. We entered the restaurant and were seated at a nice table. The décor was tasteful and elegant. The lighting was just what you would want for a romantic date night, but I was beyond nervous and extremely awkward. The food looked wonderful, but I probably only consumed five bites the whole night because of the discomfort I was feeling. The evening was shared in good conversation and getting to know this strong, Christian man. "Perhaps this is how dates are supposed to be and I will get used to it," I thought.

He shared his stories and talked about his life on the mission field. He had been recently divorced, although that was not what he had wanted. He said that his ex-wife had lost her way and ended their very long marriage. After leaving the mission field, when his life was falling apart, he found employment in the financial industry.

He was doing well, but he was brokenhearted over his loss and the effect it had on his two children. They were now young adults and living on their own. I listened to his stories and he listened to mine. At the end of our evening, he asked if he could call me the following day, and I told him I would be delighted to hear from him. I had a full day planned the next day and made my way back to the home of Jeremy and Elizabeth. They were having my niece, Jamie, spend the night and they were waiting up for me to tell them all about my evening and how my first date had gone.

As I described the date and shared some of the stories the gentleman had told me about his life, former wife, and children, Jeremy and Elizabeth realized that they knew the man. Jeremy said, "I was actually in his house when he was married!" They told me that they approved of him, but I was still uncertain. They affirmed that he was a good man and that his former wife had truly had an emotional breakdown and left him and her former life, consequently. His ex-wife had been a former teacher at the high school Elizabeth had attended.

The following day, I had a wonderful success in one of the transactions I had been working on. A house that I had under contract to purchase and renovate was sold to a buyer for a great profit without me having to do the renovations. I had shared my potential strategy for achieving that outcome with my date the night before and he had agreed to pray for me. I hadn't heard from him yet, but I sent a text with a picture of the sunset that evening and told him that our prayers had worked. God had come through for me in the deal. He immediately called me and asked me if I wanted to have supper with him the next day. I agreed.

The next date was just as unsettling as the first. Although we spent hours sharing our stories, I felt that all I had with him was a Kingdom connection. There was nothing about this man that sparked a sense of belonging or destiny. We bid each other good night and, two days later, I wrote to him and told him that I felt we were not truly a good match. He agreed and that was the end of our acquaintance. I felt deflated and unsure. Now I understood why my daughter hated dating so much. You expend so much energy and time trying to bond with someone and, when it isn't the right connection, you dread marching up that hill again and trying it with someone else. This was my feeling after just two dates with one man. How was I ever going to successfully discover the one God intended for me? Again, I remembered His question, "Do you trust me? Have I ever failed you?" Indeed, He has never failed or forsaken me.

The next week I met an old friend on the North Carolina coast. I was working on a house I had renovated and staged to sell located in Southport. He had a beach house near mine and we had arranged to meet and spend the day catching up on life. He had gone through a separation after a marriage of over thirty years. I dearly loved and cherished both he and his wife and the time we had spent in sweet fellowship together so many years earlier. We had known each other through our mutual service in the worship band at a church we attended together for several years. During our time together, as I poured out all of my fears about the dating realm and my trepidation he said, "Jan, I know you loved Del with all of your heart. Next time you find love, though, look for someone more like you. Del was your opposite. Find someone who will share the same interests that you have and do things with you." He told me that he thought the lack of shared interests had contributed to the end of his marriage of more than three decades. I was saddened by the end of his union, but thankful for his desire to impart his insights to me.

His words struck a nerve, though. I thought, "He is right. Del did life for us, not with us." Although Del was always delighted to send us out and hear our stories, he seldom joined us on our exploits. There were times that I was lonely and times that people actually thought I was single because I attended many social functions alone. I pondered the words of my old friend and considered them in the light of my recent first date. The man I had gone out with had a temperament more like Del's. He was analytical and perfectionistic. Perhaps that is not what I needed for my second act.

A few days later, I connected with a man on Christian Mingle who was delightful. His name was Keith. He, too, was divorced and had his marriage end when his wife left him for another man. He was a prison chaplain and also worked in a children's home in his hometown in the mountains. Although we had a great deal in common, and he met all the criteria for my manifesto, I realized that my life and my career were centered in my town and his life, ministry, and young daughter were all in the mountains where he was raised. I couldn't picture myself moving there, nor could I be the reason for him leaving his established ministry, home, and family to come to me. After many hours of phone conversations, I told him that I felt we didn't have a potential future. I told him that I would be delighted to have him as a Kingdom connection, but I didn't want to waste his time or mine thinking we had a romantic future connection. He was very kind and understanding.

The next day, Keith called me. "I know that you have ruled out us having any kind of future together, but I feel strongly that God wants you to come away and have a rest. I am offering you my place to rest in. I can stay with my sister, Vickie, and you can have my house." His thoughtfulness and generosity were touching. "You can let me show you the wonders of my part of the state," he offered. I had been weary and, as we had talked for many hours and I told him how rigorous my schedule had been, Father nudged him to encourage me to rest. The combination of the insomnia I had suffered since Del's death and having not one, but two, demanding businesses was wearing me down.

"I can't stay at your place and put you out," I told him, "but I will get a room up there and come for a visit." The next weekend, I did something completely out of my comfort zone and headed to the mountains. I had booked a room in a town I had never been to but had heard about for the thirty-plus years I had called the Carolinas my home. Etowah was lovely and peaceful. The hotel had a nice restaurant associated with it. That Friday night Keith met me there and we ate and talked until after midnight. He was as delightful in person as he had been over the phone, and we made plans to meet the next morning.

He borrowed Vickie's car for our outing to make me more comfortable since his normal mode of transportation was either his motorcycle or his truck. His sister had graciously loaned him her car when she learned of his dilemma.

I did more hiking that day than I had done since leaving Ireland. We were up and down all over the mountains. He introduced me to waterfalls and vistas that stirred my heart and drew me closer to the Creator of this earth. Although He had used this brother in-the-Lord to issue the invitation, the Originator of the invitation was my Father in Heaven, Who had created all of this beauty for us to enjoy.

We went back to his home after I was comfortable with him. Keith's house is very rustic and has a moving stream that emits the loveliest sounds as the waters pass over the rocks, worn smooth by years of surrendering to the melting snows. A screened porch overlooks the stream and wildlife abounds at its edges. From this picturesque backdrop, we continued to learn more about one another's lives and share our hearts.

As we sat on the porch and he shared the story of the betrayal and heartache he had experienced after his wife of many years had left him and his children, I was moved with compassion. He spoke of the many nights he and his children had gone to sleep through their tears, longing for the life that had been stolen from them. I longed to help him find a way to peace and to make an alliance that would bring him the companionship he desired. After his initial loss, he had remarried a woman who had been an even greater disappointment. I saw, from his loneliness, that when you are in transition you are extremely vulnerable. I spoke a secret prayer in my heart. "Father, when you bring me my next love, can he please be a widower instead of a divorced man? I am not judging these men,

Father. I just know that I want to be married to a man who lost his wife for reasons outside of his control. I want a widower who had a successful marriage. I don't want to deal with the brokenness of all these shattered marriages. Please, hear my heart, Father. I trust You. I know You will not give me more than I can bear." I remembered that prayer a few days later when Father delivered what I asked for and so much more.

The next morning, I met Keith in Asheville where we were joined by his lovely daughter, Janie Lynn. We enjoyed the Sunday morning service at his church. The three of us had lunch together afterward, and then I made my way back to Charlotte. The weekend was memorable but far too brief. I still longed for a true rest and for my next adventure.

Chapter Ten: Free to Dance

My next adventure followed just a couple of weeks later. Vickie, Keith's sister, invited me to come up and visit for her birthday weekend. Vickie and I had become friends on Facebook through her brother. He had said, "You need to send my sister a friend request. You two would really get along well." She was a strong Christian who loved to sing in her church worship band and she loved her family fiercely. She had moved back to Brevard to be with her mother during the final days that her matriarch was on the earth. Her husband had made the sacrifice of letting her go to her hometown to find a house for them to retire to, even though he had been transferred to a new location with his job, yet again. He knew that he had only a couple of years left before retiring and that Vickie needed to be with her mom more than he needed her to be with him at his new assignment since it was going to be so short-lived. The gift of time had been so precious to Vickie. She didn't know how little she would have left to spend with her mom, but she was thankful for all the moments and memories she had been given. I saw that her birthday was coming and sent her a private message through Facebook asking if her husband, who was working at his job in Houston, Texas, was coming home to celebrate with her. She told me, sadly, no. He wasn't coming home until the holidays. His schedule wouldn't allow him to be there for her birthday.

She later messaged me and asked me if I would like to come and spend the weekend with her. She told me that her cousin's band was going to be performing at a dance near her house. Her plan was to spend her evening at this social gathering with her cousin and the attendees. "Sorry. I don't dance!" I told her.

"Neither do I!" she exclaimed. "That doesn't stop me from getting up and enjoying myself." I had to laugh. "These old guys don't care if you've got the moves. Most of them are just happy to have someone who is willing to dance with them. Come on. Say yes!" she encouraged.

Something in me thought, "You know what? I have nothing to lose." I told Vickie, "I will come. I will try not to embarrass you." The idea of not having any constraints appealed to me. I realized as I reflected, that so many of the decisions I had made over my lifetime had been decided by how Del would feel about them. Would I embarrass him? Would I bring shame or dishonor to him? What would he think if he saw that I was doing something that wasn't done perfectly? Understand, Del didn't put these constraints on me. I did it to myself. My strong desire to never do anything that would disappoint him or make him think less of me is what drove me. As I considered this paradigm shift in my thinking, I was excited to have new experiences and decided to allow myself to enjoy the freedom and an escape from a prison of my own making. Only Father God deserved to have the power to influence the decisions I was embracing. He wasn't concerned about whether I executed something perfectly. He was more concerned with my motives than my actions. He was more concerned that I not miss a thing I had for Him or He had for me.

During that time, I won a bid for a house that was located in Brevard, North Carolina. This was the same area where I was meeting Vickie that weekend. I had put $1,000 down as my earnest deposit and planned to view the property while I was in the area to see her. The most I would lose was $1,000 if the property was not a good value, but this transaction represented an opportunity to make a good profit. (Buying homes, sight unseen, was how I had purchased several others over the months preceding this offer. This risky strategy had proven to be a reasonable gamble to take since many of the houses were beyond my ability to drive to within the time I had to make a decision as to whether or not to purchase.)

On August 10th (the ten-month mark from the date of Delbert's death), I received one of the emails that typically came every morning from Match.com. They usually were the ones with ten perfect matches that came daily. I would briefly scan them and hit the delete button ten times. (As I shared earlier, ten is the number for wholeness or completion, Biblically speaking. Del passed on the tenth day of the tenth month of the year around 10:00 a.m.) In the early hours of August 10th, I saw a man's profile that touched my heart. It read similarly to mine, stating that he was looking for a woman who was chasing after God. If she was on that path, she might find him there as well. I had written something eerily comparable in my online description about my quest for a new mate. The next thing I noticed was that he was a widower. He had three daughters and a son. I have three sons and a daughter. He had lost his wife in 2013, just as I had lost Del. The dating profile on each of these sites sets parameters that must be met that include height, distance from the subject, age, etc. His profile stated that he was looking for someone five feet five inches or more and no more than fifty miles from his location. So, I knew I wasn't a match.

Somewhere off in the distance, I could hear a haunting Irish voice from a jaunty driver on the other side of the ocean saying, "Your second time around is going to be greater than your first!" I decided to reach out and offer this widower the same hope I had been given two months earlier. I wrote in a private message, "I am so sorry for the loss of your wife. It has been a walk of faith to go forward without the person you expected to grow old with beside walking with you. Father God is faithful...I wish you joy in your journey." God is truly the God of multiplication and not division. He never wastes a thing. I sent the message and simply asked for blessings upon him.

A few hours later I received a message back: "I have received hundreds of condolences since I lost Debbie. Your message touched me like no other. Thank you." I was happy that the message had been received and had encouraged him. I went on with my day and didn't think more about it, as I had often received this sort of quick message that didn't lead to any further contact with prospects on various dating sites.

Not long after this, I received another message from him about my investment business. He told me that he had a small nest egg that he wanted to invest in real estate, and he wanted to discuss this idea with me. He asked if I ever did business in South Carolina. I told him that there were certain geographical locations within South Carolina that I was knowledgeable enough about to help guide him. Much would depend upon where he planned to invest. (I was thinking about the property I had won the bid on in Brevard and how it might prove to be something we could invest in together if it weren't too far from his location.) Because he was no longer a dating prospect, but rather a business contact, I gave him my business cell number and told him he could call me to discuss this matter. I would be available later that day after church. I didn't follow my established protocol of sending my manifesto as I had with other suitors because I no longer considered him a suitor.

I studied his name, Dale. My husband was Del, short for Delbert. Here in the South, folks often called my late husband Dale. He would attempt to correct them and say, "It is Del. Like the farmer in the Del." They would smile and say, "Oh, I see, Dale!" He would give up and just let them call him Dale.

I studied the profile further. This not-so-perfect match's last name was Nealis. My last name was Teel but was often misspelled, Teal. Because of the misspelling of my name, we had branded my real estate firm with the color teal which is on our signs, logos, and often in the clothing I wear. I considered the similarities but then dismissed them. One of the things that Match.com does is make a personality profile for you and assign you a color. It then tells you what temperament type, or color, you best align with. I felt that Dale's color personality was all wrong for me. My guard was down, and I settled into the conviction that this was going to be a Kingdom connection and, perhaps, we would do business together.

After church, I had lunch with Kathy East and her husband, Joe. I drove her home with Joe driving ahead of us separately so that we could have girl talk. I caught her up on the men I had met and the dates I had been on thus far. I told her about the widower who was supposed to call me to discuss business later that day.

As Kathy and I were sitting outside of her home chatting, my phone rang. I didn't recognize the number, which is not unusual given my line of business. I answered the call through the Bluetooth in my van, "This is Jan Teel with Teel Realty. How may I help you?" This was my standard greeting for all incoming calls if I didn't recognize the number.

"Hey! This is Dale Nealis. I told you I would be calling you after church," came the voice from the other end of the Bluetooth link. I continued talking to him over the speaker with Kathy listening. We started our conversation by recapping how our respective church services had gone that day. We then segued into the subject of real estate investments. He told me about his past experience as an electrician for almost twenty years in Washington, D.C. before feeling drawn to go to seminary to study for the ministry. While attending seminary, he owned and operated a painting and handyman service to support his family. He later moved to Greenville, South Carolina to work in the maintenance department at North Greenville University so that his children would be positioned to attend a university for free as a benefit to his working there. He had been pursuing his doctorate in ministry while employed there as well.

At the start of our conversation, I thought this communication was solely going to be about business, but it was quickly becoming personal. I didn't know how to tell him that I was in my van with Kathy and that she was privy to our conversation. Instead, I told him that if he would call me later that evening I would be free to talk at length. The thought passed through my mind, however, "Wouldn't it be something if the person who was beside me when I lost my first love was here beside me when I met my new love?" I dismissed the thought, telling myself that this guy was all wrong for me.

I ended the conversation and Kathy immediately said, "Jan, he sounds perfect!" with great enthusiasm.

"What?" I asked skeptically. "The only reason this guy has my number is because he wants to learn about investments. He is nothing like Del. He is just going to be a business partner, not a romance."

"I don't know, Jan," she said, shaking her head. "I feel in my spirit like there is something here." I pondered her words and thought, again, about how fitting it would be for her to be the one beside me if this did, indeed, develop into something more. "He could be a great life partner for you with his construction skills and heart for ministry. Seems like a perfect fit," she suggested.

Later that night Dale called again, and we spoke for hours. (I didn't yet know that this was extraordinary for Dale since he was typically an early riser.) I told him about how we lost Del and how I came to be so heavily involved in the real estate investment business. He shared the shock of losing his wife who had gone in for hip replacement surgery. The morning she was scheduled to go home, she lost her life to a blood clot. Her death was sudden and stunning in its swiftness. His young family was left with a hollowness that my family knew all too well.

Dale told me that he and Debbie had started their family late in life compared to Del and me. Their youngest, Josiah, was only fourteen years old when Debbie died. They had homeschooled, so he lost not only his mom but his teacher and his very best friend. Dale and his children were still trying to figure out a new rhythm to life and finding the process challenging.

As we continued sharing over the course of the next few days, we saw more similarities in our stories. Since God was always speaking to me in numbers, I was especially tuned into some of the dates and times he shared. Del was four years older than I. Debbie was four years older than Dale. Debbie died on March 9, the birthday of my granddaughter, Leah. Del had his fatal heart attack on October 9, Dale's birthday. (Dale had also lost his mom on his birthday many years earlier.) The date on the manifesto I wrote when I had returned from Ireland describing the man who would be in my act two was Debbie's birthday, June 30.

Dale had expressed an interest in pursuing a relationship, but I told him we were wrong for each other. I insisted this was just going to be another Kingdom connection with a brother who had similar values and interests and that we were too much alike. A romantic connection would be fraught with conflict and would never work. "According to your profile parameters I am too short, and I live too far away," I reminded him.

He said, "Are you kidding me? You would miss out on a potential relationship over a couple of inches of height?" He was indignant. "Filling out that profile was one of the most awkward things I have ever had to do. I just picked numbers. I don't even know how tall Debbie was. I just knew she was right for me." His voice was pleading for understanding of the difficulty of being put into such a painful place. I laughed at his comments as I remembered how inept I had felt filling out a preference list for a potential mate on each of the dating sites. He was right; it felt like a shopping list, not especially romantic.

Dale had left his home and career in Maryland and the Washington, D.C. area to pursue the study of theology. The pursuit of that study had taken his family to the Dallas/Fort Worth area of Texas, where he attended Southwestern Baptist Theological Seminary and received his master's degree. After five years there, his mentor and friend, Dr. Kenneth Hemphill, arranged an interview for Dale for a position at North Greenville University in their maintenance department. This would require a move to South Carolina, but they saw the wisdom in taking the position, as it would come with the benefit of allowing his children to receive a degree with no tuition fees. Dr. Hemphill told him, "The pay isn't great, but every time one of your children attend the university, it will be like getting a bonus." He and Debbie had been in survival mode during their years of seminary training and had no savings set aside for their children's higher education. This lack had been a concern for him and he felt this move would be prudent. He loved being surrounded by people of faith and the thought of providing an opportunity for an education for his children was enticing. Debbie had agreed it was a great opportunity. This move would also take them back to the East Coast where they felt more at home.

As we talked for those endless hours in the week following our initial conversation, he told me that he was willing to relocate again if there was a door God was opening to him. If he needed to move to pursue a career in the area of real estate flipping, that was a possibility that he wasn't afraid to follow. He said, "I would rather be a doorkeeper in the house of The Lord than to own any other house. I have been without a permanent home ever since I responded to the call to pursue ministry. Wherever He leads me, I know He will provide for me." I considered his words but hoped I could find a project we could do together in his area that wouldn't require his relocating again.

I looked on the map to see where the new house I had won the bid on was located. I found where I was going to be meeting Vickie in a few days and then where I thought Dale might be in proximity to those two targets. I asked him, as the day approached for me to go to see Vickie in Brevard, if he wanted to meet for coffee at a Starbucks. "The house I am going to look at is in Brevard. Is that anywhere near where you live? We could meet for coffee and then, perhaps, go see the house I may buy if it isn't too far out of the way."

"I can meet you in Hendersonville," came his reply. "That is on your way to Brevard and only about forty-five minutes from me. I will find a Starbucks there," he offered. He sent me an address, and we scheduled our rendezvous for that coming Saturday at noon. (I was meeting Vickie around seven o'clock that evening.) We continued to stay in constant communication as the hour approached, and I was feeling more and more like he was thinking of this as more than just a casual cup of coffee. I was thinking that we were just going to have some memorable conversations and share our common experiences as recently single parents, grandparents, and lonely hearts. I looked forward to having time with someone who could so closely relate to what I had been feeling after my loss.

One day that week, preceding the upcoming meeting with Dale, I had to shorten one of my classes at the YMCA (where I did water aerobics three mornings a week) because of an appointment to show a house to a client. As I was rushing through my hair and makeup routine, attempting to make myself presentable for my showing appointment, I grabbed a new curling iron I had purchased and started using it on my hair. I smelled a strange odor and thought that, perhaps, I hadn't gotten all of the chlorine out of my hair after my time in the pool that morning. I continued curling my hair by bringing the curling iron around to the front side of my head, curling my bangs under when, to my horror, my bangs melted onto the curling iron and crumbled away into ashes with a heinous odor. I was dumbfounded and horrified. What had just happened? I reached around to the back of my head and felt the spot where I had first applied the curling iron, only to discover that there was no hair there either. It, too, had melted away to ashes. I couldn't believe this was happening. I looked at the reflection in the mirror and wanted to just burst into tears at the image staring back at me. Short, tiny pieces of hair were protruding from the top of my forehead where bangs had once framed my face and from the crown of my head where the malfunctioning curling iron had first been introduced. The first thought that came to me in that moment of horror? "This is not the worst thing to ever happen to you. You lost your husband. That kind of sadness is something to cry about. The ruin of your hair is just something to deal with, lady. Don't cry over something so trivial." My self-imposed pep-talk was helping me in those first moments of dismay.

As I was trying to figure out how to deal with the mess I had just created, the phone rang. It was a fellow real estate broker/friend calling from the St. Louis area. "Hey, Jan! How are you doing?"

"Actually, Richard, I am doing terrible. I just burned off my bangs and a big chunk of the crown of my hair and I am supposed to be meeting a client in just a little while to show a house. I don't know how I am going to show up looking like this!" I lamented to my Midwest colleague.

"Oh, my goodness! What happened?" he asked sympathetically. I told him about my shock at the malfunctioning new curling iron. "I'll tell you what," he said, "I think you should just pull your hair back, put on a pair of jeans and a baseball cap, and own it! I think one of the sexiest things a gal can do is show up in jeans and a baseball cap!" he suggested.

"Spoken like a true sports fan," I replied. "I am also supposed to be meeting a new client this weekend in the mountains and going to a dance. I don't know how I would look in a baseball cap and jeans for those two outings, but I don't think it would evoke confidence in my professionalism or look very becoming."

"Trust me!" he encouraged. "The baseball cap and jeans are a winning combination." I appreciated his compassion and encouragement. After our conversation, I hung up and called my hairdresser and told her of my dilemma. She told me to come straight over and she would "fix" it. I drove there, sporting a baseball cap as Richard had suggested.

She greeted me warmly and said, "Let's have a look." As I removed the cap and she could see the damage, her eyes began to fill with tears. "Oh, Jan! I am so sorry!" she exclaimed in horror.

"Look! I have managed to not break down and cry over this fiasco. I need you to just try to do what you can and tell me it will grow out and everything will be fine or tell me to buy a wig, but don't you dare cry, or I am going to lose it," I warned her.

"Okay. Let's just shampoo this and see what we have to work with," she encouraged as she attempted to come up with solutions. After shampooing, she split the remaining hair between the front and back of my head, in an effort to cover the crown with some of the longer hair in front of it and cutting in very light whisper bangs for the fringe near my forehead. The final outcome didn't look great, but it was far nicer than where I had started when I came in that afternoon. She said, "In a few days the hair will begin to flatten out where it has been scorched. When that happens, we are probably going to need to cut it again to encourage it to come back from the trauma."

"I am meeting a new client this weekend," I told her. "I am also supposed to go to my first dance too. This does nothing for my self-confidence," I said, as I stared into the mirror in front of me trying to picture myself dancing around in a hat, as Richard had suggested in our call earlier that day.

"Tell me about the new guy. Is this a date? Is he taking you to the dance?" she asked.

I told her about how I had sent Dale a message online after having been paired with him on Match.com and how that had transitioned into a business opportunity. "This guy is not going to be a suitor, but I still don't want to show up looking less than my best," I said. "He isn't taking me to the dance. The sister of another guy I know has asked me to come to the dance." I told her how I had come to know Keith and his sister, Vickie.

"So, is Keith going to be at the dance, too?" she asked, curious about the dating activity into which I had suddenly been immersed.

"No. I don't think so, but I am not sure. I think it will just be Vickie and me and a few of her friends, but I suppose Keith could be there. If that is the case, that makes me even more aware of how badly I feel with my hair singed and my ego bruised," I added jokingly.

I went back home and tried on several hats, trying to see how I could manage the lack of hair without looking like I was suffering from a medical condition. While immersed in my closet, I heard the front doorbell ring and went to answer it. As I opened the door I saw a man holding a Carolina Panthers ball cap. I had opened only the interior door, leaving the storm door locked, and I said through the glass, "How may I help you?"

The man on the other side of the door smiled warmly and said, "Richard asked me to buy this for you and drop it off. I am his brother. I live here, and since he couldn't be here to get it to you, he asked me to act as his courier and pick this up for you with his greetings," he explained.

I unlocked the door laughing and said, "That is wonderful! Did he tell you what happened with my hair debacle this morning?" I took the hat as he extended it toward me.

"Yes, he did. That is why he sent me on this little errand for him. I hope it helps," he offered.

"Thank you so much for doing this for me. That was so thoughtful of you, ...and Richard," I added.

"You are welcome," he said with a big smile as he made his farewells and returned to his vehicle. I returned to my bedroom, pulled my hair up into the ball cap, snapped a picture, and sent it to Richard with my thanks. The gift warmed my heart in immeasurable ways as it spoke to my Heavenly Father's provision, even in the tiny details of my life. He even cares about my sense of self-confidence and had met me in this minutia the way He had met me at every turn in my life, but especially since Del had been taken so suddenly.

The days that followed found me purchasing several more hats for the collection I felt I would likely need in the coming months as my hair grew back. I chose one of those to wear for my meeting with Dale that Saturday and for the dance that would follow.

I arrived at the Ingles grocery store in Hendersonville that had a Starbucks located inside. I positioned myself outside of the store entrance to look for Dale's approach. He called my cell and said that he had arrived a little early and decided to explore an apple orchard up the street. He said, "Hey, after we grab our coffee, we can go pick some apples from the apple stand and sit out here on the front porch of this place in these rocking chairs and visit. What do you think?" I thought it was a splendid idea and was delighted that he had been so proactive in finding us a memorable place to share our time together.

As I took up my post outside the Ingles and awaited Dale's arrival, I kept watching my cell phone for new email or text messages. A burden of my given profession is that I can't be away from my mobile office for more than short periods of time. If someone is presenting an offer for one of my listings, I need to be available to respond. I was trying to catch up on everything that needed my attention before our visit so that I would be able to carve out a couple of hours of uninterrupted time. My head was down as Dale made his way across the parking lot. I wasn't sure if I would recognize him from the thumbprint-sized pictures I had seen on the internet, but as I looked up beneath the brim of my new, black, straw hat, I could see a tall man dressed in cowboy boots, nice jeans with a large belt buckle, and a colorful plaid shirt sauntering toward the entrance with a playful swagger. He glanced at me sideways as he was about to enter the store. I smiled and started to approach him. "Hey there!" I ventured. "Dale?" I asked.

"What were you doing?" He responded with a warm and mischievous smile. "Hiding behind a post so that you could run if I looked too scary?" he jokingly questioned.

"Already this guy is reading my mail," I mused. I just laughed, but the thought had crossed my mind that I wanted to size him up from a safe distance and sort through what my gut was telling me about this man before engaging him too intensely. Of course, that is not what I told him. "I was just waiting for you before I went inside," I responded. "I wasn't sure I would recognize you."

"So, you aren't going to run?" he asked, teasingly.

"Not until after I have had my coffee," came my reply.

"Fair enough!" he replied, as we stepped inside and headed for the coffee shop located front and center in the grocery store.

"Cute hat!" he commented. I had told him about my hair fiasco and was thankful that he had acknowledged my effort to conceal my embarrassment.

"Thanks!" I said. "I have an entire collection now. I have a feeling I am going to need them for a long time."

"Well, you wear it well, but you don't have to keep it on for me," he offered.

We continued toward our Starbucks destination inside the store. I started a conversation with the barista after I noticed her name tag and asked her if she knew the meaning of her name. Researching the meaning of names was something I have been doing for several years. Since many people do not know that their names have significant meanings, I love sharing with them if I happen to know the meaning. In the case of our barista, I did know. I told her the meaning of her name and said, "Do you know that every time someone calls you by your name they are speaking your destiny?"

She said, "No. I had no idea. That is amazing." She grabbed another young man who was working with her there and demanded, enthusiastically, "Tell him what his name means!" I looked at his name tag. The young man was named David. Thankfully, it was a common name and I happened to know its meaning as well.

"David, your name means 'beloved.' In the Bible, it was said of King David that he was a man chasing after the very heart of God. That is what God desires from you too. He wants you to be a man who chases after Him."

David shook his head affirmatively and said, "Cool!" I told him that when someone called him by name they were calling out his destiny. Dale listened as I spoke with them while they made our coffees. He also encouraged them to learn what God was calling them to be and I was pleased that he didn't think the entire exchange was strange.

Dale suggested we leave my van and just take his up the road to the apple orchard. He said it wasn't even five minutes from where we had picked up our coffee. Although I might have had reservations had we not spent so many hours over the phone getting to know one another, I felt at complete ease going with him. Again, at this point, I felt no particular attraction to Dale. I had no romantic notions toward him. My guard was down, and I was comfortable in my own skin knowing that this was just going to be a relaxed afternoon in the company of someone who belonged to the same club as I did. It was a club that neither of us had asked to join. We were inducted without our permission. It is the club for those who have lost their mates too soon. The term "widow" or "widower" is foisted upon you without regard for your resistance to the title. Carving out a few hours to spend with another heart who understood the complexities and sorrow of this burden was a gift I intended to treasure.

As we walked across the parking lot toward his vehicle, the unexpected happened. Both sudden and breathtaking, one simple gesture almost made my knees buckle. Dale simply reached over and took my hand in his as we walked along the path, and in that moment, something inexplicable happened inside of me. My spirit leapt within me and I began to shake, internally, as I have experienced from time to time when I was having a Divine encounter with God. An internal dialogue began between me and my Maker. "What is this?" I asked God, silently. "What are you doing with my heart? You and I both know this guy is all wrong for me!"

That quiet voice that had led me so gently asked of me once more, "Do you trust me, my daughter?" I tried to still my churning insides and not give away the turmoil that was raging within to this man who held my hand. Perhaps this was just a gesture of kindness he would have extended to any of the ladies he had been courting, I assured myself. His gesture was meaningless, I argued. Yet, what had started out as a casual afternoon was suddenly taken to a different place in my consciousness. My senses and my guard were now on high alert.

As we reached his van he said, "The air conditioner isn't always reliable in here. I hope you don't mind."

"Why don't we just take my van?" I suggested. "You can just drive it instead," I offered.

"Okay. If that is what you prefer," he acquiesced. We walked a few feet further to where I had left my Toyota Sienna parked, and he escorted me to my door.

"Finally," I thought. "Something feels like it is back in my control again." The ground became more certain under my feet as we settled into our respective seats in my mobile office. Maybe this spark of hope, provoked by his touch, was just a sense of longing. Maybe it was just a passing emotion? Maybe I was just responding with tumultuous emotions because I missed the touch of Delbert's hands holding mine, I reasoned.

After only moments, we pulled into the apple orchard. A picturesque setting with rolling fields surrounded the little apple stand. Facing the road there was a deep porch with white rocking chairs where one could sit and enjoy the view while sipping the cider (or, in our case, the Starbucks coffee). One could also enjoy other delicious offerings such as apple fritters, apple pastries, and all things apple one might imagine at the beginning of the apple harvest season. On this perfect day, it wasn't too prohibitively humid as the Carolinas can be in mid-to-late August. The gentle breeze was a kind friend to us as we made our purchases. I had chosen a special gift for my friend, Vickie, whom I would be joining later. I bought an apparatus that both peeled and cored apples. This tool would be an ideal gift for her since she lived in the apple-infused part of the Carolinas. I also bought one for myself as a memento to take home to remember this special outing. I thought my granddaughters would enjoy slicing their apples with this unique find. Dale purchased fresh apples to share with his family later. We sat on the rocking chairs to get further acquainted, face to face.

As we retold our stories once more and continued exploring our acquaintance deeper, Dale made it abundantly clear that he was not out for a casual afternoon. He was out seeking a mate. He wasn't seeking a romance. He was seeking a heart connection that would take him into the next chapter of his life. At times, I felt I was being interviewed. He asked me many questions. Some were completely inappropriate for my sense of protocol and decorum, yet, they were refreshingly honest and sincere. At one point he asked me, "So, are you a good kisser?"

I laughed and said, "I don't know. My husband thought I was and I thought he was, but what did we know? We never kissed anybody else. We thought we were brilliant!" I responded, but his question set ablaze a whole new set of self-doubts and a sense of vulnerability. I had never even considered that I might be a bad kisser. I had never contemplated just how inexperienced Del and I had been as childhood sweethearts or how that fact might impact my ability to navigate in this new world into which I had been launched.

Dale reminded me a little bit of my son Joel, whom we had nicknamed "Mr. Inappropriate" for his frequent, no-filter commentary on life. He was funny, and he was earnest. Joel also had those qualities and the similarities caused my heart to be less guarded. I knew how to deal with this temperament. I had raised a son with this kind of heart!

We talked a lot about the possibility of doing a few real estate flips together if he wanted to pitch in and do some of the work and oversee some of the projects while I financed the work and then we could split the profits in an agreeable manner. Our hours together flew by as if they were just minutes. We drove up to the house in Brevard to check out whether or not it was a viable candidate for my flipping business. The listing had stated it was in Brevard, but it was, in reality, up a torturously twisted road that was seventeen miles outside of town. We went from paved road, to gravel road, to dirt road. The house was a gorgeous log structure with amazing views, but I knew that the cost to bring it up to date and make it a good investment would be too high, given how far out a contractor would have to come to do the renovations. Then there was the additional burden of how remote the property was from any amenities. This location would not be too appealing to the broader market.

What did strike me during our time viewing the house was how thoroughly Dale was investigating it for me. He climbed under it, around it, and through it. He told me what his experience had been in finding contractors willing to make this kind of a trek to do the work. He felt they would add an exorbitant fee to the total cost just to cover all their commuting expenses. I agreed with him and, reluctantly, decided this one had been a waste of $1,000 because it didn't fit the blueprint for my typical flip. I knew I would have to let it go. I was so very thankful that God had provided a partner to view it with me so that I could make that decision with more than just my own opinion. I was also hopeful that we could find another opportunity that would be more suitable.

As we made our way back from our adventure to go on to the next appointments we each had later that evening, Dale said something I was not at all expecting. His words left me feeling simultaneously warmed, confused, and completely questioning my self-assurance. He said, "I dated a lot before Debbie and I met and were married. Since Debbie's death, I have had a lot of dates, too. I know that you have not dated a lot." He glanced towards me as he was driving down the mountain to see how that had landed.

I thought, "Is this a contest? Is he telling me I am naïve?" Aloud I said, "You are right. I have dated very little. I guess I am just getting started." Internally I said, "And if you only knew how much I hated it…" I felt that his introduction to the dating topic was just beginning and I waited to hear the rest of what he had to say.

We arrived back at his van, which we had moved to a location closer to where he had an appointment that evening. He turned to me, with sincerity in his eyes, and grabbed my hands. Instantly, there was that ridiculous feeling in the core of my being again. "Stop it!" I told myself. "Focus. What he is saying is important."

"Here is the thing," he began. "I want you to go back to Charlotte and date a lot. I want you to have an opportunity to meet a lot of men. Then, when you become as convinced as I already am that this thing that we have has been put together by God, I want you to call me. I would like to see you again. Maybe next time I can come to Charlotte?"

"Okay?" I didn't know what else to say. I was taken aback at how completely vulnerable he had left himself. I could have shot him down or told him I had no interest in seeing him again, much less a feeling that God had Divinely orchestrated our meeting. I said, "Well, you have certainly given me lots to think and pray about!" We did, at that time, have a few moments to pray together. We invited God to guide us by His Divine Spirit and show us if we were supposed to pursue this relationship further as merely friends, or as something more.

After our brief prayer, I got out of my side of the van and walked around to the driver's side once more where Dale tucked me safely inside and said his goodbyes. He headed to his van and I started putting my next destination into the GPS, with more to think about and process as I made my way to the first dance of my entire life.

I arrived at my meet up with Vickie, a bubbly, gracious, red-headed darling. She introduced me to several of her friends at the dance club. Most of those in attendance were middle-aged and older. The man who managed the club welcomed me for an evening of fun and dancing. I told him, apologetically, "I don't really dance."

"I am sure you will be fine. Some of these folks love to teach newcomers how it's done!" he assured me.

The band played mostly oldies that evening. The memories these songs produced evoked a sense of nostalgia and longing for me and, I'm sure, most of those in attendance. I danced that night with various partners. One was in his nineties and he was extremely gracious and kind to this novice. He was also a very fine dancer. The experience was sweet and one I will never forget. Vickie said, "See, I told you they don't care. They just want someone who is looking to have a good time. There is no pressure here."

The manager of the club came up to me after a few of the dances and said, "I thought you told me you can't dance. I think you meant you don't dance. You look like you are dancing to me!" he declared.

"Thanks for the encouragement. I am feeling very much like an actress pretending she dances," I told him.

"I think that is all any of us can do," he said with a wink and a smile.

During one of our brief breaks, I asked Vickie, "How does your husband feel about you dancing in the arms of all of these other men when he is out of town?"

"He doesn't really care," she shrugged. "He knows my heart belongs to him and, when he is in town, he joins me. These folks know that I love my husband and I am just here for the exercise and the music and the fun. It sure beats sitting home alone on a Saturday night," she explained.

As I moved from partner to partner throughout the night, my thoughts were carried back to the encounter I had just experienced with a tall stranger in cowboy boots who had made an extraordinary declaration to me only hours before. I kept wondering what it would have been like to have danced in Dale's arms. How would we fit together? Would we fit at all, I wondered? What was he doing at this moment, I questioned?

Our evening was cut short, abruptly, by an explosion in a transformer outside of the dance club. We heard a loud bang and then everything went dark. Most of the dance club patrons went outside to investigate and determined that the party was now over. The power company would take some time to restore such a major outage. Vickie and I decided to go back into town and grab a late dinner at a local diner.

During our time together getting to know one another, Vickie told me about her family and extended family. She told me about how she had met her current husband after the breakup of a very unhappy marriage. She also shared that she was disappointed that I had not given her brother more of a chance in my life. I explained to her, as I had to him, that the logistics just weren't there. I needed someone who was either already located in the Charlotte region or was ready to move there. Unless I fell in love with a rich man who wanted to take care of me as his wife, I had two businesses I needed to keep running and a family who meant the world to me located in that place. For a man who didn't already live in the Charlotte area to consider moving there just to pursue a relationship with me would be an extraordinary thing. "Was Dale that man?" I asked myself as we continued our conversation. I was anxious to get to Vickie's house that night to have quiet time with God to pray and really pour my heart out.

Vickie had hosted me for more than just a birthday outing. She had hosted me for a transition into the realm of possibilities I had never considered before. As I lay in her guest room that evening, pouring my heart out to my Heavenly Father, I told Him that I wanted Him to explain the sensation that had overtaken me as Dale had taken my hand in that parking lot when we first met. "Father, You know exactly what I need. You have promised me that You will guide me. I need Your guidance now more than ever. I don't want to be moved by my emotions. I know that I am vulnerable, and I have seen what happens to vulnerable people when they are hurting. Please help me to hear You clearly and know that I have heard You."

I considered Dale's words about me not dating a lot. He was right, of course. Del and I hadn't really dated as most couples do. We dated as two people who had grown up together. Del was the only adult man I had ever kissed or been intimate with and the thought of giving myself to another was daunting. Even a first kiss with someone other than Del made me feel uncertain and full of dread. As that thought passed through my heart, I considered how candid and unfiltered Dale had been earlier in the day. I thought, "I wonder if he would be willing to be my first kiss after Del? Would it be too weird or out of order to ask for such a thing?" In my mind, I was thinking that the awkwardness of a first kiss could be put aside. Just as I had gotten over the hurdle of my first date a few weeks earlier, maybe getting over the hurdle of that first kiss might also help ease some of my dating anxiety. "Father God, may I ask Dale to kiss me?" I prayerfully asked.

In response to that question, the Lord gave me a picture of a stone. He reminded me of the stories in the Bible where important things had happened during the pilgrimage of the people of Israel. When something happened of significance, they would often build an altar of stones from the ground in that place as a memorial to the Lord and as a marker for future generations. As a token, the participants would take a smaller stone that they could carry in their pouches and mark it to remember this place and to show their children as they recounted the story of how God had met them in a certain place. The generations that were being told these stories might never visit the place, but their ancestors still told the stories and the stones were the prompter to a memory and a testimony. I felt that God was giving me a yes, but that He was also telling me that this needed to be memorialized in some fashion.

Early the next morning, I sent a private message to Dale asking if he could meet me later that day if I headed back home by way of his area. The distance was about the same as the route I had taken coming up the day before, but the drive would be mostly interstate instead of back roads. He immediately responded affirmatively and gave me the address of a place near his home where we could meet after church that day.

I went to church with Vickie that morning. She introduced me to more of her family and to several folks who attended her church. One young man she introduced me to had been homeless just a few years before and was now fully engaged and being used mightily by God. After the service, this young man approached me. "May I tell you something that I was sensing during our service that I wanted to share with you?" he asked.

"Of course," I encouraged him.

"I don't know what you do for a living," he said, "but I feel like I am supposed to tell you that God is going to use you in more than just houses. You are going to have influence over towns and cities too. I feel like God said it isn't just about houses," he said.

"Well, thank you for that word. Did you know that I am a real estate broker?" I asked.

"No, ma'am!" he answered enthusiastically. I think it meant a lot to him to feel that he had heard so clearly from God.

These were words that you take and put on the back burner and just wait to see what God does with them. I was encouraged that he had singled me out and given me such an important message.

Vickie and I went out to lunch that day to continue celebrating her birthday and reinforcing the bonds of our new friendship. She gave me dating and sisterly advice and graciously looked after me until I made my departure. I told her about my night of turmoil and all the questions my heart was asking God. I told her about the jaunty driver's words in Ireland and the secret sense I had when he had turned 180 degrees around to face me and deliver that word about my second time around being greater than my first. He hadn't said it would be better. He had said it would be greater. To me, that meant that it might be more impactful. I also felt that my new love would be 180 degrees different than my former love. Nobody could be like Del was. I had told him that almost nightly. He wasn't replaceable. That meant my next love would need to be cut from a different mold so that there would be no comparison. Instead, he would be a completely new kind of man. Dale certainly fit that equation. I was both excited and timid about what the balance of my day would hold.

Chapter Eleven: My Huckleberry Friend

After leaving Vickie in Brevard, I headed for the small town of Landrum just off of Interstate 26 and south of Brevard. Dale had sent me the address for yet another Ingles grocery store that had a Starbucks inside. Dale was there waiting for me when I arrived this time.

We greeted each other far more warmly and with less guardedness at this meeting. "How was your service this morning?" I asked as we made our way inside to grab our coffee treats.

"It was fantastic!" came his enthusiastic reply. "We usually have an evening service, but we were doing something special this afternoon and skipping the evening service, so I am free for the rest of the day," he explained.

I was pleased that we would be able to spend time together without the impending concern about schedules that had to be met. My top-of-mind request for a first kiss was going to be a delicate dance for me and my emotions had me reeling. "That is good. We can take our time," I remarked. "I would just like to be heading back home before it gets too dark, if possible." The area of upstate South Carolina was unfamiliar to me. I wanted to be in an area I was accustomed to before the sunset. Fortunately, it was August and the extended sunshine was going to allow us hours together, getting better acquainted before darkness enveloped us.

"What did we order yesterday?" Dale asked as he thoughtfully perused the Starbucks menu. "This isn't a place I come often."

"You had a caramel Frappuccino, I believe. Did you enjoy it?" I asked.

"Yes. Let's do that again." He zeroed in on his choice and I ordered my usual poison: a mocha Frappuccino, decaf, made with a lactose-free alternative, hold the whip.

With drinks in hand, we headed out to a small truck Dale owned for a tour of his town of Landrum and the surrounding area. Leaving my van behind was a stretch for me. Delbert used to say that my van was an extension of my person, as was my cell phone. Since a minivan has been a rolling office for me for so many years, it is hard for me to relinquish control and just be a passenger, but on this day, I felt a new liberty to let someone else hold the reigns and this freedom was invigorating.

As we settled into his truck, Dale turned to me and said, "What should we do first?" in excited anticipation, as if we were going on a great escapade. His enthusiasm was encouraging and infectious.

"Oh, boy!" I thought. "Is he going to think I have a screw loose when I ask him to take me somewhere to find a stone? Father God, if this man is a part of my destiny, I trust You to show me, somehow, today. I don't need to date a lot of men. I just need to know the man You have chosen for me. Please show me today, Father," I prayed.

After taking a deep breath aloud I said, "I need you to help me find a stone."

"A stone?" came his intrigued response. "What kind of stone?" He seemed genuinely curious and up for the adventure.

"It needs to be a natural stone, not carved out by human hands. It just needs to come out of the earth, unaltered," I explained. I remembered the stories in the Bible where the Israelites had been told that altars made to God were not to be made of human carved stones, but from the natural stones they found in the land.

Dale pondered for a moment and said, "Hmmm . . ." Then, a look of revelation came across his face, as if he knew what I was trying to do. "We can't get this stone from South Carolina. It has to come from North Carolina, and I know just the place."

"Okay," I said. I didn't yet follow his logic, but we were both up for the quest. He turned the truck toward a little town called Tryon, just across the border into North Carolina. Dale told me there was a large park in the small town where annual barbecue festivals were held. (Barbecue prowess is a matter of great pride in this region of our nation.) He took me through the rolling topography of the mountain foothills toward the park. We drove through the little towns of Landrum and Tryon. Both were filled with thrift stores, novelty shops, and little diners. To me, they were filled with the promise of an adventure that I hoped perhaps to enjoy on another occasion when my mission wasn't so specific.

The day was beautiful, with abnormally mild temperatures (for August) continuing to grace my time away from Charlotte. The skies were brilliant blue with huge, white, puffy clouds that highlighted the depth of color in the surrounding visage. I was thankful that we weren't experiencing the more oppressive heat that typically accompanies a summer day in the South and the outdoors felt refreshing.

As we made our way into the park, Dale pulled the truck toward a lovely stream that wound its way through the area. We got out and meandered toward its edge. I could hear the gentle sound of the moving water as it tumbled through the landscape.

"I think we can find some great stones in there," Dale suggested, pointing to the crystal clear, glistening stream.

"You are right!" came my delighted reply. "They will be smooth and perfect." I wanted a stone I could write the date and place on with a permanent marker. I had pulled a stone out of Galway Bay in Ireland on Delbert's birthday, writing the date and place on it. I considered it one of my greatest treasures from my time spent there. The marking of Del's birthday in Ireland had been a momentous occasion, as I felt this would be.

I took off my shoes and made my way into the cool, refreshing waters of the flowing brook. There were a few children splashing upstream with a man I assumed to be their dad. We headed toward a shallow area (with lots of potential stones of remembrance) and began harvesting our crops from the clear waters. Dale was wearing his boots and I was concerned that he needed to remove them. When

I suggested it, he said, "No way! I am a tenderfoot. I can't walk on those rocks like you are doing." Instead, he demonstrated his physical agility by walking over the rocks, positioned above the surface of the brook, carefully navigating as he pulled up his treasures. He would pick up one and show it to me, "How about this one?" he would ask.

"No. It is too dark. I wouldn't be able to see the writing on it." He would continue searching and pull up another for my critique. "No. That is the right color, but it is too heavy. The stone has to be small enough that I can carry it in my pocket," I explained.

With new directions, he began to find multiple stones that were candidates for my purposes. After a short time, he and I both had our hands filled as we gingerly stepped across the stone covered waters and up the shallow embankment. We took our newly acquired finds to a picnic table nearby and began to sort through them. "I need a permanent marker," I said, as the thought occurred to me that I had nothing to write with.

"I've got it!" Dale said as he ran back to his truck, opening the glove box and retrieving a black marker. He came back to me with a look of accomplishment on his face, carrying the last element needed to complete our task. "I'm your Huckleberry!" he declared playfully. (Dale is an avid fan of the Western movie, *Tombstone*, in which Doc Holiday refers to himself in this way. I would only learn later that the meaning of *Huckleberry* is, *a man uniquely qualified for the task*.)

I just shook my head and laughed. "You are brilliant! That is exactly what we needed."

As we sorted through the rocks looking for the best candidates to write upon, Dale finally asked, "So, are you going to tell me what we are doing here? I mean, I think I may know, sorta what you are doing. You want to tell me exactly what this is about?" he asked, leaning back against the picnic table and stretching his long torso, cowboy boots extended, as if ready for a story.

Before I launched into the narrative of the children of Israel and how they would collect memory stones from the altars they built on their journeys in the wilderness and the Promised Land, I asked him, "Why did you think we needed to come to North Carolina for the stone?" I was hoping he would have been given some sense of what was to come.

"I will tell you later," came his simple answer. I felt he was discerning the direction I was going with my explanation. Maybe I just hoped that I would be spared the full awkwardness of the revelation I was about to divulge.

Having been a theologian for more than a dozen years, and a follower of Christ for even longer, he was familiar with the practice of the children of Israel. I told him about collecting the stones at Galway Bay for Del's birthday and carrying them back across the ocean as my sacred treasure. He listened intently, shaking his head in understanding. He told me that he had a few of those himself. "So, I feel that our meeting, and this day, are extremely important. I felt led, after prayer, to mark this occasion in a special way," I explained.

He nodded in agreement. "That is why I had us come to North Carolina when you said you needed a stone, instead of where we started today," he interjected. "I felt that you wanted to do something special and I wanted it to be in the state of North Carolina, where we met. I don't know exactly why, either. It just felt right," he said. His sensitivity made it easier to continue.

"In my prayer time last night, I considered your question about if I thought I was a good kisser. It really made me think about how uncomfortable my first time could be sharing a kiss with someone other than my late husband. Do you understand?" I asked, hoping he would see how difficult this was for me.

A look of sympathy washed across his face as he responded, "I am so sorry. I didn't mean to make you feel bad. Something comes into my brain and I just say it. No brakes and no filter!" he declared.

"Please forgive me for hurting you. I was just being playful. I didn't mean for it to upset you," he continued apologetically.

I quickly tried to explain, "I know you weren't trying to hurt me, but you did get the wheels turning. It is part of why I wanted to meet with you today. I know this is going to sound like a really strange request," I proceeded, timidly, "but I did pray about it and I felt like God said it would be okay, so here goes." After a deep breath, the words came tumbling from my lips as quickly as I could say them. "Would you be the first person to kiss me? I just want to have that behind me and I felt like I could trust you with this request." Now it was out there, and I waited (what felt like an eternity) before receiving his reply.

"I'm sorry," he said. "I wish I could, but I just can't do that for you." He seemed genuinely sad and I felt like an absolute fool.

"Okay. I understand. It was a lot to ask," I tried to regain some of my lost dignity as I started berating myself, internally, for even conjuring up such a bizarre request. Had I misread him the previous day, and all of the days before, I wondered? Had I breached a protocol I didn't know existed in the realm of dating?

As I was processing a stream of emotions, none too pleasant, he continued in a more playful tone, "Yeah, I just can't kiss you because I would ruin you for any other man!" he boasted, with a bit of a swagger and a sideways grin. I began to laugh, and my laughter was a blessed relief. I could now see that the playful side of him was expressing itself and he was attempting to inject humor into the matter.

"You are pretty pleased with yourself, aren't you?" I responded. He had a boisterous laugh and the tension of the moment was broken. The idea of a first kiss was put completely out of my mind now and I decided to just let it happen at a natural time instead of being in a hurry to just "get through it."

We continued talking for hours, once again, as Dale shared some of the story of his struggle with loneliness after Debbie had died. He called his stories his "Hall of Shame," and felt compelled to tell me about what he had gone through in recent months. He explained that he wanted me to know everything about his past because, if we were going to have a future, he wanted all the cards on the table. He held nothing back as he explained how he had fallen into a relationship that had been shameful to him and had left him feeling unfit for ministry. "When you are used to sharing everything about your day, your thoughts, your wins, your losses with someone and that someone isn't there, you are so vulnerable."

He had been faithful to his wife for twenty-seven years but had been weakened by her loss and the state of vulnerability that had left him prey to a situation that made him leave his job and his studies. "When a woman starts to talk to you about things going on in her life, just as a friendly conversation to begin with, and she is thrilled to have someone truly listening to her and responding, it can lead you to places you have no business going. Now I understand why we are told during seminary training the importance of having another woman in the room when we are counseling, or having the door open between the place where you are counseling and the place where other people are gathered. It is so important to have that accountability," he said, shaking his head with regret. "Doc Hemphill warned me that I was playing with fire, but I thought I could handle it. Turns out Doc knew what he was talking about." (Dale told me that Dr. Kenneth Hemphill had been one of his dearest mentors and a father figure in his life.)

After he had fallen prey to this seduction, he left the pursuit of ministry. He sought Dr. Hemphill's counsel and told him. "Doc, I am disqualified for ministry. I can't preach or be used by God," he lamented.

"What do you mean?" Dr. Hemphill responded.

"I have failed miserably. You warned me. I thought I could handle it, but I blew it!" he had confessed.

In loving compassion, his spiritual father had responded, "Brother Dale, if that were the case, none of us could preach." Dale had been heartened by his mentor's reassuring words and had only recently been picking up the pieces and trying to put his life back on track.

Dale's revelations about his struggles only made me feel more drawn to him because there was an honesty and a strength in him that were being revealed in the admission of his failings. One of Delbert's most valued qualities (to me) was his undeniable integrity. He never lied to me. I always felt secure in his words, never second-guessing the honor of the man. I felt like the honesty and transparency Dale was demonstrating reflected the same endearing characteristics as those of the man I had lost only ten months earlier. My heart was being gently massaged by God, and I was sensing His hand in this connection as every hour passed.

Dale drove me back to Landrum, where he resided in a parsonage beside a Baptist church. The parsonage had been his home with Debbie and his children when she had passed away. I met his sixteen-year-old son, Josiah, for the first time. Despite the awkwardness, Josiah was amiable and pleasant. I considered the weight of becoming a stepmom and the mother of a teen-aged son, once again. Having raised three sons, I felt I was up for the challenge, but the stereotype of the stepmom scenario was a bit daunting. Delbert used to say, "It never costs anything to try things on, mentally. Picture what it looks like. How do you feel wearing that image, emotionally?" I heard his wise counsel, even as I sat in the home of this widower and his son. "Do I have what it takes to become a stepmom?" I wondered. "Is this part of what God is calling me to do in this second act of my life?"

The hour was late, and I knew that the sunset was inevitable. As much as I was enjoying my time of Heavenly connection, I wanted to be on the road before that happened, so Dale returned me to my van where we had left it at the Ingles earlier. Dale turned to me and asked, "Why don't you take off that hat? I haven't seen you without it yet."

"No," I insisted. "Just look at my old pictures on Facebook and you can see what I look like without it," I suggested.

"You know it doesn't matter to me what your hair looks like. Right? You understand?" He then began to quote one of his favorite country song lyrics about a man who professes his love for his mate, whether she has hair or not. As sweet as his declarations were, I wasn't ready to shed the hat yet. He finally surrendered to my wishes regarding my hat staying in place.

Although it was hard to break away, the time came for my departure. I was finding, moment by moment, that my heart was becoming Divinely entangled with this man's. We had known each other so briefly, but it felt like I had known him my whole life. I had always had good male friends during my childhood and into my teen years. From Delbert's brothers to my next-door neighbor to the young men at the church where we had met and married, I had been blessed with so many great friends of the male persuasion. As we spent these hours together, I was feeling this same sense of kinship with Dale that I had experienced in so many of those relationships from my youth. There was something of the eternal in the bond that was inexplicable. I questioned and, often, resisted the feelings that were overwhelming me.

As we said our goodbyes, and both wondered where this road was taking us, we did share our first kiss (with my hat still firmly planted on my head). I don't want to "kiss and tell," but he hadn't lied to me earlier in the day when he said his kiss would have a lasting effect. The earth moved . . . Heaven applauded . . . and I was ruined for any other man. This moment we shared was more than a simple kiss between two lonely hearts. Truly, it felt as though this were a Divine appointment I was experiencing. The stone of remembrance was, indeed, appropriate for this intimate moment that was shifting the course of my life.

I drove home, filled with more questions than answers, but alive with hope and a joy that was displacing my sorrow. There were many logistics that would have to be considered if we were going to develop a meaningful relationship that led to a shared life. I knew I couldn't move to Landrum. Dale's employment there wasn't something he was seeing as a long-term position. Both my real estate brokerage and investment businesses were extremely demanding. I could see Dale fitting into the position of a partner. He was qualified to act as a project manager for the house flips I was doing, minimally. Sorting through the transition for Josiah was the single most critical part of the equation. That transition, too, needed to be carefully managed. Out of all eight of our children, he was going to be the one most profoundly affected by this developing story.

In the days that followed, I had run into a problem with the contractor who was working on the flip I was doing at Ocean Isle Beach. He had a timeline that was being strongly compromised, as the work he had assured me would be completed in a timely manner was not being addressed. My sister and brother-in-law, Linda and James Mason, had planned a mini vacation to join me at the beach house in just a couple of weeks, and the place was not as far along as it needed to be so that we could use it for our vacation. I shared my dilemma with Dale. He said, "I have a toolbox and a fix-it gene. Josiah and I would love to come and help you with the place if you want us to." I called my contractor and told him of the offer of skilled help. He was relieved to have the support. I was thankful to have more face time with Dale and Josiah to get to know them better.

A few days later, we met at my home and continued on to Ocean Isle Beach and the construction zone. I had sold a house in Southport, North Carolina a few months earlier, a property which had been fully furnished. I moved the furnishings to the Ocean Isle Beach house, once it was far enough along to accommodate the items, without too much of a mess. The house was acceptable for us to use it for our lodging, but it was not ready for company. An abundance of projects still needed to be completed. Dale and Josiah pitched in with great fervor. The beleaguered contractor had taken on more than he could manage and was thankful for the assistance. We worked together each day with the crew. Josiah managed to get in some fishing, one of his favorite sports, as we kept working down the list of items needing attention.

We attended our first ocean-side church service, held on the sand dunes near the Ocean Isle Pier from Memorial Day through Labor Day every Sunday morning. The morning worship service was a refreshing way to meet the day, with the roar of the waves behind us as we sat between the sand dunes, lifting our voices to Our Maker. The service was led by an older couple. They sang a few standard hymns with a portable sound system to project their voices above the roar of the surf and the seagulls. Dale leaned over during the worship and whispered, "I can see that being you and me someday, leading worship and sharing the Word." Again, my heart was swelling as I was picturing a future with Dale and his family. In my vision, I saw his family merging with mine in sweet harmony. Our temperaments were not aligned as mine had been to Delbert's. His ways were so different from what I was used to dealing with in the only love I had ever known before now, but I felt the peace of God in my soul about this new beginning.

Josiah had school on Monday, so we packed up Sunday afternoon and headed back to my home, encouraging our contractor that we had faith in him and we would be back the following weekend with my sister and brother-in-law. He assured us that he would be finished easily with all of the assistance we had given to him.

I called my children and invited them to come to the house that evening to meet Dale and Josiah for the first time. Most of them had agreed to do so and I looked forward to him meeting them as well. I was proud of them and wanted them to see what I saw in him. Dale and I had a conversation about how he should conduct himself, physically, while in their presence. "Is it okay for me to hold your hand in front of them or do I keep my distance? I don't want them to freak out, but I want them to know I am serious about their mother."

I considered his words. "I don't want to pretend this is casual. You should hold my hand and stand beside me," I encouraged him. "They are going to feel uncomfortable at first, but they need to adjust. I don't want to ease into this and have them shocked down the road when we begin to discuss a future together. It is like taking off a Band-Aid—the quicker, the less painful," I reasoned.

Having both lost a spouse, we were all too familiar with the fact that none of us are promised tomorrow. I was reminded of a line in a movie that said something like, "When you find out who you are going to spend the rest of your life with, you want the rest of your life to start now!" That was the sentiment I was feeling. I wanted my new life to start now. We were adults and we knew the Voice of God. Although we knew how easily many folks in the midst of grief could fall for the wrong person, we had each sought the Lord for His guidance and kept feeling His leading in this matter.

My adult children had some pretty tough questions for Dale, interrogating him just as a father might probe a prospective suitor for his daughter. They wanted to know his intentions and his prospects. The warm, engaging family I had been so pleased to introduce to this man with whom I was envisioning a future never made an appearance that evening. In their place, a gathering of brokenhearted souls had assembled, too overwhelmed by the reality of a new man coming into their mother's life and assuming their father's role, one that they weren't yet ready to accept.

After Dale left that evening and headed back to his home in Landrum, I was crestfallen. My children were frightened about my intense feelings for this man to whom they had just been introduced. One of my sons said, "When I saw him holding your hand I kept thinking that Dad was going to come around the corner, offering everybody a mocha and being really angry about this guy holding your hand. I know it isn't going to happen. Dad isn't coming back, but it just felt that way to me," he said, struggling to communicate his discomfort and displeasure. "I want you to be happy, but this is way too fast. You need to slow down!" he insisted. Those of my offspring who were present expressed the same dismay and discomfort to varying degrees.

Most of them took an instant dislike to Dale, not because of who he was, but because of who he was not and what he represented. The introduction of a new man into Mom's life meant the absolute acknowledgment that the one man they would love and cherish for the rest of their days was truly no longer going to be a part of the picture. They weren't ready to wrap their heads around this new paradigm and they fought it every step of the way, sometimes giving in a bit, only to pull back.

The next weekend, I drove to Greenville. Dale's family was going to be celebrating his granddaughter's birthday. He felt it would be a good time for me to meet two of his daughters, Dana and Kaitlyn, who lived in the area. A friend of his worked at a lovely hotel in Greenville and he acquired a room there at the employee rate. After the rough greeting he had received from my family, I wasn't sure what my reception would be as I made my way to Greenville for the weekend. I was hopeful but guarded.

The celebration of his granddaughter's birthday took place at the home of his oldest daughter, Dana, and her husband, Chris. They were joined there by many friends and Chris' family. The gathering was a sweet celebration for their little cherub, Bethany Ellen Loper, referred to by those who love her as "Ellie." The Lopers were kind and warm toward me, although I know that my physical presence was a bitter reminder that the object of their maternal affections was absent. I sat in the living room of their cozy home and glanced at the pictures surrounding me. There were pictures of Debbie everywhere. Dana looked just like her mom. I was also struck by how much Josiah and Dana favored one another, both reflecting their mom's face, her smile, her dark, curly hair, and her lovely blue eyes.

Kaitlyn came to the party a little later in the day, and I spoke with her as well. She kept a safe and guarded distance, but she was cordial. She adored her niece and her affection was clear. They lit the cupcakes and encouraged Ellie to blow out the candles. They called Amanda, the only missing sibling, in California so that she would feel included in the celebration she was missing out on at her great distance.

Following the party, Dale returned me to my hotel where we talked for hours. We had been in constant conversation since the beginning of our courtship. We both knew how challenging the transition was going to be for all hearts, especially for Dana, who would be losing the constant companionship she had enjoyed with Josiah, who visited her home regularly and adored Ellie. Josiah, too, was going to be asked to make, yet again, a life-altering change. He had been through so much in his sixteen years. They had all lost the very heartbeat of their family when God called Debbie home and here I was, a stranger, suggesting that their patriarch and their little brother relocate to accommodate my lifestyle.

As we talked well into the morning of the next day, struggling with each decision and praying for guidance from above, Dale pulled me into his arms and asked me to marry him. If I had any doubt about his commitment to the change, it was answered with that question. He simply looked at me, through tears, and asked, "Marry me?" His proposal wasn't an elaborate production but was as seamless and natural as the entire courtship had been. My heart said this felt right, like the Divine hand of God had picked up the baton and began conducting the symphony to accompany our second act.

I said, "Yes!" and we continued to seek God's cover over our union.

I looked forward to the coming weekend when we would meet up again at Ocean Isle Beach. I would have the opportunity to introduce Dale to my sister and her husband. I had hoped that all of my family would see how truly happy this newfound love was making me, displacing my sorrow and redeeming my sadness. The next weekend, James and Linda were flying in for their short beach getaway. We drove down to the house at Ocean Isle planning to meet

Dale and Josiah there. We were also going to have the privilege of joining James' dad and stepmom, Ray and Kaye Linebaugh, who were going to be in Wilmington, North Carolina, less than an hour from our beach house that same weekend.

Ray and Kaye were there to attend a Marine Ball and reunion of veterans from Ray's First Battalion 9th Marine Unit. He had been a veteran of the A Company in that distinguished group of soldiers. These men had been referred to by the enemy in Vietnam as "The Walking Dead" because they took so many bullets and just kept coming at the enemy. Ray was a chaplain to the unit now, and he and Kaye had invited us to attend as their guests for the evening. Jeremy and his wife, Elizabeth, also joined us for our time at Ocean Isle Beach.

When we arrived at the house, we were met with a note from the contractor we had helped so feverishly just two weeks earlier. The note said he was sorry that he hadn't been able to complete the job. The place was still unfinished, but much further along than it had been during our last visit. We were disappointed that what should have been a delightful vacation was, by necessity, going to have to be a working holiday. Everyone rolled up their sleeves and set to finishing the list of items still incomplete and in need of immediate attention. James put up ceiling fans on the back porch; Dale finished plumbing installation and setting up appliances. We were all like busy ants on a hill, scurrying to complete the task of having a lovely home to enjoy the weekend. Many items would have to be completed by a professional contractor later, but for the time being, we set the place in order so that we could relax and take in some ocean breezes and prepare for an elegant ball later that evening.

We finally made it down to the ocean to take in the sand and the surf later in the afternoon and set up a huge beach umbrella to shelter us from the searing heat and scorching sun. We had purchased some boogie boards for those who wished to go out into the deep waters and play in the surf. Jeremy and James ventured into the waters, and Josiah joined them. Watching his son skittishly approach the deeper waters, Dale turned to me and said, "Josiah has never ventured that far out before. He must trust James and Jeremy to rescue him if he gets into trouble," he mused. I was heartened to see him bonding with the two men. I was, once again, picturing myself as the stepmom to this young man and considering that this assignment was a part of the mission God had for me in the very near future.

As Dale wandered back and forth along the shore, sometimes joining with those frolicking in the water and sometimes collecting shells along the beach, my sister turned to me and started sharing her first impressions and her concerns. She was trying to be open-minded but, like my children, was fighting the sorrow of having lost her childhood hero and trying to picture this interloper taking his place. They were such very different men, it was hard for her to envision the connection. "James and I can see that you are happy. We just want to be sure you don't rush into something you are going to regret. I mean, what do you really know about him, other than what he has told you?" Her questions were honest and sincere. She wanted to protect me. She desperately wanted my children to be at peace with my choice as well. Linda had been bonding with Josiah during her brief time with him and had expressed how much she liked him. I told her I just didn't know if I would be a good stepmom. "If it comes to that, you will be great. You have lots of experience and I have no doubt he could use a woman like you in his life," she assured me.

"Josiah is one of the greatest concerns I have in this entire equation," I told her. "Dale and I are heading toward marriage. This impending union means that Josiah will have to be uprooted, once again. I don't know how this transition is going to work. He has already been through so much. I think he will have a better life with us at Serenity, but I don't know if he is going to see that for himself. I think he may resent me and resent his dad if we pull him out of the school where he is attending, putting him into yet another school after all the changes he has already had to manage in the past two years."

"I agree. It won't be easy, but I know God will show you what to do and when to do it," she assured me. Dale returned to our shady shelter on the sand, and our conversation moved on to other matters, as he got to know my little sister better while the rest of our group continued exploring the sand and the sea.

The evening soon arrived. With the assistance of Elizabeth, I prepared to go to my first ball. I felt a little like a late-blooming Cinderella and Elizabeth was acting as my fairy godmother. I wore the same formal dress to the ball in Wilmington that I had worn as the mother-of-the-groom in Jeremy and Elizabeth's wedding just two years earlier. We took the obligatory photos before setting off for our destination at one of the hotels along the Cape Fear River in the downtown area of Wilmington.

We were escorted into an elegant ballroom where we had a lovely meal, set to the sounds of soft music in the background. We chatted over our meal and got to know a few of the folks to whom Ray introduced us throughout the evening. After our dinner, the distinguished guests gave inspiring speeches, evoking a sense of pride and patriotism that is seldom heard amidst the din of noise and cynicism we often encounter in these troubling times. At one point in the evening, Ray leaned over and said, "No other unit in the history of the Marines has ever been engaged in combat for forty-seven consecutive months. This group holds that record. Further, no other unit has been more decorated or held more medals or suffered more casualties. We had a casualty rate of over 76 percent!" he proudly shared. Ray wanted us to have a sense of the enormous heroism of the people among whom we were seated. He was so proud of his fellow comrades. He wanted us to understand both their heroism and their trauma as he divulged some of the history of what earned them all those medals, and what led him to become a chaplain to this group of men. We were honored to be his guests and to learn, firsthand, about this history from those who had lived it.

As the meal was completed and the speakers finished their inspiring speeches, the dance floor was cleared of some of the food and drink tables. An entertaining D.J. put on more upbeat music than the quiet dinner music we had listened to earlier in the evening as we enjoyed our meal. He now cranked up some livelier tunes. Disco lights were put in place, and I finally had the chance to move on the dance floor with Dale and experience what my heart had longed for a few weeks earlier when I had attended my very first dance. It was invigorating and awkward, simultaneously. Dale had been an avid dancer when he and his late wife first met. He enjoyed dancing and was excited for a chance to share the experience. He led me through each dance and boosted my confidence so that I was willing to get outside of my comfort zone, trying some new steps.

Josiah attended the ball with us that evening and loved to dance. He got up on the dance floor, showing all of us his smooth moves and prowess at the art. Dale told me that Josiah's sisters all loved to dance as well, and so had his late wife. Dancing was clearly in their genes and Josiah appeared to be having a good time. He began to bond with my family, taking to the dance floor with Kaye and Linda a few times throughout the evening. The older generation was being schooled by this young man and just trying to keep up. Watching him shine in the midst of the gathering was delightful, although he was one of the youngest people present. I was thankful that he had been exposed to the moving stories from the men who had fought for our freedom, and I was thankful that he was having a chance to get to know the people who might one day be his aunt and uncle.

After the ball, we all drove out to Wrightsville Beach so that Ray and Kaye could actually see the ocean. They lived in Colorado and didn't make it to the shore often. Being this close to it, they didn't want to miss the opportunity. We walked along the shore and then along the pier located on Wrightsville beach. The evening air was infused with the smell of salt and the sea, and my heart was infused with hope. I had just attended my first ball. I was with my sister and her husband, who had been some of my lifelong dearest friends. I was walking alongside a war hero, and I had a new love in my life actually experiencing it all with me along with his son.

I contrasted this scene in my mind to what life would have been like had Delbert still been with us. He would not have come to the beach or attended the ball, much less danced with me. He never wanted that kind of attention. He would have loved the stories and the history being shared, but he would have enjoyed it far more from a secondhand telling of it rather than having to be in a crowd. How differently this evening had gone for me than it would have, had life not developed, through the losses and gains handed to me. Father God was teaching me to look at life through a different lens. He was inviting me to see it from a Heavenly perspective where we learn to trust Him, even when it seems He hasn't answered our prayers. I was catching glimpses of what life could be like in the future as I surrendered my fears to His loving hands and allowed relationships to unfold as Heaven had prepared.

I had waltzed through this evening with new hands guiding me and new arms holding me. These arms that held me had also learned to navigate through losses and gains and look for Heaven's meaning and purpose for his new chapter. My Huckleberry friend was here to do life with me. He was, by definition, "a man uniquely qualified for the task!" We would continue to trust God for His sovereign heart to steer us into a new beginning. Dale's life verse is Proverbs 3:5,6: "Trust in the Lord with all your heart; lean not upon your own understanding. In all your ways acknowledge Him and He will make your path straight."

Chapter Twelve: Beauty for Ashes

As a real estate professional, I have had less than a handful of times in my decades-long career where a buyer fell instantly in love with the first house they saw. When they do, I am uneasy and will encourage them to view other options to be certain that they are making an informed decision, especially if the home they have chosen differs dramatically from the criteria they had given to me as a guide for helping them in their search. My aim is to be certain they don't suffer from buyer's remorse because they limited their choices. On those occasions where some of my buyers have found their desired homes quickly, however, once I have shown them their other options, most have gone right back to the first one with which they fell in love. This is true, even when the home is completely different from what they set out to purchase when they first pictured their abode. They somehow just know, intuitively, that the object of their affection is the place for them. Because I know the market better than the average buyer, I want to be sure that they look at the house from every angle and choose the very best option for them, based on the context of looking at many options with the desired features and price point they have been targeting.

To want to know all our choices is human nature, whether it is the menu at a restaurant, the options for a new car, the vacation opportunities at our beck and call, or a home for sale. In the dating world, it is no different. We want to know who, out there, is most suited to our desired set of criteria. In our culture, dating a person becomes like glancing over a menu at a restaurant. We ask the waiter, "What do you recommend?" In the same way, we may ask our friends or family, "What should I look for in a potential mate?" or "Where shall I look for a potential mate?" Everyone has a set of criteria that is driven by their personal tastes. If the waiter at a restaurant spouts off the list of his recommendations for the best sushi choices on the menu, he loses me. I am not a fan of sushi. His tastes can't steer me toward what I am craving.

* * *

When it came to dating, I had to delve deep into the counsel of God. I sought the wisdom of my pastor and his wife, Mark and Julie Appleyard. I sought the counsel of the elders in our church, including Scott and Lori Clifton. As I have always done, I also turned to Linda and James Mason, who had met Dale and his son and had loved Delbert as a dear brother. I called upon my dad and my mom and told them what my heart was saying regarding the unfolding relationship with Dale. As each of these hearts had walked with me through the most painful chapter of my life, they were now poised to stand beside me as I took on a new beginning and to pray with me, earnestly, for wisdom to hear from God in these matters and the courage to follow His path for me. Choosing Dale was very much like the scenario where my buyers chose a house so different from what they started to search for in the beginning. It is completely natural for those who had known Del to expect that my next love would be like him. Dale was his complete opposite. For those who loved me and had known me as the duo of Del and Jan (or Dad and Mom), it took some adjusting to picture something so radically different as the union of Dale and Jan. The names may have been similar, but that is where the similarity ended.

The speed at which our relationship was developing was troubling to our children. They each had their own reservations about the potential union. We, too, knew that it was moving fast. I was like that home buyer who had found the right match without spending a lot of time looking at other homes. My children were like the real estate professional who encourages you to slow down and look at all your options before making that offer to purchase. For me, there was no reason to keep looking at other houses. I had found what I had been searching for and I was ready to move. Dale, too, felt peace about moving forward.

Initially, we spoke about marrying in January during the semester break for Josiah's sake. This would give my children a chance to get to know the Nealis family and for Dale's family to get to know the Teel clan. We started down that path, confident in this good strategy. As our itinerary unfolded, however, we were told by Josiah's counselors that our plans could seriously hurt Josiah's schooling because his class schedule in Landrum was on a different calendar than the schedule in our area. If we were going to change his high school, they felt it needed to be done immediately to assure that he wouldn't lose any more ground in his education. He had already had a serious setback when he lost his mother so unexpectedly, and we didn't want him to be put at a disadvantage, once again.

My birthday was coming in a few days and my youngest, Jeremy Luke, agreed to escort Dale and me to St. Louis to observe my first birthday without Del in the company of my siblings and parents. This gave my siblings and parents a chance to all meet Dale. They had been counseling me for weeks about the unfolding relationship, and now they could meet him face to face. Dale told me that he sincerely wanted to ask my dad for his patriarchal blessing upon our union. I was touched by his willingness to seek such a blessing from my father.

At the first opportunity, we traveled to their home, about forty-five minutes from my brother's place where we were staying, along with Jeremy. My parents live in an old high school that was converted to senior living apartments. Their apartment is located on what used to be the old stage and prop room. If you knew my parents, you would know how appropriate it is for them to live on a stage. My mom, especially, has always loved performing, mostly gospel music. She plays the guitar and the bass and sings for senior meetings.

My parents greeted Dale warmly when we arrived, and they sat down to catch up on what was going on and to visit with Jeremy. My dad and Jeremy have always had a very special bond and Dad knew how much Jeremy was struggling with this new paradigm, as all my children were. While some of the family were visiting, Dale and I followed my dad into the hallway of his apartment. There Dale asked him for his blessing upon our union.

"Sir, I love your daughter. I want to marry her and spend the rest of my life with her. I would sincerely love to have your blessing, and I know it would mean so much to Jan, too."

My dad just shook his head in agreement. "You have it. I am just so glad to see that she is happy again. I know you have both been through a lot and it is all going to be okay," he assured while patting both of us on our shoulders.

"When the time comes, I know it would mean the world to Jan if you could walk her down the aisle and give her away, once more," Dale added.

"I am not sure if I can do that, but if these old legs will carry me, I will try," he quipped, smiling broadly.

"We haven't set the exact date yet," I added, "but when we do, I really need you to be standing beside me if there is any way you can make it happen."

Dad put his arms around both of us and began to pray for us. All three of us wept bittersweet tears. Dad had watched so many of his friends lose their spouses over his lifetime. He had lost his own mom when she was in her early sixties to cancer. His dad had remarried in less than a month after my grandmother's passing. Dad said he never resented it. He knew how fleeting life truly is, and that you must grab life while you can.

"Whatever happens, you two are going to be just fine. You are adults. Your kids are going to learn to accept this and they will be happy for you, eventually. They know how hard it has been for you to be alone. You have to make the right decision for you, and it can't be driven by what your children think or feel. I understand they are having a hard time with this, but they will get used to it and see that it is the best thing for their mom not to spend the rest of her life alone," he assured us.

Our quiet few minutes in the hallway of Dad and Mom's apartment were the highlight of my visit to St. Louis. My sister Linda had plans for almost every moment of our time there, making that birthday one of the most memorable of my lifetime, but that precious moment in my dad's embrace was priceless. His complete acceptance of Dale and his support of me through this season of transition boosted my confidence that I was heading in the right direction.

The struggle to know how to proceed over the next few weeks took on a new wrinkle when I asked Dale one day before our trip to St. Louis about his studies for the doctorate program at North Greenville University. "What would it take for you to finish your courses? What is it that you are lacking?" I asked.

"I need to do one more seminar and then write my dissertation," he replied. In my ignorance, I thought that didn't sound too daunting.

"So, when is the next seminar you would need to take?" I asked.

"The end of September and first week of October, just a few days from now," he explained.

I thought that wouldn't work with our current timeline. I asked, "When is the next one?"

"Two years," came his reply.

"What?" I was astonished. I didn't understand the doctorate program schedule and thought it was similar to other courses of study. I was to learn that I was misinformed.

"I don't think they would let me in at this point anyway," Dale explained. "There is a large amount of reading and preparedness that is required. I would have had to be accepted a long time ago. They would likely not let me in now." He looked sad and somewhat dejected as he shared the dilemma. "I think that ship has sailed. I gave up on it and I may never be able to go back at this point."

My mind was reeling with this new information. I was considering the probability that once Dale made a move to our region, he wasn't likely to pick up his studies and go back to the books in two years to finish his degree. I pressed on with my questions.

"You are so close, and you won't be able to get in for two more years?" I asked, incredulously. "What if you quit your job in Greenville and just focus on your studies so that they will accept you? Could you at least ask them?" I saw a spark of hope in him beginning to rise. My wheels were turning. "I can support us if you will help me with my business. Josiah can transfer to the new school, and you can go back to your school."

My brain was firing on all cylinders as I thought of the possibility of getting Dale back to the place he had been before his loss had derailed his plans for getting his doctorate. This new option felt right for both of us. We weren't sure, immediately, what it would mean to our strategy for the wedding, but we decided to explore further.

Dale called the school and talked to them about whether it would be feasible to still get into the upcoming seminar session that was critical to his timeline for achieving his goal. The Dean of the Graduate School of Christian Ministry at North Greenville University told him that what he was asking for was highly irregular, considering the mountain of papers he would have to write in only two weeks and the reading he would have to complete before the beginning of the classes. They stated that they would consider it if he did nothing but focus on writing the necessary papers and reading all the required materials prior to the beginning of the session and meet all the expected prerequisites that the other doctoral candidates were also completing. The mountain of study and preparation to be completed in such a short time seemed daunting, but Dale assured him that he would quit his job and focus fully on the task before him. They agreed to allow him to come onboard and get back into the program if he would dedicate himself to catching up.

I had a client in need of someone to do work on one of her rental properties during this time. Dale could quit his job in Greenville and make more money in three days of work with her than he would clear in weeks at his present employment. This job afforded him the funds to pay the rent on his home in Landrum and keep up with his other expenses. He came to our area and started working on that job while writing his papers and doing the reading needed for his upcoming seminar at North Greenville University. During this time, we also began to arrange for someone to come into his home and start preparing to auction off his belongings and the items he had shared with his late wife there in South Carolina. He asked all his children to go through the house, again, and take anything they wanted from their household. Josiah started preparing for the transition too, saying goodbye to his friends there and aligning his studies for a new high school experience.

The date for our wedding was moved up, much to the chagrin of my children, from January to November. Once Dale had quit his job and started working on his degree and Josiah had started attending the high school in my area, there was no way that waiting until January would work any longer. We scrambled to make wedding arrangements and set up a flight for his daughter Amanda to come in from California. I had envisioned all eight of our children standing with us at the wedding as these two clans became one new clan in the eyes of God and the witness of our friends and family.

During this unfolding new dynamic that was being added to our course of life (Josiah's changing schools, Dale's going back to school, my preparing my home to house a new husband and a teenaged stepson), an anniversary loomed before us. The one-year anniversary of Del's death was quickly approaching. Needless to state, this was an especially tender time for all of us. All the firsts following his death had been like a minefield we were all trying to navigate through without triggering an explosion that would be harmful to our hearts, already so fragile from his loss.

Dale's birthday was coming up on the ninth of October, just one day before the one-year anniversary of Del's death. Del had suffered his fatal heart attack on Dale's birthday. It took us twenty-eight hours to conclude that he was no longer earthbound and to release him to the other side of eternity; therefore, his death certificate reads 10/10 and not 10/09, as it could have. These two competing dates presented a challenge for my heart as well. (Ironically, Dale had lost his own mother to heart failure on his thirty-sixth birthday, almost twenty years earlier.) Everything in me wanted to redeem that week and make it something less tragic, less mournful. We discussed having a private ceremony to get married a couple of days before the ninth, as this would allow Dale and I to have a little time together as husband and wife before Josiah moved in. We could have the public ceremony with all our family the next month when everyone could come to watch us renew our covenant with our loved ones as witnesses, and my dad could walk me down the aisle.

My plan, although well intended, became the landmine I had done everything I could to avoid. I wasn't expecting that my simple suggestion would blow up and cause a meltdown among my children. They read my actions as a betrayal of their dad's memory and the one-year anniversary of his death. No matter my logic or reasons, they only saw this as an act of disaffection. After much deliberation and confrontation, we tabled the discussion of marrying earlier than November. The damage to relationships, however, was done. Several of my children felt that I had broken trust with them and I, too, felt that some had broken trust with me. None of us could fully communicate our deep distress to one another. We each mourned the loss of Del in our own way. I was clumsy and uncertain through this season. I felt like there was a tug of war going on in my heart. I knew that Delbert would be so happy for me to find love again, and I believed that he probably prayed for this very thing. I was experiencing the joy of new love, while simultaneously experiencing a profound longing to see Del again and tell him all about what was going on in my heart and in this family that we had created together. Why couldn't he just step over onto this side of life and drop some pearls of wisdom onto his family, so we would know how to move forward?

My sister, Diana Johnson, who had stayed with me during the time immediately following Del's death, came to stay with Dale and me during this time while Dale was making this transition to avoid the appearance of any impropriety. Dale was in one wing of the house, while Diana and I stayed in another wing. She was given the opportunity to get to know this man who was going to become her brother and my husband. Josiah also made the move to our house and Diana spent many hours with him as he was transitioning into his new school.

Elizabeth, who had acted as my fairy godmother and one of my dating coaches at the beginning of my dating profile search, had helped me formulate a plan regarding the wedding. She helped with concepts and vendors. (She has acted as a wedding coordinator for several years professionally.) Her initial consultations helped me form a plan of action and spurred me to hire a full wedding coordinator as the day approached to take some of the burdens off me since I was finding the burden of running two businesses and trying to assimilate these two men into my home a bit daunting.

The entire subject of the wedding was proving to be too much stress on my family unit. One of my reasons for considering a small, private ceremony before the day of the wedding was because my pastor was not going to be able to be there for the actual event since he had a prior commitment that put him in California on that date. The elder who had done premarital counseling with us was going to be with him and was also going to miss the ceremony. We considered whether we should just do the private ceremony the Saturday before all our family came in for the big celebration. I wanted to have the person who was acting as my pastor during this tender season to be the one who performed the ceremony that would seal my covenant with Dale. The man who had kissed the head of my beloved Del when he had parted the earth was the one whose lips I wanted to pronounce us as husband and wife. Whether others couldn't, or wouldn't, understand my reasons, it felt like this was what we were meant to do. Dale was supportive no matter what I wanted to do in this matter. As I deliberated the possibility, two of my children specifically told me that they didn't want to know if I had a private ceremony. They said that if I did it, that was up to me. They would just see me at the wedding scheduled for November eighth. One of my children had stated that he wanted to know if we were going to have a private ceremony and wanted to try to be a part of it if that is the way we wanted to go. The fourth child didn't express a preference either way.

As the date was approaching, Dale and I discussed our desire for a private ceremony with Pastor Mark officiating before the public service that would follow a week later. Our son and his wife, Jeremy and Elizabeth, had done the same thing when they had been married in 2012. (They were married in our backyard exactly seven days before their big ceremony in Spartanburg, South Carolina, for reasons that they felt compelling.) The elders who had done our premarital counseling, Scott and Lori Clifton, offered to have a small service in their home on November first, with only my sister, our pastor and his wife, Julie, and the Clifton family in attendance.

I called the one child who had expressed a desire to know if we decided to do the private ceremony and told him of our plans. His heart was clear, but he said he didn't feel free to be there at this one. He would be there for the public ceremony a week later. He thanked us for waiting to get married beyond the week of the one-year anniversary of his dad's death and for showing deference to the feelings of our family a few weeks earlier. I appreciated his support and was warmed to feel that all hearts were clear, and I had kept my promises to all of my children.

On November first, a chilly, rainy day, Diana, Dale, and I assembled in the Clifton's home. We stood before a hearth with a glowing, warm fire, surrounded by the few attendees and lots of candles lit for the occasion. Just outside the window of the family room, there were two chairs poised to look upon the proceedings from the other side of the glass. Those chairs were for Delbert and Debbie. The place was thick with the presence of the Lord. We felt like we were bumping into angels in attendance. Perhaps it was just the "cloud of witnesses" we read about in the Word of God (who have gone before us to the other side of eternity). Whatever these presences were, the place was rich with sweetness. As we stood before our pastor and made our covenant vows, there was not a dry eye in the place, not even among the teenaged boys who were there acting as witnesses. The memory was tender and incredibly moving, too precious to fairly convey through written words.

The following week, my family began to come in from Missouri, followed by Dale's family. One of our fix-and-flip houses that was almost completed in Indian Trail served as a great place for the Nealis Clan and Lopers to assemble so that they could have much-needed face time and bonding during the days leading up to the big wedding. We set it up with temporary furnishings, much as we would for staging to sell, and it worked out brilliantly for all of them.

A flurry of activity ensued as we finished final preparations for the big event and the rehearsal dinner that would come the day before the wedding. We decided to have that meal catered (by my amazingly talented neighbor Sheila Rhoney) at our home so that there would be more time for bonding between the siblings on both sides. The highlight of that evening was when my sons began to harmonize with Dale's daughters, bringing songs of worship before Heaven's throne. All I could think about was how delighted Delbert would be to hear these sweet voices harmonizing in his home. He loved good harmony better than anyone I ever knew. He was the one who taught me how to harmonize, and I taught my children in turn. Hearing Dale's daughters lifting their voices in sweet worship with my children just couldn't have produced a happier heart inside of me.

At one point during the evening, my brother-in-law, James said, "All you need to know about the man you are marrying is right there." He nodded toward the girls singing harmony. "The fact that they know those songs and they are worshiping says a lot about the way they were raised. It sure makes me feel even better about the man to meet his family and see what they value." My heart was so touched by that loving confirmation from yet another one of my family members.

"Thanks, James. I appreciate you noticing," I said, sincerely.

"You know Del would have loved this," he said.

"Yes, he sure would have, and I think he does. I think he hears this and so does Debbie," I said.

"You're probably right about that," he acknowledged.

The next evening, Dale and I were publicly joined in holy matrimony as my beloved friend and former pastor, Reverend Barry Taylor, officiated. My dad walked me down the aisle and my heart was overflowing with joy. Father God remembered my quiet prayer, spoken as my dad had escorted me down the aisle to my late husband's casket. I remembered whispering in my heart, "This is wrong!" I remembered the fleeting thought that I had, in that moment of overwhelming grief, that perhaps one day my dad would be able to walk me down the aisle to a new love. At the time, it seemed like a far-fetched notion. My dad was getting older and so was I. The thought that I would be walked down an aisle and given away by my dad like a young bride was just too wondrous to imagine. But, God ... His Word constantly challenges us with the question, "Is there anything too hard for Me?"

We had a sand ceremony to represent the merging of two broken families into one new family. Dale had purple sand, and I had teal sand. Each of our children and grandchildren had a small vial with their names written on it. Several of the children participated in the ceremony. They added the sand that represented each one of them or their children to their respective parent's vase.

After our children had poured their sand into our two vases, Dale and I merged our two vases into one new larger vase. This act of merging the grains of sand is to prophetically declare that, as it would be almost impossible to go back and sort through each grain of sand and separate it from the new mixture, so it would be with this new family. Let nothing separate us from one another and from the new destiny He has created for us to walk into.

The reception began for us with a first dance, something I had never experienced at my first wedding. The song I chose was so perfect for the two of us. We danced to a very old classic entitled "And I Love You So," performed by Perry Como. The words couldn't have suited us (especially me) more perfectly. The words speak of the long, lonely nights and the fact that life began again, "The day you took my hand."

The fact that my life felt like it started over the day Dale made the simple gesture of taking my hand made the lyrics to this song seem perfectly suited, as they produced a poignant moment and powerful memory. We had both lived through the pain of long, lonely nights where the shadows seemed to follow us, and the nights held us captive. This pain was soothed by the infusion of new love and new hope. The book of life is brief, indeed, and we knew it all too well.

Our wedding reception was lovely, filled with people who were there to celebrate this miracle of God giving us beauty for ashes and the oil of joy for mourning. He truly did turn our mourning into dancing and lift our sorrow.

We didn't get the choice of going through life without our first loves, the mates with whom we had parented these amazing children. We didn't get to say, "No, thank You, God. I don't want a different mate. I choose to continue to share my life with the mate You gave me originally." We received the "instead" of The Lord. We were invited to partner with Him and believe that He really could give us an amazing second act. The jaunty driver in Ireland had released the words in June of that year: "Your second time around is going to be greater than your first." Greater doesn't mean better. It can mean that we can have a greater influence, a larger impact. We can't fully know what the greater is, but we can seek Him and His Kingdom in every way during this second act.

Our dear friend, Lori Clifton, was given a prophetic word for us before the wedding. She released it over us as a toast during the reception. We have used this declaration as a guide and a reminder that the grace under which we are living is His gift. The reminder of these words keeps us grounded and humble.

"This day I release over both of you: Extreme Grace that yields Extravagant Hope! Hope! The absolute expectation of something good.

No longer shall despair, disappointment, and disjointedness reign unopposed. You have been anointed with Extreme Advantage—you didn't fight for this, but it is yours to lose if you don't fight to maintain it.

It is yours to lose by being unaware of such Extreme Favor and Grace that yields Extravagant Hope.

Your new beginning is intended to be a display. Extreme Grace... Divine Influence on your hearts with the reflection of the Divine through your lives.

I release EXTREME GRACE, supernatural Spirit-Filled Grace, that shifts atmospheres and alters outcomes of all! I release EXTREME HOPE . . . the absolute expectation of the goodness of God in and through you!"

These words were the mantle under which we were anointed by God as we walked into this new chapter of our lives. They resonate through the ages and propel us forward to live each day as the gift that it truly is to us. We try not to waste a moment on regret, nor to do things that will evoke it. There have been challenges as we have navigated through belonging to a club that none of us ever wish to join, the club known as widows and widowers. As I previously stated, membership is not voluntary, and the fees are beyond cruel.

When Dale and I sat down to talk the very first time, he noticed that we have matching scars on our left wrists in almost the same place. These were from childhood injuries, but they reminded us of how similarly we have been marked by the loss of our spouses. Both scars are on the hands that also once wore the wedding rings that reflected our covenant with our late spouses. We now wear the rings that symbolize our marriage covenant to one another as we face a future neither of us imagined, void of our first loves, but filled with fresh love and a new purpose.

As parents, we sometimes wonder if we have the capacity to love a second or third child as much as we have loved the first one. What we quickly learn is that love isn't divided with an additional child, it is multiplied. With each new life joined to ours, we have a new love that accompanies it and our hearts are expanded to allow for each addition. The same is true of this new marriage. God has filled our hearts with a new home for the love He has inspired. Like those marks on our wrists, we carry a reminder of our first love, but the pain isn't as acute as it was in the beginning.

Since losing Del and Debbie, Dale and I have been invited into the lives of others who have suffered a similar loss. We have been able to assist them in the disposition of their houses or their belongings as real estate professionals. More importantly, we have been able to do what the Word of God tells us to do: 2 Corinthians 1:3-5, "Praise be to the God and Father of our Lord Jesus Christ, the Father of compassion and the God of all comfort, Who comforts us in all our troubles, so that we can comfort those in any trouble with the comfort we ourselves received from God."

May the journaling of your loss bring you comfort. May you find hope in the telling of how He has turned our mourning into dancing and given us beauty for ashes. May He inspire you to look for His Heavenly touch throughout all your days. May you learn to lean into Him, as never before, in every challenge and in every celebration, listening for His Voice and receiving His assurance that He has a hope and a future for you (Jeremiah 29:11) and that, perhaps, "Your second time around is going to be greater than your first!"

Conclusion

As I am putting the finishing touches on this manuscript and preparing to send it to my editor and friends for review, I am seated on the screened porch of our home in Ocean Isle Beach, North Carolina. This is the place where most of my book has been written and rewritten, just as I had envisioned when I bought this place before ever meeting Dale and his family.

Our family has continued to grow as we have added both a grandson, Noah (whose name means "comfort"), and a granddaughter, Grace (whose name means "the unmerited, unearned favor of God"), through Chris and Dana's family. My youngest kiddos, Jeremy and Elizabeth, added their first child, my grandson, Elric (whose name means "wise ruler"), to our tribe in January 2018.

As we watch our families grow, we can't help but be reminded of how much we miss sharing such precious moments with Del and Debbie on this side of eternity. Birthdays, new births, graduations, weddings, new houses, new adventures, all experienced without the chance to share with the two people who would have relished each momentous milestone with great joy, validated our victories, and comforted us in our defeats.

Dale and I recently returned from Ireland where we toured many of the places I had traveled before meeting him in 2014. My first trip was to mark Del's first birthday in Heaven and Father's Day. I had spent the day in Galway Bay, pulling stones from the water. This time, I was accompanied by Bethany and A.J. as well. Although we traveled to many of the same places I had visited previously, this trip was very different from my first one. The startling difference in the weather, for one thing, showed me just how remarkable my first journey had been, as on this trip we encountered typical Irish weather. The days were often gray and rainy.

The only hotel we knew we would be returning to on our return journey was the Ashford Castle. As far as we knew, all the other hotels would be different. This trip was going to take place during the observation of Debbie's birthday on June 30. On that date, our coach pulled up in front of the very same hotel where we had spent Del's birthday in 2014. This time we were pulling stones from Galway Bay and thinking of Debbie. We didn't plan for this timing. God just sent us another sign that we were where we needed to be and doing what we needed to be doing. The booking of that same hotel was just another one of the many kindnesses He has visited upon us to assure us we are in the center of His Divine path for our lives.

If you have traveled with me through this grief journey, you are aware that I have had one constant in my life. Without the love of my Heavenly Father, I don't know if I could have come back from the sea of sorrow upon which I had been sailing. His love has buoyed me and sustained me. His goodness is too infinite for the limitations of my mortal tongue or vocabulary.

God is still writing my story, as He is still writing yours. I have been blessed with the EXTREME FAVOR and EXTREME HOPE that my dear friend released over me on my wedding day, but that hope and favor have been with me all the days of my life, just as the Originator of the hope and favor has been with me. As you are continuing your life journey, I encourage you to invite Him into your story. He is already there, but He is awaiting your invitation to officially participate in a way that you can see Him in the numbers, the dates, the colors, and every tiny detail of the fabric of your life.

Abba, Father, I am asking You to bless the reader of these words with an infusion of supernatural EXTREME HOPE and EXTREME FAVOR that will totally shift the atmosphere around them. Where there is sorrow, replace it with joy. Where there is despair, replace it with encouragement. Where there has been a loss, replace it with the knowledge that Your goodness is more than enough. You are so, so good, Father God. Let those who are reading these words encounter You in a new and joyful revelation. Let them trade the spirit of heaviness and sorrow for garments of celebration. Give them beauty for ashes and the oil of joy for mourning. Let them exchange weeping for dancing, in the name that is above all names, the name of your dear son, Jesus. Amen!"

As the final words are being added to my conclusion, a lovely hawk just swept down from the sky over the waters of Lake Joel.

Perhaps it is a coincidence, but I will receive it as another hug from Heaven. Keep your eyes open, beloved, Heaven is speaking.

Epilogue

Early in the morning on January 25, 2017, I received a text message from Amanda Houseknecht, one of my real estate clients and a beloved friend. She and her family have been woven into the tapestry of my life for many years. I have often referred to them as my "tribe." The text read: "Please say a prayer for Justin's dad. He had a massive heart attack last night and is now in ICU. They are keeping him sedated but are concerned about brain and kidney function."

This text message began a series of days that led to me reliving the loss of Del in a more healing manner than I ever could have designed. I was swept into the unfolding of the loss of the beloved daddy of the Houseknecht Family, Keith Houseknecht. His parting was eerily similar to the loss of our beloved patriarch. Father God was setting me up for a glimpse of the haunting prophecy spoken by an Irish jaunty driver, "Your second time around is going to be greater than your first."

Keith's battle lasted five days, during which time I traveled to and from the hospital where his family had assembled, offering prayers and making intercession. I was firmly fighting, in the realm of Heaven, for a different outcome than that which my family had suffered. My faith in the goodness of God is unwavering. My absolute conviction that He can still heal and Divinely reverse the damage incurred by a massive heart attack is not shaken. Upon this occasion, however, He took Keith home.

As Lori, Keith's wife of more than thirty years, stood outside of the ICU room, knowing that all the life support keeping Keith's body functioning was going to be disconnected, she looked at me with tear-stained cheeks and a regal beauty. She asked, "Will you speak at his service?" A strength and grace were cloaking her, and she was glowing with the presence of a Sovereign God Who was carrying her, just as He had carried me three years earlier. I recognized the Grace that was now flowing from Heaven to earth and covering her like a mantle.

Although I knew speaking on such a tender occasion would be one of the hardest things I had ever been required by God to do, my mission was certain. "I would be honored," came my reply. I would comfort others in the same way that I had been comforted. I had watched this family contend for their beloved dad, husband, brother, and friend to return to them. I was powerfully connected to their grieving, not just sympathizing, but empathizing. I had stood beside them at every turn and with each disappointing report we were given through the course of the long hours from the time he first began his battle. I would be there for them as little, or as much, as they requested. All other tasks would be suspended. My business would keep until these critical moments were navigated with my beloved friends, my tribe, the ones with whom Father God had joined me to through Divine connection.

The night before Keith's service, Lori's brother called me and asked if I would give an invitation to those in attendance, who might not know the One in Whom we have placed all our hope, to open their hearts and receive Jesus as their personal Savior and Lord. I had never given such an invitation before. I had never given a eulogy before or spoken at a funeral, not even at Del's. My children had spoken at that time, and I had been relieved to just sit and let others handle all the matters surrounding his service.

Now, I was being called upon to pay it forward, to use the message of God's goodness that had been delivered at the homegoing celebration for Del to inspire hope in the mourners for Keith as well. I knew that if Father God was putting me in a place to speak, He would fill my mouth with His words. As I prayed and prepared for the message, I considered the fact that the services would be held at the same funeral home and the same chapel where Del's had been held. I would be standing at the podium where Del had been eulogized by his children. I would be looking upon Lori as she was seated in the same place where I had been seated. Could I do this without completely falling apart?

I heard the Voice of God whisper to my spirit, "Count the days!" I counted, just as He instructed, and the words unfolded before me as the ships of a sail unfurl in surrender to the winds that embrace them, opening them fully to propel the vessel forward.

As I stood before the congregation of mourners and comforters who came to honor the legacy of Keith on that date, Thursday, February 2, 2017, I delivered the following message:

"It is my honor to grieve with you on this day of farewell to your beloved patriarch. It is also my joy to celebrate with Keith the occasion of his graduation and reward for a life well lived. God's Word tells us that, 'To be absent from the body is to be present with the Lord' (2 Corinthians 5:8). He also says that, 'Precious in the eyes of the Lord is the death of one of his saints' (Psalm 116:15). That scripture always gave me pause. Then, one day, I understood that it was precious because they could be with Him with absolutely no restraints. In our mortal bodies, we cannot see God, because His goodness is so immensely glorious that our flesh couldn't bear it.

These two conflicting moments in time seem to be colliding with one another. A joyous celebration has just begun on the other side of a veil that we cannot see through with our earthly eyes. On this side of eternity, our eyes are swollen from the tears of loss and sorrow; on the other side, there are no more tears. Heaven is inviting you to see from a higher perspective on this occasion. Heaven would invite you to picture just how gloriously happy your beloved patriarch is now in the space of his Heavenly Homeland. He loved you all so much. He was so proud of each of you. You are his legacy and his greatest accomplishment.

Lori, he was still smitten with you every day of his life and in awe that you would have chosen him as your Boaz. His sons all made him beam with pride as he shared their stories and accomplishments. He bragged that his daughters were the fairest in the land and treasured each as a princess and a fragile flower to be cherished. He positively beamed when in the presence of the grandchildren, who knew him as Pop Pop. There was only one love greater than the love that he held for each of you, and that was the love that he held for his Creator. Lori told me that when Keith was in a Gospel music group, they sang about Heaven so incessantly that one day she said, "Don't you ever sing anything about this side of Heaven?" He truly loved singing about his Heavenly Homeland. Only the powerful call of Heaven could have separated him from you. This separation is only temporary, however. He has just walked a little bit ahead of you to prepare a path. He is looking forward to the day that he can show you around Heaven and introduce you to his Beloved Heavenly Father. He will now be present with you in a different way. While it is true that you will no longer feel the warmth of his arms, or hear his laughter, or listen to his prayers, it is also true that those prayers for you are still effectual and will continue until the day you walk across the threshold of Heaven and join him on the other side.

It is altogether fitting and noble to allow the waves of sorrow you are feeling to give way to your tears of grief, for there is a time to mourn, and this is that time. The book of Ecclesiastics tells us that there is a time for every occasion under Heaven. The New Living translation isn't as poetic as the King James, but it communicates in vivid language the wisdom of timing.

There's a Right Time for Everything

New Living Translation

'For everything there is a season, a time for every activity under heaven. A time to be born and a time to die. A time to plant and a time to harvest. A time to kill and a time to heal. A time to tear down and a time to build up. A time to cry and a time to laugh. A time to grieve and a time to dance. A time to scatter stones and a time to gather stones. A time to embrace and a time to turn away. A time to search and a time to quit searching. A time to keep and a time to throw away. A time to tear and a time to mend. A time to be quiet and a time to speak. A time to love and a time to hate. A time for war and a time for peace' (Ecclesiastes 3:1-8).

Time will be your friend and your adversary in the unfolding days that lie before you. I can tell you that, as I was preparing to deliver these words, I counted the number of days from the time that my late husband had his fatal heart attack to this day. Del's death was similar to Keith's. It was sudden and life-altering. We contended for his return to us after his heart had initially stopped beating for twenty-eight hours. His call to Glory happened exactly 1212 days ago today. The number twelve is Biblically symbolic of Divine order and the Family of God. So, just a little over 1212 days ago, I was seated where you are seated today, in this very chapel, listening as my beloved husband of forty years was eulogized by his children. There was a grace that carried me and my family that was inexplicable and beautiful, as we surrendered to the intimacy that Father God was calling us to enter. We experienced what it means to have peace that passes understanding.

In the beginning of our grief journey, we counted the hours from his departure, then it was days, then weeks, then months. Now we count the years. The good news is that, although I counted the number of days to determine how long it had been up until today (to give you context), it is something I no longer do, because Father has lifted me above the anguish of the loss. Grief is not something you get over, but it is something you get through. In the beginning, a song, fragrance, movie, book, or place will trigger waves of sorrow that you feel will certainly take you under. Eventually, that trigger of sorrow will be replaced by a winsome smile as a memory comes over you and you realize your heart is healing. Nobody will ever replace Keith in your lives but, little by little, you will find comfort and peace as Father turns your mourning into dancing and gives you beauty for ashes.

For those of you who do not know me, I am connected to this family (and the extended family of the Meyers) through houses. I have served as their real estate broker and been abundantly blessed to be promoted to this tribe as a faux aunt. It is humorous (and somewhat prophetic) that I am connected to the Houseknechts through houses. I always felt that, with a name like Houseknecht, these folks should be real estate agents, or builders, or architects. What I learned, when doing research on the meaning of their name, however, was that the origins of the name Houseknecht means, 'steward of the house.' The word 'steward' is indicative of someone who is managing another person's property. Keith was a steward of the family with whom God had entrusted him. He knew that they were a gift from God and he raised them in the fear and reverence of the Lord. His greatest desire was to see all of his children and grandchildren come into an intimate relationship with their Heavenly Father.

Lori asked me, following the revelation that Keith would no longer be with us on this side of eternity, how to address the subject of faith. How could a loving God take their husband, father, and grandfather? We had all prayed and contended. We had anointed him with oil. We had believed that our good Heavenly Father was well able to restore Keith to wholeness and deliver him back to us again.

God's Word tells us that, 'Without faith it is impossible to please God' (Hebrews 11:6). I know that the demonstration of faith that was exhibited in the days following the initial report was stunningly beautiful to God. There aren't many things we can present to God as a gift, but His Word tells us, 'The trying of your faith is more precious (to God) than gold' (1 Peter 1:7). We don't know what all of this means, nor can we sort it all out on this side of eternity. I can assure you of this one fact, God is GOOD. His love is ALWAYS GOOD.

The author, Max Lucado, wrote an article my daughter, Bethany, posted on Facebook following the death of her father. In this article, Max recounted how his two young daughters had different bedtimes because the youngest needed more sleep than her older sister. As he would carry the younger one to bed at night, her older sister would protest that he was taking away her playmate and she wanted to keep playing. Why was he being so mean? He told her that her little sister was tired and that he wasn't being mean, he was giving her little sister what she needed. He knew that, as a loving father, he had to let the little one sleep and go ahead of her sister, even if her older sister couldn't understand it. Perhaps our Heavenly Father has just taken our loved ones to bed a little early because they were tired. There is a song that my late husband used to love with the lyrics, "When you can't trace His hand, trust His heart!" I have learned to trust His heart and He has never failed me. He has not always answered my prayers in the way that I would have hoped, but He has never forsaken me, nor will He.

As a personal testimony, let me tell you what I have experienced. Bearing in mind that every journey is individual, yet the expression of Father's abundant mercy and provision is something every child of God can expect to inherit. On the very day that my late husband was afflicted with a fatal heart attack, there was a man sitting in the foothills of the mountains, a little to our west, observing his first birthday following the death of his beloved wife of almost thirty years. He was still counting months. His birthdate was the seven-month mark from the date of his wife's passing. God had already orchestrated a second chapter for each of us but, in our immense sorrow, we couldn't see His hand of provision. I can tell you we have experienced what it means to see beauty come from ashes and the oil of joy come from mourning. There isn't a day that goes by that the absence of our spouses isn't felt, but there is also not a day that goes by that we are not astonishingly aware of Father God's goodness in giving us this gift. We couldn't see it immersed in our grief. My husband, Dr. Dale Nealis, has not replaced my children's father, but he has become a friend and confidant to those who have chosen to embrace this gift. I don't know what the future will hold for each of you, but I know that God has a good plan for you, and you are not fatherless, for He will never leave you nor forsake you. Lori is not husbandless, for He will be a husband to the widows.

I asked Keith's children what their father's favorite candy was, and they told me it was Good and Plenty. I want each of you to picture your favorite candy. It is in the package, just as this one I am holding. It hasn't yet been opened. Suppose you had never tasted that candy before? How would you know if it was good? You must unwrap it and put it on your tongue and take in its sweetness to know that it is good.

God's Word tells us to 'Taste and see that The Lord is GOOD' (Psalm 34:8). This is what I am asking you to do today. I am asking you to extend your faith and do as your Creator invites you to do. He is inviting each of us into a Divine encounter with His love and His goodness. Keith is experiencing that in ways we can't begin to fathom. His sincerest desire would be to know that all of those who have come today to honor his legacy and comfort his family would accept the invitation to come into an intimate relationship with Him. This isn't about a religion; it is about a relationship. Keith was the steward of his house and his family. He has now entered into his reward for his faithfulness. Father God is inviting you to follow the pattern that Keith set, as he followed the pattern of the son of God, Jesus Christ."

Author Bio

Jan Teel-Nealis is an entrepreneur, owner of two successful real estate businesses, speaker, and writer. After the sudden death of her beloved husband, she turned to her love of writing again to heal her broken heart and inspire her loyal followers on social media. Teel-Nealis found love the second time around in a supernatural fashion, marrying a widower and blending her family of four children with his family of four children. Jan and her husband, the Reverend Doctor Dale Nealis, reside in Charlotte, North Carolina where they are active in their church, couples counseling, and teaching. They partner together in real estate adventures, hold marriage encounter weekends, and assist in bereavement counseling. They are infusers of hope and healing for the hurting.

If you enjoyed this book, please leave a review of it so that others may find it and enjoy it as well.

APPENDIX: Numerical Meanings

One: Unity, Singularity, Uniqueness

Two: Witness, Division, Difference

Three: Divine Fullness, Completion, Perfection, The Trinity

Four: The Number of Creation, Earthly Completeness

Five: God's Grace and Preparation for What Lies Ahead

Six: The Number of Man, Release from Bondage

Seven: Completeness and Perfection

Eight: New Beginnings

Nine: Divine Completeness

Ten: The Completeness of Order or Wholeness

Eleven: Disorder and Chaos

Twelve: Divine Order and the Family of God

Thirteen: Redemption and Blessings

Fourteen: Deliverance

Fifteen: Covenant and Favor

Sixteen: Love and Loving

Seventeen: Indivisible Love, Vanquishing the Enemy, Victory

Eighteen: Life or Slavery

Nineteen: Faith in God's Perfect Judgments

Twenty: Waiting and Expectancy

Twenty-One: Time and Spiritual Maturity

Twenty-Two: Sons of Light

Twenty-Three: God is With Us, Abundance

Twenty-Four: Heaven and the Heavenly Servants

Twenty-Five: Grace, Favor, Redemption

Twenty-Six: God's Love and Adoration, the Name of God

Made in the USA
Middletown, DE
23 December 2018